Jenny Rees was born in 1942 on the Wirral in Cheshire. A journalist since the age of eighteen, she learnt the rudiments of reporting on the *Hackney Gazette* in East London and went on to work for the *Daily Herald, Radio Times, Daily Mail* and *Daily Express*. She left the *Daily Telegraph* in 1994, after eight years on the staff. Currently editing *The Charming Small Hotel Guide to Southern France*, she lives in London and has two sons and two grandchildren.

'What makes *Looking for Mr Nobody* memorable is Rees's moving account of her own attempt to come to terms with her father's "secret" . . . her poignant memoir gives a rare insight into the experiences of families whose fathers joined the ranks of "Stalin's Englishmen" . . . Jenny Rees now probably understands her father better than he did himself' CHRISTOPHER ANDREW, *Sunday Times*

'Resolute but tender' JEREMY TREGLOWN, *Times Literary Supplement*

'A sensitive voyage of discovery' TOM BOWER, *Daily Telegraph*

*Jenny Rees*

Looking for

# MR NOBODY

The Secret Life of

## GORONWY REES

First published in Great Britain in 1994
by Weidenfeld & Nicolson

This paperback edition published in 1997
by Phoenix, a division of Orion Books Ltd,
Orion House, 5 Upper St Martin's Lane,
London, WC2H 9EA

A catalogue reference is available
from the British Library

ISBN 1 85799 225 3

Printed and bound in Great Britain by Butler & Tanner Ltd,
Frome and London

*For my children, Sam and Benjamin*

Illustrations appear between pages 152 and 153

The photographs mainly come from the Rees family. The photograph of Oleg Tsarev was taken by Jerry Bauer.


The Public Record Office, Kew, allowed me to use Crown copyright material (FO 1049/113) which is reproduced by permission of the Controller of Her Majesty's Stationery Office.                    J.R.

# Acknowledgments

When I conceived the idea of writing this book, I was worried that many of those who could help me might find talking to me about the past a painful experience; I need not have been so anxious. On the contrary, those who knew my father seemed to take a great delight in remembering their absent friend and his ways, which made our conversations particularly enjoyable for me. They, too, had kept him in their thoughts and without their insight I could not have achieved the task I set myself. Others who had bumped into him at certain periods of his life had also retained very vivid memories. I am extremely grateful to the following for their understanding and their patience under questioning:

Walter Allen; Lord Annan; Lady Ayer; Sir Isaiah Berlin; Micky Burn; Sally Chilver; Nigel and Maria Clive; Professor Richard Cobb; Robert Conquest; Margaret and Owen Cowell; Catherine Dove; Sir Stuart Hampshire; Mary Hardy; Lord Hartwell; Emyr Humphreys; Lord and Lady Jay; Melvin J. Lasky; Mary Morgan; David Rees; Sir Patrick Reilly; Alun Richards; Nat Rothman; Shiela and Michael Sokolov Grant; Sir Stephen and Lady Spender; Diana Trilling; Nick Willey; Sir Edgar Williams; Victoria Woollard; Mark Wyndham; Sebastian and Margarete Yorke.

For their assistance in my research, I should like to thank Professor Kenneth Morgan, Mr Daniel Gruffydd Jones and Dr Ted Ellis, of the University College of Wales, Aberystwyth; Lord Greenhill; the Rev. J.E. Wynne Davies of the Presbyterian Church of Wales; Christopher Andrew; Rupert Allason; the late Robert Cecil; John Costello and Oleg Tsarev; Michael Rubinstein; Lucy Gaster; the London Library; and the Public Record Office, Kew.

I cannot name Dr X, but his help was invaluable.

My sister, Lucy, and my brothers, Daniel, Thomas and Matthew, agreed to let me go ahead with my project although I knew that at times they had reservations; I am deeply indebted to them for their moral support and for sharing with me their own recollections and feelings about my father's life. None of us sees any other person through the same eyes, and without their blessing I could not have proceeded alone.

I am also grateful to Derrick Hill who has, for two years, listened to me talking about my father with impressive tolerance and good humour and cheered me up along the way.

My employers, the *Daily Telegraph*, to whom nothing is a surprise, kindly released me from my duties so that I could write this book, and my colleague on the paper, David Twiston-Davies, gave me the vital introductions I needed to enter the world of the 'wilderness of mirrors'.

I owe a great debt of gratitude to Jacqueline Korn of David Higham Associates and Ion Trewin of Weidenfeld and Nicolson whose early faith in my idea and their subsequent encouragement made this book possible.

# Prologue

'Moscow! Moscow! To Moscow!'

Irina, from *The Three Sisters* by Anton Chekhov

There was a light scattering of snow in Moscow when I arrived. It lay fresh and white on the roof of the university that I could see from the back windows of the hotel in Tsverskaya Ulitsa. I did not know what to expect; everything had happened so quickly. Shortly after the long-awaited message from Tsarev had come chattering out of the fax machine, a stern-looking man at the Russian Embassy handed me my visa and I was ready to leave London. I had stepped into a surreal world.

The flight to Moscow was like something bound for the Yukon: the aircraft was packed with 'know-how' from the West in the form of geologists, metallurgists, fitters and pipelayers, with attendant cooks and kitchen hands, setting off for the distant oil and gas fields of Uzbekistan and Azerbaijan. My prospecting was of a very different nature. They were going forward, I was going back, back more than fifty years to see if, somewhere in the KGB files, I could find a clue that would help me finally solve what had become for me an all-consuming mystery – had my father been a Soviet spy?

In May 1951 two diplomats, Donald Maclean and Guy Burgess, disappeared, alerting the world to the greatest spy conspiracy this country has ever known. Their defection to Moscow was also responsible for turning the dramatic and unwelcome spotlight on my father, who, in the thirties, became one of Burgess's closest friends, and was drawn into the secret world of the Cambridge spy ring. From the time Burgess and Maclean vanished, Rees was under suspicion and the exposure of his connection with them was to have a profound effect not only on the rest of his life but also on our family.

Nor did the rumour and innuendo end with the death of my father in December 1979.

It may seem inconceivable that I, the eldest of his five children, could not be certain about his role. But my father was a complex man who revealed very little and I knew that only by setting out on a journey – that would ultimately lead to Moscow – could I discover what I had to know about his secret life.

On my first morning in Moscow I had an appointment to see Oleg Tsarev, a writer and consultant to what is now known as the Russian Intelligence Service. I telephoned beforehand to let him know that I had arrived and he told me the route I should take if I wanted to walk from the hotel to his office. For five years Tsarev had been a KGB agent in London, and he gave me directions like a spy: 'You go through Dzerzhinsky Square and keep walking along the boulevard ... as soon as you pass the Polytechnical Museum, you turn left into a street named Maroseyka ... then take the fourth turning on the right into a little lane called Kolpachny Pereulok ... you will be walking downhill ... on the left-hand side is a three-storey mansion ... blue-grey ... the door is painted shiny black ... press the bell ... I will be there waiting for you.'

Grey and black hooded crows were pecking in the snow among the birch trees in the gardens of the large houses in the street as I passed on my way to the shiny black door. I felt a sense of elation as well as apprehension. Would Tsarev solve the mystery that had haunted me for so many years? Would what he knew help me to make sense, finally, of the extraordinary course of my father's life?

I pressed the bell ...

# 1

I was content with a private fantasy of my own
in which I figured as Mr Nobody ...

From *A Bundle of Sensations* by Goronwy Rees

When he died, my father left a legacy that perfectly fitted him: a modest collection of papers and manuscripts in two brown cardboard boxes; ten books, including two volumes of autobiography; and notoriety. To many people, Goronwy Rees, though no Byron, meant 'mad, bad and dangerous to know'. But, alas, there was no sealed envelope containing an explanation of why his life had taken such a bizarre course.

I last saw my father a few weeks before he died on 12 December 1979, in a room at Charing Cross Hospital in west London. His handsome face, which plays such a significant part in the events which make up this strange story, was hardly recognizable; his skin so tautly stretched across his pure-bred Celtic bones that the features I knew so well had more or less gone. He was very ill and in pain but managed to hang on just long enough to reach his seventieth birthday on 29 November. He did not, in the words of his one-time drinking companion, Dylan Thomas, the Rimbaud of Cwmdonkin Drive, 'rage against the dying of the light'. It was a bit too late for that. There was little left to rage against and, according to one of my younger brothers, Daniel, who was with him when he died, he rather regarded death as his last great adventure. Nobody can remember anything very clearly about those last few days except for his final words: 'What do I do next?'

They had taken the police guard off my father's bed some days before he died. So many extraordinary things had happened by then that I felt almost numb and could not muster any further surprise when it was suggested there had been intruders who wished him harm. Holed up in his hospital bed, protected from the newspaper reporters prowling the corridors, my father had witnessed his life come, in a sense, full circle. They were not so much his chickens which had come home to roost as large, black flapping crows. On the television in his room he had watched his old enemy, Anthony Blunt, dramatically exposed as a spy, and nothing could take away from him, in his dying days, the sweetness of this particular revenge. More than forty years after my father's friend, Guy Burgess, had confided to him that he was a Comintern agent and that Anthony Blunt was working for the Russians, too, a score had been settled, but at a terrible price.

In the years that followed my father's death I often found myself, in the course of my work, at memorial services, listening to those lines of Canon Henry Scott Holland – 'Death is nothing at all; it does not count. I have only slipped into the next room ...' – which mourners find so comforting. But as I heard them again and again, my thoughts wandered and I found that the good canon's words made me feel uncomfortable in the context of my father. I did not want him in the next room. It was too close. As I gradually realized, time had not done its job for me. My father's death had left me with a confusing muddle of jumbled and disordered images from the past, from my childhood and from my family life, out of which, however hard I tried, I could make no sense. I wanted to think about him very much, but it disturbed me when I did. My mind would dart here and there, producing, in an irritating way, one image after another, yet there was never one place where I could peacefully rest or which offered me respite. I think I was cross with him. I felt that, instead of a treasured familiar keepsake of the kind which helps others to look back on someone they have lost with love and a balanced and mature sense of mortality, all that my father had left me was a mystery.

Why had his life, which had apparently begun so full of promise, gone so disastrously wrong? What had happened and why? How could someone, once regarded as one of the brightest and best of his generation, have made quite so many mistakes? Was it a strange, dark, Welsh affliction of self-destructiveness, or was my father forever damned by his association with Guy Burgess? I had to know, for I found myself in what was to me the absurd position of being unable to give my own children an accurate account of their grandfather's life, as well as being left in such turmoil myself. But I had to move quickly in order to find what clues were left. I had to open up the two cardboard boxes of his papers that had been shut away for nearly fifteen years. I needed to find his friends and his critics – many of whom were his contemporaries and so already well into their eighties – to help me in my search for some kind of explanation.

As a guide to how to go about solving the mystery, I took A.J.A. Symons's book *The Quest for Corvo* – a record of how the author became a literary detective and tracked down the truth about the self-tormented life of Frederick Rolfe, author of *Hadrian the Seventh*. Symons's quest had begun in 1925 in the garden of a house in St John's Wood, where, over a glass of Valdepeñas, he was first introduced to the work of Rolfe, alias Baron Corvo. My quest began on my fiftieth birthday in March 1992, when, wondering what I should make of such an event, I found myself gazing at a photograph taken at my parents' wedding in December 1940. My mother, Margie, a little over twenty, with her hat smartly tipped down over her pretty face, is smiling radiantly at her husband, Captain Goronwy Rees of the Royal Welch Fusiliers. They both look so wonderfully happy as they stand there, arm in arm, for the photographer.

As I began to determine the course of my search, I realized it was going to take some time. Quests of the kind I had in mind are not the same today as they were when Mr Symons set off on the trail of the real Corvo in the late 1920s; few people, particularly academics, can be induced to write a good letter of the kind sent to Symons and which lend such character to his work of literary detection; one is left with the telephone and the tape recorder as inferior tools of the trade. At times I felt like a spy myself as I added more and more to my file on my father. Often I wished for a 'control' to whom I could report on my progress and who, with a wealth of experience in the field, might help me with difficult assignments. For my head whirled as I set about searching for the scattered pieces that could still be retrieved of my father's life and shuffling them around to see if I could make any sense of them.

When, in the summer of 1993, I embarked on my journey to solve the mystery of my father's life, I found that a surprising amount of what I had stuffed away in the inner cupboards of my mind came flowing back. As I drove around the country visiting his friends and contemporaries, the clouds of cow parsley in a Wiltshire lane reminded me of how much he loved to walk, often five or six miles, on his own and in all kinds of weather; a room in an Oxford college, filled with books, could so easily have had him sitting in the large armchair in the place of my interviewee; in the Public Record Office at Kew I felt my heart thump when I saw his small, neat, rounded handwriting on a confidential document. I could hear his voice again – so Welsh when he was angry and so persistent in argument – and the refrains of songs from the curious repertoire that he would sing to himself as he went about his daily business at home. They reveal so much about him: 'The bells of hell go ting-a-ling-a-ling-, for you but not for me

'...' and Brecht's 'Alabama Song', 'Oh, show me the way to the next whisky-bar, oh, don't ask why, oh, don't ask why ...' I recalled how upset it made me, when I was small, to hear from the bathroom the sounds of him singing 'We're poor little lambs who have lost our way, baa, baa, baa, We are little black sheep who have gone astray, baa-aa-aa'. He would always put plenty of emphasis on the plaintive cries of the creatures. I found it heartbreakingly sad for I did not like the idea of any animal being lost.

As these images returned, I could not help but observe how important he had been to me and how, as a child, I had absorbed so many aspects of his life. Fathers, whatever the cut of their coat, *are* important to their children, though, in the background, I can hear my father dismissing that as banal. As I set off on my quest, I wondered if I was being disloyal to him, poking about in his past, prodding those who had been close to him to remember things they might probably rather forget. Was it not better to let sleeping dogs lie? But the trouble was that the dogs were not sleeping; at fairly regular intervals they would leap up from their prone positions beneath the table and bark, furiously, as yet another book was published of the kind which the London Library files away under *Science – Miscellaneous – Spies*, with my father's name in the index. There he would always be, this one-dimensional person with a funny, unpronounceable name, though he was seldom more than a footnote. Nobody ever had any conclusive evidence that he was significantly involved in the Cambridge spy ring, but the suggestion was there. After his death, these allegations became more and more fantastic. I picked up a tabloid newspaper one morning to find, under the sensational headline 'Confessions of the Welsh Red', that Rees had apparently maintained contact with the KGB until at least 1964; another book made the claim that he had handed Anthony Blunt the plans for D-Day. None of this seemed to make sense to me. Countless thousands of words have been written about the conspiracy and there are certainly thousands more to come. I did not want to be caught out by any more barking dogs. Whatever I discovered about my father, I felt, could not be worse than not knowing the truth.

The matter was further complicated because, for almost as long as I can remember, our family life was troubled. My father was an enigma to me. I loved him, as daughters do love their fathers, but he was a distant, often severe figure and I had difficulty in feeling close to him. To me there was a hidden, secret side to him, and that secretiveness,

I felt, hung heavily over our large, otherwise busy and lively household, as I was growing up with my sister, Lucy, and my brothers, the twins Daniel and Thomas, and Matthew. At times there was also a pervasive sense of fear. I was nine years old when, in 1951, Guy Burgess disappeared with Donald Maclean and my family went through its own '*Annus Terribilis*'. Nothing was ever to be the same for us again. Guy, in his absence, seemed ever more present; he seemed to haunt my parents. However, at home very little was said to enlighten us about the series of disasters that followed. I remember becoming wearily familiar with the expression '*pas devant les enfants*' as my mother and father retreated behind their closed doors.

My father wrote most elegantly about his life in two volumes of autobiography, *A Bundle of Sensations*, published in 1960, and *A Chapter of Accidents* which contained an account of his friendship with Guy Burgess and was published in 1972, seven years before he died. I was eighteen when, in 1960, I first read *A Bundle of Sensations*, my father's reminiscences of his childhood and adolescence in Wales. My father was fifty in the summer of 1960 when the book came out, his first for more than ten years, and it seemed as if a particularly turbulent part of his life was over and that, at last, our luck had turned. Three years before, he had resigned as Principal of the University College of Wales in Aberystwyth, the small seaside town where he had been born, after a row over a series of articles which he wrote about Guy Burgess for a Sunday newspaper. His academic career, which had begun so brilliantly at Oxford, was in ruins and, to many of those who had known him, he had committed the unforgivable sin of betraying a friend, even though that friend was a spy. He was out in the cold and, as Robert Conquest once put it, 'fell in less than half an hour, from riches, dignity and power'. But there was worse to come. Just as he and my mother were trying to start all over again, with five children and very limited finances, my father was knocked down by a car and, in his words, 'came as near death as is possible without actually dying'.

However, by the time *A Bundle of Sensations* appeared he was just beginning to establish himself in a new role as a professional writer. He had made a good recovery from the road accident and we were settled in a Victorian house in Highgate, north London, which my mother, with her gift for gardens and interior decoration, had transformed from something dark and dreary into a light, bright home for us all. I was fascinated by what I read, for my father's childhood could not have contrasted more markedly with ours. In his book I could recognize little of the person who, when I was small, was my 'Daddy' and who had, by then, become Rees, for that was what my mother called him and I copied her. She had decided that Goronwy was really not a fit name for anyone, silly, even, and his own family's shortened version of 'Gony' was even less acceptable to her.

At home, Rees spoke very little about himself. It was therefore a curious experience to read about his childhood in the 'priest and professor ridden' little town in Wales, from which we had all so rudely been ejected, in words that were, for me, almost shockingly intimate and revealing. We had never been treated to stories from him that began 'When I was a little boy ...' We knew that he considered talking about oneself to be 'boring' and that boring others was, to him, among the most serious of crimes. Unless one had something to say of a personal nature that was extraordinarily interesting, then it was better left unsaid. Indeed, I realized, thinking back, that possibly one of the reasons why people used to say my father was 'unusual' was because he did *not* talk about himself. One of the abiding influences on my life has been his crushing response to most of my admittedly feeble attempts to contribute to discussions: 'You are simply making a statement about yourself. It is not interesting.' These were the intellectual disciplines of Oxford, of course, of which I knew nothing, but I was astonished to read so many sentences in his book that contained the word 'I'. '*I*' was pretty important to *me* at that time. Being eighteen, I was very wrapped up in myself, and being the eldest of five children I had pioneered the way in introducing my father to the exacting and tiresome traits of adolescence.

My sister, Lucy, was eighteen months younger than I; my twin brothers were four years younger than she and moving fast up the track to trouble. My youngest brother, Matthew, was only six. Our house reverberated with the thuds of doors being slammed and the shrill and furious sounds of teenage tantrums. It was a very difficult period for my father who, of all the ages of man, liked sweet-smelling babies who did not answer back, or the company of adults like himself. He was profoundly short-fused, uncomfortable and unsympathetic with the 'in-betweens', or so it seemed to me. Just as my father was having a difficult time in 1960, so were we, for the first time, coming up against his anger – an anger that could turn him into someone as frightening as his own father, a Calvinistic Methodist minister, had been to him, although in quite a different way. For my own childhood, unlike his, had been unusually unhampered by paternal influence or interference.

My father was a kind of non-participating member of the family; our busy household revolved around him, but he seldom joined in. I usually found this a most satisfactory arrangement because of the freedom it gave me, but as I was growing up I became aware, without regretting my own circumstances, that other families, on the whole, were not the same as mine. There was, of course, one very clear distinction; my father was an intellectual and a very impractical one. It had come as quite a revelation to find that my friends had fathers who repaired the engines of their cars, mowed lawns, sailed dinghies, or had 'dens' in the garden shed where, with hammers and vices, they made useful wooden objects. This was all very new to me. And there was something else. From quite an early age, I felt that something separated us, the children, from my father and mother; there was something more important than us. It seemed to me that they had a secret of some kind, a secret that they talked about behind closed doors and which, however many keyholes I listened at, I could never fully grasp or understand.

I knew that Guy Burgess, whom I remembered well from my own childhood, was in some way a part of this secret, for he had lurked behind the two major incidents that had upset our family life so far: his vanishing act in 1951 and our hurried retreat from Aberystwyth when my father resigned in 1957. But I really knew very little more and had become accustomed, as it were, to the presence of The Secret, which was, I sensed, an almost organic component of our family life. I sometimes resented the way my mother would always put my father first, and became angry when I could not manage to find a way to gain her attention. I had by then, I think, formed the impression that dramatic things happened to my father, that he was accident-prone and needed a careful eye kept on him. My mother behaved as if he were a very special person who needed most of her time, her attention and her love, and, as I had absolute trust and faith in her, I did not doubt her wisdom. What I remember most clearly is never being quite certain that I could be proud of my father, which I wanted to be, and the feeling of frustration this gave me. My mother's overwhelming concern and care for him seemed, at the same time, to send out conflicting messages that although my father was special it was not something to shout about from the rooftops.

Looking back now, I realize that the constant factor in our family life was a kind of anxiety, a general feeling in the air that something was wrong. It was pervasive, it was often oppressive. I was an imaginative child and I was curious. Putting together little bits of what my mother said, remarks and fragments of telephone calls that I overheard, I gathered that The Secret was, somehow, related to the past. It was as if, before he married my mother, my father had had another and quite different life that we were not to be told about. I always hoped that my mother would confide in me, but she never did. There was something in her manner that made me feel absolutely certain that, whatever it was, it was not my business. It was better for me if I did not know.

However, I think I can say that at the time I read *A Bundle of Sensations* I was happy at home. The underlying anxiety was not new to me, and while my personal antennae were constantly primed to pick up the slightest speck of information that might carelessly come my way, I simply accepted this as a natural part of our family life. That summer I had just returned from Paris, where I had been sent to learn French. I was growing up and looking forward to getting a job on a newspaper and, for a while at least, my parents appeared to be safe from the disasters that had plagued us. This is how I like to remember my father and I have kept in my mind a very clear picture of him at that time.

Given the difficult task of making a resumé of Rees's life for the *Dictionary of National Biography*, his friend, the philosopher Freddie Ayer, described him as an author, journalist, man of business and university administrator. I think of my father as a writer; whatever else he was engaged in, his daily habits rarely changed. He wrote and he read. He had a particular way of reading. He would sit, with his legs crossed, in one of our armchairs – with a loose cover made by my mother and often resprung and buttoned by her, too – and hold his book in his left hand and a cigarette in his right hand, so that the smoke wafted around his head, and one of our cats would more often than not be draped around the top of the chair back. On a small table at his side, there would be an ashtray and often a glass of whisky. For as long as I can remember my father got through about a bottle of whisky a day and three or four packets of cigarettes. As he read, he coughed his smoker's cough from time to time. Because of our calamities we were always moving house, and the first thing my mother did, when the men began to lift the furniture out of the removal van, was to arrange the chair and little table for him and there he would sit oblivious to whatever was going on around him. The understanding was that Rees should never be disturbed. Breaking away from whatever else was going on in our large and bustling household, one of my favourite things was to put my face around the door of the sitting-room and see him sitting reading in his little oasis of calm. His stillness and concentration gave me a sense of security; as long as he was there I felt all was well with the world.

And, of course, somewhere in the house was his desk. Precisely where depended very much on our financial situation. When the going was good, as it sometimes was, we had a house large enough for my father to have a study. When the going was not so good, as was more often the case, he wrote at a desk in the sitting-room. If he was working on something, he went directly to his desk straight after breakfast every morning, with *The Times* – in which he did the crossword – under his arm, and he stayed there until lunchtime when he went to the pub. In the afternoons, he read; later he would leave the house to go out for another drink and the evenings were his time for talking and arguing with friends. My father found arguing exhilarating. He argued as if he were fencing; standing back, positioning his foil, waiting, and then lunging to close in on his victim. He was happiest when he had, through skill and alertness, managed, so to speak, to get himself in the thrilling position of pressing the end of his foil into the soft and vulnerable flesh of his adversary's neck, like Errol Flynn in his swashbuckling films.

He wrote on Oxford foolscap pads of lined paper, on which he made few corrections, as if he had clearly ordered whatever he was writing beforehand, in his head. When he was writing something long or substantial, he was particularly withdrawn and lost in thought as he worked out his themes and his ideas, which meant that when we saw him at mealtimes – one of the few times one could count on a sighting – he was more often than not absent, although present, physically, in person. He had small shiny black pocketbooks in which he made notes and added and subtracted sums of money – such as how much would remain of a publisher's advance once he had deducted monies owed or whether he could afford to pay the Inland Revenue, a problem that played a large part in his life. His handwriting never changed, I have found letters that he wrote while an undergraduate and the writing is exactly the same as it was in the letter he wrote to me just before he died, telling me he had cancer and did not have long to live. He kept the top of his desk immaculately tidy and free of unnecessary clutter. Noël Annan, who was an intelligence officer with my father in the Control Commission in Germany in 1945, remarked, when I met him to talk about my father, that it had been the same then. Noël remembered this feature so vividly that he got up out of his chair and gave me a demonstration.

What was baffling was the contrast between the order and discipline which Rees imposed upon his intellectual activities, his reading and his writing and the arguments which he conducted with such precision, and the chaos that frequently seemed to prevail in other aspects of his life. Perhaps he had unconsciously allowed the Calvinistic Methodism of his childhood to stay with him where he felt it was acceptable and unintrusive, while throwing it out altogether in most other respects.

My father had very few material possessions that he considered his own. Apart from the hundreds, if not thousands, of books which we carted about with us from house to house, he travelled light. In the two cardboard boxes which I opened after his death, I found no letters, apart from a few written to him in those final days in hospital; among the contents were manuscripts and book reviews, contracts and articles that my mother had typed for him, some depressing bank statements, and receipts from Chez Victor, one of his favourite haunts in Soho. I also came across some scraps of paper on which he had carefully written shopping lists to remind him of what my mother had asked him to buy: bread, Whiskas, washing-up liquid . . .

Opening up the boxes, I remembered joking with my brothers in the past about the improbability of my father being a spy, because he was so useless at the basics of life. He would light tipped cigarettes at the wrong end and never knew his own telephone number. He could not drive a car, though at quite a late stage in his life he did manage to learn how to boil an egg. We would giggle as we imagined how he might deal with the job of having to deliver some very important piece of information to a dead-letter box. How would he get there? Would he find the way? Surely he would lose the package? It was a release to us to be able to laugh at him. It helped to make light of the whisperings, of which we were only vaguely aware, that our father was a spy.

We regarded him with a certain amount of awe, both because he kept himself so distant and aloof from our family activities and because of his flashes of temper. I was also well aware of how charming he could be when he wanted to be and was enthralled by his intellectual gifts. He was tremendously handsome and I will not be persuaded by the view that this is ever a handicap to anyone. Superficially, I suppose, Rees had all the components necessary for what is often called 'a charmed life'. Before the events of the 1950s his good looks, his cleverness, and his ability to speak to anyone of any social class made him welcome wherever he went. I loved looking at his face; in simple terms of aesthetics it gave me enormous pleasure and enjoyment. My youngest brother, Matthew, once said that Rees's intelligence was like watching the sun come up on a glorious morning. I think his attributes, and my mother's attitude towards him, inspired in all of us a sense that we had, somehow, been blessed in having such a father.

He and my mother were passionate gossips and both had a very sharp, dismissive way of talking about people they did not like, which amused and entertained me. There was no question that my father could not answer, or so it seemed to me; he was like having my own university, my own personal fount of all knowledge. Due to the turbulence of our family life, I had been to six schools and had remained a fairly blank sheet as far as education was concerned. My father, who had no difficulty in passing examinations himself, showed little patience with those, like me, who found them hell. Only my sister Lucy showed any sign of fulfilling the scholastic ambitions my father may have had for any of us. In fact it was very difficult to know what he wanted, for he used to say that he only liked women who were 'unmarred' by education; in that, I felt sure, I must have had his approval. I considered myself fortunate that if I wanted to know about Thomas Mann or Joseph Conrad or the Duke of Wellington, my father was there to instruct me.

My mother's protectiveness and the dramatic events of our family life had, in a sense, shrouded my father in mystique. But at the time I was first able to read about his early life in *A Bundle of Sensations*, my father shone like a blazing star in my small firmament. It was, therefore, absolutely shattering to me to learn from his foreword to that book that he thought of himself as 'Mr Nobody', a man without character, a man without qualities, a person without a sense of 'self'. I was horrified. What did he mean? I knew perfectly well who he was; I saw him every day, and was all too aware of his character and his qualities. What was the matter with him?

He wrote that he was always slightly bewildered and surprised when other people took it for granted that they possessed what is usually called a 'character', for he had never been able to find anything of the sort in himself. In the course of his life, he explained, this had been the source of many misunderstandings, since other people persisted in expecting of him a kind of consistency which, he felt, they had no right to demand. It also made him feel inferior, he said, as if everyone else had something he lacked, rather like an extra arm or leg. Apparently it was a view that had come to him when he was very young and it had remained with him over the years. He wrote: 'As a child this did not worry me, and if, indeed, I had known at that time of *Der Mann ohne Eigenschaften*, the man without qualities, I would have greeted him as my blood brother and rejoiced because I was not alone in the world; as it was, I was content with a private fantasy in which I figured as Mr Nobody.' He did not want a character, he did not want an 'I', he said, he had no need of it. But already, at a very early age, this notion of his created difficulties. When he was punished for breaking the rules and conventions of a society which depended upon what he described as the 'fiction' of an individual and responsible 'I', he was unable to explain that, in his case, there was no 'I' to be blamed.

However, he continued, he was not alone for long in his no-man's-land. At Oxford he had discovered the philosopher David Hume. A sense of 'blinding revelation' had struck him when reading the chapter on Personal Identity in Hume's *Treatise of Human Nature*, in which Hume, just as sceptical about the self, wrote: 'Setting aside some metaphysicians . . . I may venture to affirm of the rest of mankind that they are nothing but a collection of perceptions which succeed each other with inconceivable rapidity and are in perpetual flux and movement . . .' Rees called his book *A Bundle of Sensations* in tribute to Hume, and told of how, when he read those words, he had the same feeling of joy as Robinson Crusoe finding the footsteps of Man Friday in the sand. I had no such feeling of joy when I read my father's words. I did not want him to be a leaf in the wind, tossed about by events and unwilling to take affairs into his own hands. I did not want him to be mixed-up about himself. It was too dreadful to contemplate. He does not know who he is, I repeated to myself in horror; if my father does not know who he is, who are we? The very foundation of my existence was shaken and I do not think I ever fully recovered from the impact. I was angry with him for playing, so I thought, some fey, perverse, philosophical game which I put in the same category as a rhyme which he used to recite to me as a child:

As I was going up the stair,
I met a man who wasn't there.
He wasn't there again today;
I wish that man would go away.

Fearing my father's wrath, I never raised the matter with him but brooded on it. Interestingly, I recently came across a review of the book by the literary editor of the *Daily Telegraph*, H.D. Ziman, who seemed to agree with me that this notion of my father's – that he was 'merely a theatre on the stage of which certain scenes appear' – was just not viable. Ziman felt that the fantasy could be dismissed, without any philosophical argument at all, merely by reading what Rees wrote: 'For it is the unity of the narrator's personality amid the diversity of his experiences which gives interest to any good biography, and this is noticeably true of his own book . . .' Ziman observed shrewdly that in Rees's collection of sketches about his childhood, the war and a hospital ward, 'the reader will notice that while the outward Goronwy Rees is assimilating himself joyfully to his surroundings, the inner Goronwy Rees is often a withdrawn and curious spectator'.

With the passing of time, I thought less and less about Mr Nobody. But he will be a close companion of my father's throughout the story I am about to tell and I believe that his complicated perception of himself, which I shied away from all those years ago, is a key to understanding his nature and possibly gave rise to the suspicions about him. This cannot be a conventional biography, of course, if it is to deal with a man who often wasn't there, and I do not claim that it is. Anyone, for example, looking for intimate details of my father's many amatory adventures will be disappointed, for this was never an area of his life about which I was concerned or even really curious. Neither have I touched, in any significant way, on his career as a writer, except to quote his words at length where they are most appropriate.

Before I started work on the book I was warned, kindly but firmly, that daughters should not write about their fathers and that, in my case, this was particularly dangerous. I am not sure on which ancient tablet of stone this edict is carved, but I have ignored it, perhaps at my peril. I suppose it means that I am presumed unable to be objective or sufficiently detached and ruthless in the pursuit of my goal. However, it was never my intention to attempt an apologia for my father's misadventures and he never sought such a thing himself. Self-pity was never one of his indulgences. I have also been admonished for being capricious and mischievous – in which case I have more of my father in me than is good for anyone, but he would be the last person to hold it against me.

My guide, A.J.A. Symons, said there were no conventions about biography 'save the sober one of truth' and that what mattered were the life and acts of man 'in all their majesty and meanness'. He said that the important thing is to try and see people as 'rare and curious flowers of character interesting both when they conform and differ from the general standards of law and virtue'. The truth in this case was always bound to be elusive, but my father was certainly a rare and curious flower and the story of what he and my mother went through together is one of the saddest I know.

# 2

*Arglwydd, arwain trwy'r anialwch*
*Fi, bererin gwael ei wedd,*
*Nad oes ynof nerth na bywyd,*
*Fel yn gorwedd yn y bedd:*
*Hollalluag*
*Ydyw'r un a'm cwyd i'r lan.*

Guide me, O Thou great Jehovah,
Pilgrim through this barren land . . .

It was Milton who wrote: 'The childhood shows the man as morning shows the day', and there is no more appropriate place to start this story than at the beginning. Today the debate is about nurture or nature, environment or genes, and in my father's case both are highly significant. It is curious that someone who has written so much about himself should have been seen, even by those who knew him well, as such a shadowy and mysterious figure right up to the end. I believe that it was because of his Welshness, perceived, over the border, as something very alien and unEnglish, wild, devious and unpredictable, a dark Celtic something that comes down with the mist of the mountains. He could not have been more Welsh.

As a child my father had his head held in the hands of a professor of anthropology, who pronounced that from its shape it was of the purest Celto-Iberian stock and of none other. He was born on 29 November 1909, in the small Welsh seaside town of Aberystwyth in what was then Cardiganshire, the youngest son of the Rev. Richard Jenkyn Rees, a Calvinistic Methodist minister, and his wife, Apphia Mary, née James. Both their families had farmed locally for generations, but the Reverend, known to my father as Dada and to me as Ganga, had been brought up in the East End of London. My father gave a charming picture of his grandparents in his second volume of autobiography, *A Chapter of Accidents*. His grandfather was a stone-mason, and his earnings were supplemented by the proceeds of a small dairy, run by his grandmother, for, together with their language and their religion, the Reeses had brought to London with them their traditional attachment to the cattle which had provided them with a living for so long. 'So that in the East End,' he wrote, 'they formed, as it were, a little pastoral enclosure, where the Bible was always on the table and the cows lowed to be milked in the byre at the back of the shop and occasionally, for their health, were driven out for a blow on Hackney Marshes . . .'

The dairy was in Hannibal Road, Stepney Green, and Ganga's father, John, was an elder at the local chapel of the Presbyterian Church of Wales, in whose records he is entered as 'Cowman'. At the age of sixteen, while still at the City of London School, Ganga received his call from God. This led him to the University College of Wales in Aberystwyth, where he graduated in classics (in those days, degrees were conferred by the University of London), and then on to read theology at Mansfield College, Oxford, where, with a First, he became one of the earliest Nonconformists to take an Oxford degree. He was given his first ministry in Pwllheli in 1891, from which he had moved to the Clifton Street Presbyterian Church in Cardiff. When my father was born, he was well established as the minister of *Y Tabernacl* ('The Tabernacle') at Aberystwyth, one of the largest and most prosperous Calvinistic Methodist chapels in Wales, which he had taken over in 1903.

In *A Bundle of Sensations*, written before Ganga died, but following our retreat from Aberystwyth in 1957, Rees went as far as he could to poke fun at the society in which he was brought up. His birthplace, he said, had the distinction of being the seat of the first Welsh university college and of the National Library of Wales and this had gone to the heads of those who lived in the town. 'So much learning was almost too much for its inhabitants,' he wrote, 'they felt as if Providence had selected them to be the intellectual leaders of their nation and this seemed only natural to them. This gave them a kind of smugness, which increased because the little town also had thirty or forty churches and chapels, mostly chapels, which gave it the astonishing proportion of one place of worship for every two or three hundred people.'

As a small boy, walking to school, he passed chapel after chapel – 'a Salem, a Shiloh, a Tabernacle, a Bethel, and a Moriah' – and it was like walking through the Middle East, he said. His father, with his large congregation of about a thousand, was a person of considerable standing in the town and, naturally, the four Rees children, my aunts Muriel and Enid, my uncle Geraint and little Gony, my father, were expected to behave in accordance with his important place in society and to set an example to other children.

I turned to my father's reminiscences of his childhood to see if I could find any indication in them that he had not been happy, but what prevails is his sense of romanticism, which colours what references there are to any disturbing elements of his early years. Photographs of him and his brother, Geraint, later a judge at the Central Criminal Court at the Old Bailey, show a couple of sturdy little boys standing reluctantly in front of the camera as if they were longing to escape from temporary captivity back to the stream where they were fishing or to roam the nearby countryside again.

Many of my father's friends were convinced that his background was somehow to blame for the way he careered off the straight and narrow almost as soon as he escaped from Wales. Voices became hushed and heads nodded knowingly as if no more need be said than the dreaded word 'Calvin'. But this did not appear to be my father's view, or, at least, the one he wished to express. Far from it. In *A Bundle of Sensations*, he explained that Calvinism, though not an easy or a comforting religion, is based on a premise that God has His chosen ones and the elect have the knowledge that they can never fall from His grace, whatever their sins: 'All my childhood, I had had the comfortable confidence that, as my father's child, I would not fail to be among the elect; it was as if I had been put down from birth as a member of my father's club.'

What Rees did not like was being punished by his father and, as an example, he recounted what had happened when he was sent out of chapel after fighting in the family pew with Geraint. His father simply ignored his existence, which, he said, could not have been 'more effective or more terrible'. 'It seemed to me that this time I had really committed the sin against the Holy Ghost, that I was beyond forgiveness, that I was expelled for ever from my father's presence,' he continued. 'I hardly knew indeed whether it was my heavenly or my earthly father who was punishing me in this way. When I saw my father in the pulpit, I hardly distinguished between him and the God whose religion he preached, and somehow I always felt that during the week God also, like my father, took time off, as it were, from the more frightening aspects of his work ... When my father turned away from me in such displeasure, it seemed as if grace had been taken away from me as finally and mysteriously as it had been given, and for days, I trotted like a puppy at my father's heels, vainly trying to make him recognize that I existed, sinful though I was.'

My cousin, Margaret Cowell, daughter of my father's eldest sister,

Muriel, told me that my father had been a cherished and much loved child. 'You see, Gony was the youngest and Apphia had lost three of the seven children she had and he made her very happy. She was inordinately proud of him.' Of the four surviving children, Muriel, named after a character in *John Halifax, Gentleman*, and my father, named after Goronwy Owen, the eighteenth-century Welsh poet, were the intellectuals and what Margaret describes as the 'dreamers'. Enid, a gifted organist and pianist, and Geraint, although also clever, possessed a greater degree of common sense and practicality.

In the years since my father's death, the Welsh side of our family has had plenty of time to reflect on his misadventures and to search for possible explanations for his often incomprehensible behaviour. My cousin Margaret felt that one of the keys was bound to be Calvinistic Methodism and the fact that my father was always thought to be more sensitive than his siblings and had found it more difficult to accept the strictness and severity of his upbringing. 'Chapel played a major part in their lives and as children they were not permitted to do any wrong because their father was the minister and looked up to for guidance by his congregation. The children had to be little angels, they had to conform. The mantle of Calvinistic Methodism is a heavy one – some carry it lighter than others and Gony may have been one of the ones who found it very hard to cope with.' Margaret's husband, Owen Cowell, who in retirement has researched into Calvinistic Methodism, added: 'It is important to remember that nonconformists make you conform.' The Welsh are familiar with the phenomenon of the 'child of the manse' becoming a rebel. Someone else I know who comes from the same background described it as 'stifling'.

In his memoirs, my father alludes to the problems of having a father who, during the week, was lovable and approachable, but who, on Sundays, transformed himself into quite another being. Ganga was a powerful preacher, as well as being an erudite scholar, and is still remembered as one of the last of the great Victorian orators of his Church. My father was 'terrified', he wrote, by the sight of his father taken over by what in Welsh is called the '*Hwyl*' – in his words 'a special form of impassioned utterance half-way between speech and song' – that possessed preachers in their pulpits. 'One saw before one's eyes a man, whom one had taken to be a man like any other man, quite suddenly transformed into a kind of witch-doctor, demoniac and possessed; it was as if, without warning, he had gone off his head. As a child I saw this happen on innumerable occasions and in a variety of forms; indeed, among our preachers, it was the rule and not the exception ... But whatever form it took, the *Hwyl* inspired fear and terror in me, and a kind of shuddering shrinking from such a bare-faced, bare-breasted display of real or simulated emotion; and also a kind of alarm, because my father also could become, whenever he chose, a victim of this kind of possession. I resented it because in my heart I felt him to be a great man, too good for this kind of thing.'

The articles of faith of Welsh Calvinistic Methodism were drawn up in the house of a grocer, draper and corn merchant in Aberystwyth in 1823 and my father's father was a leading light in the movement. The great back wall of Tabernacl rises above the road between the station and the harbour like a cliff-face. Although it is a little shabby and down-at-heel now, it was built to seat a congregation of 1500. At its opening in 1878, the ceremony lasted from midday on a Tuesday until late the following Sunday; eleven ministers took part and nineteen sermons were preached. In a book on Aberystwyth, published by the local newspaper, the *Cambrian News*, I found the following comment on the religious mood of the town at the time of the opening of Tabernacl: 'Aberystwyth now contained a very large number of Methodists indeed, and their leaders were men of great influence in the town, too influential for the peace of mind of moderate dissenters ...' During my grandfather's first ministry in Pwllheli, he had supervised the building of an English chapel, so associating himself with the Calvinistic Methodists' far-sighted new 'English cause', of which he became a leading figure.

The policy of holding services in English had been adopted by the movement because it was felt that Welsh was a declining language and might soon be dead, leaving the chapels with no congregations. Naturally, the decision caused divisions: some felt that encouraging English 'causes' would only hasten the death of the Welsh language; others felt that the Calvinistic Methodist tradition would be weakened. But the main opposition, apparently, was on the grounds that many of the English adherents were middle-class congregations made up of the prosperous local tradespeople and professionals, and not truly 'missionary', and that when English churches were built they turned out to be grander than the simpler Welsh ones. By the time my father was born, the great tide of the Welsh religious revival that swept the principality in the nineteenth century had turned, but the social status of the minister had been unaffected. 'Ours was a theocratic society, ruled by priests and elders; they formed a sort of unofficial Sanhedrin, which exercised an absolute dictatorship over the morals and behaviour of the town,' Rees wrote. 'My father shared in the respect and devotion which was shown to all ministers of religion; they ranked in society even higher than Professors at the University College, being less learned perhaps but more holy, and being armed moreover with all the authority of the law and the prophets...'

My cousin Margaret described the ambiance of the manse in Aberystwyth where my father spent the early part of his formative years as 'loving, but strict'. It was a Welsh-speaking household, of course, and my father told me that he did not start to speak English until he was eleven. There may not have been very much money, but theirs was a society in which education was status, and the Reeses had plenty of that. The house was spick-and-span, and the family had a maid. My father was privileged. In his memoirs he said that, in retrospect, these had been years of 'intense happiness' for him. He felt secure and safe and cherished at home and he remembered with pleasure how he and his brother would set off with billycans and haversacks to wander along the cliffs overlooking Cardigan Bay and to swim and to lie on the sandy beaches indulging in their favourite pastime, reading. 'Our precocious education in Biblical criticism had made us passionately, inordinately, fond of reading any book that was not the Bible and did not require a commentary,' he wrote. 'Our preparations for our excursions always began with a walk into town to buy our supplies and visit the Public Library to borrow enough books to last throughout the day. Then we walked home, only our desire to read our books was so urgent that we read them as we dragged at snail's pace through the town, holding them before our eyes as we walked, so that sometimes when we reached home the book was already finished and we were no better off than when we started.'

The Rees children were infused with a strong sense of social conscience and no one set a greater example to them than their mother, Apphia. She always had time for others, so my father said. She established a successful and busy women's group at the chapel, but my father wrote, lyrically, of another side to her. 'My mother had an instinctive and an intuitive sympathy with all the unfortunates, the eccentrics, and the failures of life; they were her own form of release from the intolerably oppressive respectability of the chapel and, sometimes to my father's irritation, she attracted them as flies to the honeypot. So that to the back door of our house flowed an endless stream of fantastic and disreputable characters, never seen in chapel, who called in the certain confidence that they could depend on my mother's inexhaustible love and charity. Such creatures, gypsies, tramps, drunks, the outcasts and ne'er-do-wells of the town and the wild country beyond, often in rags and always penniless, offering for sale worthless objects which my mother always bought, performing useless services which only my mother could have invented for them, were an assurance to a child that somewhere outside the walls of the chapel there existed another world of fabulous freedom and adventure.'

In later years Rees would quote a poem by D.H. Lawrence, that, he said, reminded him of his mother:

> Softly, in the dusk, a woman is singing to me;
> Taking me back down the vista of years till I see
> A child sitting under the piano, in the boom of the
>     tingling strings
> And pressing the small, poised feet of a mother who
>     smiles as she sings.
>
> In spite of myself, the insidious mastery of song
> Betrays me back, till the heart of me weeps to belong
> To the old Sunday evenings at home, with winter outside
> And hymns in the cosy parlour, the tinkling piano our
>     guide.
>
> Now it is vain for the singer to burst into clamour
> With the great black piano *appassionato*. The glamour
> Of childish days is upon me, my manhood is cast
> Down in the flood of remembrance, I weep like a child
>     for the past.

However, there was, perhaps, another side to Mrs Rees. My cousin Margaret told me that she had once asked Geraint about her, saying that she imagined that their mother had been very beautiful and soft and gentle. She had a surprise. 'Geraint started to laugh. She was, apparently, one of the most malicious gossipmongers ever', he said.

As I have learned, my father was the most sensitive of the children and he was to remain a romantic all his life. Romantics, of course, often find that life does not live up to their expectations. Looking back on his childhood, Rees once said that if he had not been so spoilt by his mother he would not, as he did, have held pleasure as the first principle. It has also been suggested to me that this upbringing might have taught him how to lie. My sister Lucy believes that so much time in chapel gave him his writing style, his beautifully balanced sentences, composed like the verses of psalms. In his memoirs Rees himself appears unwilling, apart from asides, to make any harsh judgment on the circumstances of his childhood.

Going back over my father's early years, I thought I came somewhere near to finding out what had brought Mr Nobody into being. Calvin himself preached that the individual should not feel he is his own master: 'We are not our own; therefore neither our reason nor our will should predominate in our deliberations and actions ... We are not our own; therefore let us, as far as possible, forget ourselves and all things that are ours.' Little Gony, sensitive and imaginative, would have been steeped in the imagery of the words from the pulpit and absorbed them through every pore. Many of them were to remain with him throughout his life.

His childhood in the chapel made a marvellous subject for him to write about. He has left a delightful account of how, on the rare evenings that he and the other children did not have to be in chapel, they would play a game of make-believe in which Geraint was the preacher, conducting a service from a large armchair. Enid sat by the bookcase and 'with wonderful dexterity' manipulated the books as organ stops; Rees was the congregation, 'staring up open-mouthed as my brother went through the points of the sermon. It was best of all when he gave his own version of our favourite sermon by one of the greatest actors and exhibitionists of the Welsh pulpit. It was a sermon about Noah and the Ark, in which the preacher re-enacted the whole story of the Flood, taking in turn the part of Noah himself, then of his sons, then of the animals entering the Ark, giving to each part its appropriate dialogue, human and animal, and with wonderful and primitive realism transforming the Bible story into a drama that could have taken place in any farmyard of any little Welsh farm in the hills. This was by far my favourite game, and the element of mockery in it provided a release for nerves and emotions overwrought by so many religious exercises.'

But the life that centred around the cosy parlour of the manse and the chapel was to be brought to an unpleasant end. In the summer of 1923, at the age of thirteen, Rees left Aberystwyth with his family to settle in Roath Park, Cardiff. He felt, he recalled, like a mountain sheep being shepherded down from the hills by his father. (Just over thirty years later, our family was also to leave Aberystwyth, under very distressing circumstances, and on that occasion our shepherd – my father – had no idea of where we were going.) Leaving Aberystwyth appears to have been traumatic for him. In 1921 there had been a by-election in Cardiganshire, a stronghold of Liberalism, and my father's father, or R.J., as he was often known in Wales, had made the great mistake of dabbling in politics, which ministers were not supposed to do. In a small town like Aberystwyth, little is forgotten or forgiven, and the repercussions of R.J.'s support of the Lloyd George candidate were to be felt by my father when a later generation of those who had judged his father was to judge him no less severely.

The by-election was held because the sitting MP, Vaughan Davies, a former Conservative, had been given a peerage after representing the constituency for nearly thirty-nine years. It became clear that Lloyd George had arranged this so that a seat could be found for his young private secretary, Ernest Evans, a barrister, whose father was a pillar of Tabernacle and a close friend of R.J. The local Liberal Association objected strongly to being used to support a government tainted by the atrocities committed by the Black and Tans in Ireland, said my father.

There was a stormy meeting, Evans was rejected and the Association chose instead Llewellyn Williams, the Recorder of Cardiff, who was bitterly opposed to Lloyd George. In the end, the Liberal Party split on the issue and both men were adopted, causing havoc in Cardiganshire, particularly among Calvinistic Methodists who were Lloyd George's Liberals at prayer in Wales. Mrs Lloyd George also lent her support to Evans, who was elected with a majority of 3500, but it was reported that he won only because 250 Tory-owned motor cars came to his assistance. The Asquithian Liberals refused to use the official Liberal Association headquarters in the town and, for my father's father, things were never quite the same again.

My father wrote: 'In the eyes of many Welshmen, among whom my father would normally have been included, Lloyd George, himself a Welshman and a liberal, was a traitor to the cause with which Wales had hitherto identified its political fortunates, the architect of its defeat and the prisoner of reactionary and imperialistic forces which Wales could never look to for any benefits; he had made *il gran rifiuto* and deserved to be consigned to the deepest circle which Hell preserves for treacherous politicians. Besides, for the religious, like my father, moral as well as political considerations were involved; for like every-one else he was aware of the well-substantiated rumours of the Goat's sexual promiscuity, and indeed was well acquainted with a lady who happened to be one of his mistresses at the time. How could a minister of the Gospel, who was also a liberal, hold up such a man to the admiration of his flock?'

In Rees's account of his father's support of the Lloyd George candidate, he pointed out that R.J. had yielded to the appeal of Ernest Evans against his personal, political and pastoral instincts, and having decided to do so 'flung himself into the electoral battle with an enthusiasm and effectiveness which surprised even his admirers, shocked others and convinced many that his talents were worthy of some larger arena than Cardiganshire and Calvinistic Methodism . . .' But the victory of young Mr Evans rebounded on R.J., who, by some, was regarded, like Lloyd George himself, as a traitor to liberalism, which, said my father, in Wales at that time was a cause 'hardly less sacred than that of religion itself'. R.J. made enemies: some felt that, in preferring the worse to the better cause, he had put expediency before principle. 'This criticism came mainly from those who in their own lives would never have dreamed of taking any other course,' my father commented. 'Some thought that he had been overborne by the influence exerted by Lloyd George and the coalition; some hinted that his motive had been personal ambition and that he had been bribed by who knows what promises of future advancement.' Accord-ing to my father, what made things worse, in the eyes of R.J.'s critics, was that his intervention had been so effective: 'The Welsh admire a victor, but his success always stimulates their secret resentment, and it is the defeated Cato who really wins their hearts. Worst of all, for my father, such feelings divided even his own congregation and as their shepherd he never again possessed that unchallenged moral and pas-toral authority which had previously been his. He had plunged into the muddied waters of politics and had not come out of them unstained; he had shown himself to be, not the servant of truth but a man like other men, with the same passions and weaknesses, a brawler in the market place; his aura had been diminished and in Cardiganshire it would never again have the same brightness it once had . . . What made it worse for him was his own feeling that, as he confessed to me many years later, he had allowed personal considerations to get the better of what he knew to be right.'

So, when the opportunity to leave Aberystwyth came, R.J. took it.

Mrs Rees looked forward to the move because her youngest son could attend the excellent grammar school in Cardiff and prepare himself to fulfil her ambition that he should go to New College, in whose gardens she had once sat and judged it the 'most delectable spot in Oxford, perhaps in the whole world'. The family moved to a house in Tydfil Place, Roath Park, and my grandfather took up his new job as Superintendent of the Forward Movement of the Presbyterian Church of Wales, which was then sending out 'missionaries' into the mining valleys to entice immigrant workers from England and other parts of Wales to join the flock. Different tactics had to be used for these outsiders, for many of them did not speak Welsh and socialism was after them, too. 'A man may well turn to God, if it's a question of saving his own soul, but personal salvation does not seem an urgent matter if his wife and children are starving,' wrote my father. 'During the long years of the great depression which weighed upon South Wales after the First World War, it might well have seemed to the miners that God had abandoned them in their valleys, and if they were to be saved at all, it would only be by their own efforts; it was not surprising that the evangelical seeds sown by the Forward Movement fell increasingly on barren ground and that the con-gregations of its mission halls dwindled as conditions in the coalfield deteriorated. It was not in Jesus but in Mr A.J. Cook that the miners hoped to find a saviour; though in the agony of the miners' strike that followed the General Strike of 1926, he hardly proved to be any more effective.'

Rees found it hard to adapt to Cardiff at first. To him the sur-roundings were ugly and grey after the hills and the sea of Aberystwyth; he missed the presence of his father, who was often absent from the house on his missions to the valleys and his mother was lonely and restless now that she had less to do. He began to be afflicted by the great black moods that were to become a dominating feature of his life. He described experiencing, for the first time, 'that destructive sense of depression which reduces the whole of life to a uniform monochrome and transforms every impulse to thought or action into the meaningless reflex of a mechanical puppet'. His depressions were never to leave him and, intertwined with the peculiarities of Mr Nobody and the effects of drinking a bottle of whisky a day, were often to make him an impossibly difficult person. Even at Oxford, his moodiness was famous. In a letter written to Douglas Jay, whom he first met at New College and who preceded him by a year at All

Souls, Rees said, 'My mind becomes like a superimposed and detached observer, continually mocking me and hurting me until I could beseech it to cease all activity whatever, to be free of its ceaseless sneers ...' His early bouts of depression in Cardiff are also best described in his own words: 'It is a sense which has frequently recurred to me in later years; for those who feel it, it is so acute that it eats like acid into the texture of life, so that it falls away from one in shreds and tatters, like some threadbare garment which has worn so thin that it can no longer hold together. And whether or not it was a fact of our removal that induced my depression at that time, or whether it had its roots in deeper causes, it is true that for a year or two I underwent some mysterious form of sea–change, some hidden revolution in the depths of the self, which coloured all my experiences and made them so dark, confused, and fragmentary that they hardly seemed to be mine at all.'

Rees's early performance at Cardiff High School was so poor that his mother feared that he would be nothing better than a bank clerk. He found it hard to adapt to his new life; he said the other boys laughed at his Cardiganshire accent and his cut-down second-hand clothes, recycled by his mother. But the situation slowly improved as he lost his sense of disorientation and, by his own account, started to steam ahead academically. At fifteen, he had decided he wanted to be a writer and, more than that, he wanted to write in English, not in his mother tongue. 'I have no doubt that, in a sense, and without knowing it, I turned my back on Wales at that moment and since then I have had no reason to regret it,' he wrote. Literature was by then already becoming more important than nationality, 'a means of release from a way of life that had begun to seem cramped and constrained, and the key to some wider world than Wales had to offer'. It was, he explained, as if, in choosing the language of his childhood, he would have chosen to remain a child for ever – 'something Welshmen often do'. In leaving Cardiganshire, he had left the happiness of childhood behind, and, however hard he wished, he could not have it back again. 'The trouble was, I suppose, that I wanted to grow up and felt that I could not do it in Welsh.'

He always held up the Cardiff High School of his day as the ideal of what a school should be. There were lessons in classics, mathematics and history taught by serious, dedicated masters and the best and the brightest of the boys went on to Oxford and Cambridge to become lawyers and doctors and the backbone of the Welsh professional class.

There was also rugby football, for which my father had a talent. Any conversation about football would set him off on one of his pedantries. To him football was rugby football. There was also Association football, which could be abbreviated to 'soccer'. But rugby football was never 'rugger' and the game played with the round ball was not football. Part of the mythology that grew up around my father's reputation was that he was a barefoot boy from humble beginnings. He knew this was far from being the case. Alun Richards, the Welsh novelist and playwright, who became a friend of his in the sixties and was brought up in Pontypridd, described Cardiff High as 'virtually a public school'. 'It was extremely Anglicized and when I played football there during the war we found they had soap in the showers – the fools – when soap was rationed,' he told me. 'We stole it, of course. Perhaps some of the boys might have been a bit rough, but it was that kind of a school.' Indeed, Cardiff High had a tuck shop and its school song was 'Forty Years On', borrowed from Harrow.

My father read and read until reading became an addiction 'as powerful and compulsive as drugs'. He fed it at Cardiff Public Library with a heady mixture of Blake, the French Symbolist poets and Yeats. Rees recalled that he had tried to find some meaning in Yeats's 'combination of Celtic mythology and cabbalistic lore'. At sixteen, he slept with a rose under his pillow at night 'so that I might dream of the Sacred Rose, which is the rose of all the world, and believed that, if only I concentrated enough, I would hear the shields and spears clashing in the Valley of the Black Pig ... For I was possessed by a state of exaltation, which made me believe that in such books I might, with sufficient effort on my part, seize hold of the key to the secrets of the universe; they were not only literature to me, they were the deepest manifestations of life itself...'

One of the great influences on him at school was his history master, Dr R.T. Jenkins, who later became professor of Welsh history at the University College of Wales, Bangor. When he died in 1969, aged eighty-eight, Rees wrote a small tribute to him in *The Times*:

May I add a note to your excellent obituary of the later Dr R.T. Jenkins? I was a pupil of his for five years at the High School for Boys, Cardiff, and have counted this ever since as a very great privilege. As a teacher, he could be severe and caustic, because of the high intellectual standards he imposed on himself and on others. But boys easily forgot his severity because it was always illuminated by wit and humour and by his gift for treating history as if it were something one had just read about in the morning paper. His classes sometimes collapsed in laughter. His understanding of history was both broad and deep. His history course included, in addition to the normal syllabus, a class on Plato's *Republic*, which was an excellent introduction to philosophy, and one in universal history, which to a schoolboy opened up unusually wide perspectives. He was the best teacher of history I have ever known . . .'

During his last year at school, Rees worked harder than ever, bent over his books at the table in the parlour while his mother and father read in silence in their armchairs on either side of the fireplace. 'The crimson tablecloth on which my books were piled, the glowing light of the fire, fed by the best Welsh coal, the dark mahogany furniture and the Victorian prints on the walls, the scratching of my pen on the paper, the absolute and unbroken silence, induced in me a feeling that time had come to a stop and that we three were preserved for ever in an immobility which change could never threaten,' he recalled. He wanted his father to send him to London so that he could be apprenticed to a printer, after which he would try and write novels. That was his initial plan, he said, though he regarded going to Oxford as the 'fate or doom' that lay in wait for him. It was expected of him. His older sister, Muriel, had read history at the University College in Aberystwyth and his brother, Geraint, went to Aberystwyth to read law and then to Cambridge where he took a first, all on scholarships.

My father had already formed a view of Oxford and he did not much like the look of it. In 1926, during the General Strike, he had watched the mounted police charge the crowds in the streets of Cardiff and thought the 'sports-jacketed undergraduates', who had turned up to keep the public services going, looked 'arrogant and oafish'. He wrote, 'Oxford seemed to me the very heart of the English class system, of what we had not yet learned to call the Establishment and, as such, to be entirely alien to the romantic dreams which had begun to haunt my imagination. For Oxford, in my prejudiced view, not merely represented the opposite of what I felt to be the just and natural order of things; what was even worse, it seemed to me the enemy of those affections of the heart and those flights of the mind which are both the source and the material of life.'

Boys from his school, who had gone to Oxford and Cambridge on the strength of their football prowess, returned to Cardiff in the vacations looking different, Rees noted. 'They had adopted all the physical and mental attributes of the typical university athlete of the time, the Philistine outlook, the sporting slang, the college scarves and the Oxford bags. They had become almost caricatures of the type and their native virtues had been submerged by new affectations. The university had not broadened but narrowed them and if this was all it could do I saw no reason why I should follow in their footsteps ...' Of his political beliefs at that time he has left little record, except to say that he already thought of himself as a socialist. The General Strike of 1926 had given him his first view of industrial and civil strife and his sympathies, not at all surprisingly, lay with the miners from the valleys. He also took a small step in distinguishing himself from the crowd; he started to wear white socks.

In the Christmas vacation of 1927, doing what his parents wished him to do, he travelled up to Oxford to take the scholarship examination. He had left Wales only once before – to play football in Gloucester. On the other side of the Severn bridge he entered another country and began that part of his life during which he would never feel entirely at home either in Wales or in England. Waiting in the Warden's lodgings in New College, he experienced his first view of the products of the English public schools *en masse* as they waited with him for their interviews; they seemed to him as if they were of another race, as indeed they were. Their voices were different, their clothes were different, their manners were different. They all knew each other and they knew each other's sisters and brothers and cousins as well; they felt at home in Oxford and it seemed to Rees that it was, for them, the natural and inevitable sequel to school. He watched, warily, as they 'lounged gracefully around and gossiped to each other in a manner which seemed to me the height of elegance and sophistication'. He was not sure whether he really wanted a scholarship and, indeed, wondered whether New College would even consider him; at the same time, he was determined not to feel put down or left out. 'But though I was not sure what I wanted I was also combative and competitive and did not at all like the idea that, with all their advantages, these people seemed certain to succeed where I seemed equally bound to fail.'

His initial sense of unease was relieved as soon as he found the Warden and some of the college Fellows waiting to talk to him in the Warden's study. He was struck by their 'tone of kindness and friendliness ... the politeness of the interest with which they listened to my answers ... the air of gentle consideration ... and in those few moments the seeds of an abiding affection for Oxford were implanted in my heart.' It was, he thought, less like an interview than a 'form of seduction'. He won a state scholarship, a college scholarship and a third one from the City of Cardiff, which gave him the princely income of £250 a year, and in the autumn of 1928, at the age of eighteen, he went up to New College to read history.

# 3

O stands for Oxford. Hail! salubrious seat
Of learning! Academical Retreat!
Home of my Middle Age! Malarial Spot
Which People call Medeeval (though it's not).
The marshes in the neighbourhood can vie
With Cambridge, but the town itself is dry,
And serves to make a kind of Fold or Pen
Wherein to herd a lot of Learned Men . . .

> *Moral*
> *Be taught by this to speak with moderation*
> *Of places where, with decent application,*
> *One gets a good, sound, middle-class education*

'A Moral Alphabet',
From *Cautionary Verses* by Hilaire Belloc

Rees often said that Oxford had been bad for him; it changed him. Others have said that it ruined him, or point out that he exploited it for all its worth. Whatever else, among those staircases, gardens and quadrangles Mr Nobody came on like a young horse in training; the character that he denied he had and which was to lead him into so much trouble took shape and, despite his protestations to the contrary, he took all the fences in his stride. There were plenty of glittering prizes for him. In the autumn of 1931, shortly after taking a First in philosophy (which he said he was not much good at), politics and economics – he had changed schools at the end of his first year – he was elected to a prize fellowship at All Souls.

He left various impressions of his time at New College both in his memoirs and in a piece he wrote, months before he died, for a book published in 1979 by the Warden and Fellows to celebrate the 600th anniversary of the college. Though he was near the end of his life, there is something very youthful about the picture he painted of his time at New College. He had chosen the college, he said, because he was in love with the Middle Ages at the time and wished to live in 'daily and intimate contact with buildings that were the work of medieval hands'. Another reason was that his mother had once spent a 'golden summer's afternoon' sitting in the gardens with his father and had decided that New College was the place for him. His years at the college, he remarked, were not a period of 'unalloyed happiness': there was always a part of him that longed to be elsewhere and he felt that Oxford and the college were shielding him, too protectively, from an outside world of 'harsh realities'. But he was grateful, he said, for the 'haven' of a convalescent home that the college provided for him to get over the 'green sickness of youth'. He recalled the solid ranks of Wykehamists that confronted him for the first time; the college was like 'some kind of pheasantry where the products of the public schools were reared like game birds'. Those from Winchester College, founded by William of Wykeham, gave New College a 'certain prim, slightly self-satisfied, almost ecclesiastical air, though even then modulated to meet the demands of a secular society; to an outsider there was something inexpressibly English and middle class about it all . . .'

Other colleges produced communists, eccentrics, poets and aesthetes; New College, where the aim was moderation in all things, produced socialists. In this piece of writing my father dispensed quickly and kindly with Douglas Jay, who became a close friend, but could not resist having a dig at Richard Crossman, who will make another brief appearance later in the story: 'Crossman would certainly have been voted almost unanimously the man in the college most likely to succeed and perhaps it was because he was so efficiently organized for success that we found each other unsympathetic. Many years later, when editor of the *New Statesman*, Crossman reviewing a book of mine said that at New College he had thought me a young man on the make and I had thought him dull. It would have been truer to say, I think, that I was on a different kind of make from his, and he had thought me frivolous. Besides, I used to play rugby football for the college with him and he used to exasperate me by his assumption that rugby was a matter of brute force rather than intelligence, which offended all my instincts as a Welshman . . .'

At the start of my quest and in response to a small advertisement I placed in *The Spectator*, I received a letter from Sir Patrick Reilly, diplomat and ambassador to the USSR and to France, who was elected to All Souls in 1932, a year after my father. He went up to New College as a classics closed scholar from Winchester in 1928 and his is the first non-family sighting of Rees at Oxford that I have. 'I have a very clear picture of our first meeting,' Sir Patrick wrote. 'We were sitting fairly near each other at dinner in Hall on our first night at New College. I recorded in a letter to my parents in India that I has a strong impression that the English he was speaking was not his mother tongue. I remember that by the end of his three years at New College, he had almost lost his Welsh accent. He had tremendous charm. He was very good company and his conversation was scintillating. When I think of him now, he always has his delightful smile. He was so different from the rest of us.' That evening, in Sir Patrick's estimation, there must have been a little over two hundred undergraduates in Hall, about fifty of whom were from Winchester. If my father felt among strangers, Sir Patrick did not; there were fifteen Wykehamists in his year alone.

What was Rees like in that first year at New College at the age of eighteen? He was certainly very handsome – the 'Byronic' black curls were much noted – and he had already begun to impress with his charm and his intelligence. The rebel was to emerge later, but he had already, perhaps not even consciously, put his background behind him. Sitting at her kitchen table in Pwllheli, my cousin Margaret, who as a child listened to her family discussing the virtues and vices of my father, observed that in that one bound, from Cardiff to Oxford, he had made himself free. All the brakes were off. 'He found this wonderful freedom,' she said. 'There was anonymity, no one knew him. He no longer had to conform, he could be someone else.' He quickly broke two of the rules of his Calvinistic Methodist background: he began to drink and to smoke. Talking about this period of my father's life, Margaret's husband, Owen, said that he felt the constraints of Rees's strict upbringing had perhaps 'thwarted' him and caused some kind of 'conflict in his soul'.

The discovery that he was free was exhilarating to Rees and he undoubtedly made the most of it. But the Welsh Nonconformist culture clings and the ancestral voices keep on calling. It is never easy to escape. Emyr Humphreys, the Welsh novelist who knew my father well later in his life, has explored the Welsh identity in his book *The Taliesin Tradition*, and described Rees as someone whose Welsh connections 'caused him more pain than pleasure'. Emyr considered that along with the sense of freedom from the restraints of his upbringing, my father must also have felt disorientated. 'It would be more like a dislocation.' At Oxford, he would have started to feel the tension of having to choose between two cultures, which, Emyr told me, creates 'huge complications'. 'You can be one of two things all the time,' he said. 'You can be Welsh or you can be English. This has been a constant dilemma since the days of the Tudors and it still exists. Everyone has a choice, but if you are Welsh you have an extra choice. It can be painful. You can compare it to the medieval quest, where you are forever confronted with yet another; you overcome one and you are faced with another. If you are someone with a certain amount of genius, then you are presented with constant dilemmas throughout your life. Eventually, you can achieve some kind of peace from what is essentially a form of torment. But I don't think Goronwy ever did.' Emyr also believed that the great Cardiganshire by-election of 1921 would have left its mark on my father: 'I think by the time he went up to Oxford, Goronwy will have felt that the world of chapels was a false one and represented something that repulsed him. His father, a minister, was a man of great power and influence and the fact that he had become involved in politics far more than he should have done would have been seen, I think, by him, as a form of hypocrisy. He would have been disillusioned.'

Rees's exoticism as an outsider, almost a foreigner, appeared to have made him very interesting and novel to others. While being as far away as it was possible to be from what he categorized as EMP – English, middle class and public school – he played bridge, a useful social attribute. Indeed, the first invitation he received at New College was to play bridge with a Wykehamist who lived on the next staircase in the New Buildings. It was during a game of football that he was first 'discovered', rather like a starlet, by John Sparrow, elected to All Souls in 1929 and later Warden of the college, and seriously launched into Oxford society. To begin with, he simply watched and absorbed what he saw around him. In an unfortunate choice of words, he saw himself, he said, 'as in the role of a spy, despatched on a secret mission from abroad, which, if it were to be successful, depended above all on submerging one's real identity and achieving a kind of anonymity which would allow one to pass unnoticed even in the enemy's most secret citadels.' He became adept at assuming the manners, customs and ways of speech of this country to which he had been assigned. But, writing about Oxford more than thirty years later, he observed: 'Unlike Mr Auden or Mr Isherwood, I did not see myself as a conspirator. After all, I had no one to conspire with, and in any case one only conspires against a society of which one is in some sense a member, as I was not, I felt, of Oxford. Mine was an attitude which, it seemed to me, gave me the pleasure both of the outsider looking in, and, as I became more acclimatized, of the insider looking out; of teetering deliciously between the two societies to neither of which one was really attached.'

This passage illustrates the talent Rees had for creating drama, which is also a Welsh gift. My cousin Margaret put it most aptly when she said, 'Life was always so exciting for Gony and he made life exciting for others. He came in and out of our lives like a flashing light.' Indeed, Rees himself wrote, 'I am afraid that such fantasies played a large part in my life as an undergraduate. No doubt they played a necessary part in that process of finding out who or what one really is, and wishes to be, for which Oxford at that time, like some well-equipped laboratory in which every variety of experiment can be conducted, offered such admirable facilities. They also added a sense of excitement and elation to one's activities, as if they were all attended by the risk that at any moment one's disguise might be uncovered and oneself revealed for what one really was.' Two factors, he said, helped him to protect himself against such a danger; he was 'excessively impressionable', and quick to 'adopt the protective coloration necessary for survival in any alien environment' and possessed an 'overdeveloped' faculty which made it easy for him to assume the manners and habits of other people. Both attributes, whether they were gifts or faults, he did not know, he exploited to the full. The result was, he felt, that much of his time at Oxford was spent in an 'elaborate, and on the whole, I think, successful exercise in simulation'. There was a certain pleasure in the performance, he said, but there was also a considerable strain, which showed itself in frequent outbursts of temper, sulkiness and aggressiveness, which must sometimes have made him a difficult companion, even to himself.

But terms at Oxford were short, so he did not have to keep up his masquerade, he admitted, for more than eight weeks at a time, and then he could go home. He maintained that he did not do very much work. Instead, he seemed to have discovered the delights of pleasure. Freddie Ayer, who was at Christ Church and became a loyal, lifelong friend after being introduced to Rees by one of the hordes of Wyke-hamists, said that, at that time, he had based his attitude to life on a model conceived by Walter Pater and that Rees seemed to have adopted it, too. On the value of experience, Pater held that success in life was 'to burn always with this hard, gemlike flame, to maintain this ecstasy ...' One should not form habits, which are relative to the stereotyped world, but 'catch at any exquisite passion or any contribution to knowledge that seemed by a lifted horizon to set the spirit free for a moment, or any stirring of the senses, strange dyes, strange colours, and curious odours, or work of the artist's hands, or the face of one's friend ...' To fail to do so was to 'sleep before evening'.

That was not something Rees ever intended to do. He said he felt that only at Oxford could he have learned that pleasure is so important as to be worth taking seriously. In some notes that I found among his papers, he described how a nameless don had taught him that the pleasure principle was something which, far from being suppressed, should be cultivated and developed. But, of course, pleasure, as such, was not very highly regarded in his Welsh background; it was seen only as an accidental by-product of the pursuit of higher things. The notion that pleasure 'might be pursued, and be valued, for its own sake, is a necessary ingredient in any form of happiness and can even be enjoyed when happiness has been lost, that far from being ephemeral it could be one of the most lasting sources of satisfaction, he wrote, 'is not easy to adapt to Calvinist doctrine, nor is it one which easily occurs if life only rarely and intermittently rises above subsistence level.' Others taught him the importance of pleasure and it was a lesson he took 'eagerly to heart'. He said that not only his tutors, but his Wykehamist friends 'in whom the belief that life, if not quite real, is certainly earnest, is too deeply engrained', disapproved of his new-found hedonism. His philosophy tutor, H.W.B. Joseph, warned him about the dangers, both moral and practical, to which he was exposing himself. Rees recalled, 'He was genuinely shocked that anyone like myself could elevate pleasure to a prime objective in life ... he continued to warn me against the intellectual errors implicit in the pursuit of pleasure and to hint mysteriously that there were even graver forms of corruption to which it might lead, though what he could have known of these I could not understand, for his own life combined worldly innocence with austerity to a degree which I have never come across again in any man.'

The college chaplain was particularly distressed. 'He is *far* too great a social success,' he was heard to say, 'he will never get a First.' Rees maintained that he did not know what all the fuss was about. He regarded the concern as 'misplaced because the kind of pleasures of which I was so enamoured were innocent ones, so innocent indeed that I sometimes wondered whether they really qualified as pleasures at all.'

He met witty people, read Proust and pretended that Oxford was a kind of Paris. As a 'creature of fashion', he became infatuated with all things German, he wrote poetry and made lots of friends who shared his literary interests. 'Oxford during the late 1920s was a nest of singing birds, some of whom were to make a permanent contribution to literature,' he wrote. He met Louis MacNeice, a fellow Celt and clergyman's son, who was later to become a neighbour of ours when I was a child, and they drank and talked about poetry and football. He walked in Christ Church Meadow with Freddie Ayer who told him that he had solved all the problems of philosophy. 'I talked incessantly, went to many parties, drank rather more than was good for me, and altogether enjoyed myself almost excessively. So that my undergraduate days have retained in memory a special colour and flavour, as if drenched in some golden liquor that was only distilled at such a time and at such a place.' Douglas Jay, who knew my father reasonably well at New College, said he was very 'charming, sweet and gentle' for a large part of the time, but could quickly change to become emotional and violent. 'He would suddenly announce that he was wholly opposed to Oxford and did not want to have anything more to do with it. But it was just a mood, really. When I say violent, I mean verbally violent, and it was a little like coping with a woman when he was like that. You knew, it was best not to argue with him.'

Patrick Reilly was a member of the Essay Society at New College, of which, so he told me, my father became president. He recalled being grateful to Rees for having saved him from an embarrassing situation. 'It was the most prestigious club,' he said, 'and most of the papers read to it were on philosophical subjects. When my turn came I was not capable of talking adequately about philosophy and, being interested in architecture, I read a paper on the Gothic Revival in Britain, not a subject likely to provoke a lively discussion. I have never forgotten how kind Goronwy was to me that evening. I can see him now, standing by the fireplace, facing the audience and doing his best to make something of a discussion out of my pretty pedestrian paper.'

My father so vividly described his time at Oxford in *A Chapter of Accidents* that it is hard to improve on his version. As homosexuality and politics are both aspects of this period of his life which he wrote about in connection with his friendship with Guy Burgess, I searched in the cardboard boxes for any unpublished material relating to his undergraduate days that might be enlightening. In his memoirs he commented that women were second-class citizens in the hierarchy of the university and that it seemed to him as if undergraduates, and their elders, in those days lived in a state of sexual infantilism. The notion that men should live without women was accepted as 'perfectly natural' but he thought that under these conditions 'what men love and admire most is formed in the male image'. A 'large number' of undergraduates in his time were, he said, homosexual, and for many it was simply a fashion. In the great war between the Hearties and the Aesthetes, it was the 'flag of culture as opposed to philistinism' and a symbol of that 'intense cultivation of personal relations in which Oxford placed such faith'. It was also a flag of rebellion; to be homosexual, he said, was the easiest and most flagrant way of affronting the moral standards of the Britain of Stanley Baldwin. Rees made it very clear that he did not think that 'young men designed to form the executive and governing class of a great country should have received their higher education at institutions which were a combination of a monastery and a nursery'. His instincts rebelled against such a system of values, and he did not believe there was likely to be much of a place in it for him. He thought that it rested on false intellectual and emotional foundations and this belief separated him from his friends. 'Public schools were bad enough; it was even worse if they were to provide the standards for adult life. I felt reinforced in my feeling that Oxford was not for me nor I for Oxford.'

In his notes I found the following: 'They . . . the standard bearers of the cause of homosexuality . . . included some of the most gifted of the undergraduates, and among the dons, those who were most generous and inspiring; they were exceptions and in some curious way they proved the rule. For it was not the active practice of homosexuality which was the characteristic feature of Oxford; it was the prevalence, even among those who were least aware of it, of a homosexual attitude of mind and heart which profoundly affected people's ways of thought and feeling and continued to do so long after they had left Oxford and had become the most respectable of citizens and fathers of families . . .' It could be detected in a manner of speech, he said, handed down from dons who had most prestige and influence among the undergraduates. 'Even now, forty years later, there are certain English voices, tricks of phrase, a particular way of phrasing, which, wherever I hear them, often in the most unlikely places, strike me that the speaker must have been at Oxford at the same time as I was.' There were certain affectations of dress which proclaimed an undergraduate's loyalties; and there were particular manners of gesture, gait and comportment which displayed them equally clearly and which, he said, were the 'outward and visible signs of an inward commitment'. At Cambridge, homosexuality had achieved the status of a philosophy, encapsulated in G.E. Moore's famous pronouncement that there is nothing which everyone will grant absolutely good except works of art and personal relationships.

Rees added: 'Many of my friends were themselves homosexuals, the more so because at the time a liking for the arts tended to be identified with sexual deviation, so that to be a poet or an artist it was almost necessary to be, or pretend to be, a homosexual...'

In *A Chapter of Accidents*, Rees wrote that, on his arrival at Oxford, he had believed himself to be a 'socialist and a Marxist', a 'worshipper at the shrine of what was sometimes familiarly referred to as the MCH; the Materialist Conception of History'. He explained that his version of socialism was 'confused and incoherent', and he wondered how devout a Marxist he could be as he was an 'inveterate egoist' and had never considered how this could be reconciled with Marxism. He described his own brand of personal politics as being a kind of mongrel 'largely derived from Marx, William Morris and George Bernard Shaw' and 'deeply coloured by a kind of naive industrial populism, based upon an intense admiration for the South Wales miners and an acute sense of what seemed to me the injustices which they suffered in their lives and in their work.' If someone could have waved a magic wand, he would have chosen a world governed by the South Wales Miners' Federation. Rees's notes revealed a little more about his vision of a perfect world. There was a Welsh musical version of the Psalms, which he used to sing in chapel when he was a child and which haunted his memory:

> Who are those who are arrayed in white garments?
> They are those who came out of great tribulation
> And washed their clothes as white as snow...

His idea of revolution had a dreamlike quality: it took shape in 'the figures of men and women who had risen from the pits and valleys of Wales, like the dead from their tombs, and had been washed clean of the grime and coal dust of the dark underground in which they spent their lives before presenting themselves in shining garments before the seat of judgment at the great day of revelation'.

Rees had no idea of what he was going to do with his life. The two characteristics of Mr Nobody that his Oxford friends noticed were that he appeared to be very frivolous, despite his intellectual ability, and quite lacking in ambition. He was never to become ambitious; he never envied anyone else. At the end of his last year at New College, much to his surprise, he got a First in PPE but was told it had been a 'close thing'. In Cardiff, his success was big news. In my grandfather's diaries I found a small yellowed cutting from a South Wales newspaper:

Mr M.G. Rees of Tydfil Place, Cardiff, has taken first class honours at 21 in the honours school of Politics, Philosophy and Economics at Oxford, where he went on an open scholarship.

All in all, 1931 was an eventful year for him. He returned to New College in the autumn to take up a senior scholarship, which he had accepted because he did not know what else to do, and it had already been suggested that he try for All Souls. But at the end of August, his mother, Apphia, died of angina, which Rees later said was 'the worst single thing that has ever happened to me' and he was left dazed and bewildered. At night, in the house in Tydfil Place, he could hear his father crying out her name in his sleep. Of that time, he remembered, 'Unless one is a singularly pure character, grief, especially when compounded with guilt, confuses all one's reactions; one does not know how to respond to a situation for which one had deliberately contrived not to prepare oneself. My mother's death ... deprived me of any power to make a rational decision about the future.'

Shortly afterwards, in September, he wrote to a close friend: 'Except for a strange sort of loneliness and apathy, I am happier now. I don't suppose I shall ever be quite the same again because the world, at least for me, is different. I suppose I was foolish and thoughtless because I could afford to be then, because whatever happened I could always suddenly return home and see my mother. Everywhere, really, I depended on her and I felt that whatever I did it didn't really matter. You weren't at Oxford in my second year when I fell in love with a very beautiful and wild young man and this earned almost everyone's disapproval and a good deal of contempt ... for being, as they said, weak and drunken and going downhill. They didn't understand, but I shouldn't have behaved as I did if I hadn't been quite certain that nothing I did really mattered. Now I suppose it does. I can never suddenly leave everybody and come home as I always have done because at home will be no different from anywhere else ... The saddest thing about my mother's death is perhaps that my father's life is so ruined by it, because for him it is almost inconceivable to be without her. They adored each other and had been born within a mile of each other in Cardiganshire and had spent all their lives together...'

In a letter to Maire Lynd, whom Rees had met at Oxford while she was an undergraduate at St Anne's, lodging with the family of Warden Fisher at New College, and with whom he appears, by the nature of the letters sent to me by her daughter Lucy, to have been in love, in a rather on-and-off way, he said he felt inadequate and unable to help his father in his grief: 'I have many things left and my interests are with the living, but he has nothing. I can't do anything to help him, because I'm not like that. My family think me callous because I will not speak about her but if they would only understand the saddest thing about dying is that the dead, having gone out of existence, can have no life at all, no feelings, no rights or duties, no claims. If it were not for that it would not be sad at all. But my family do not see this and so, while missing the real tragedy, wear themselves out all the more because they grieve for her as if she were alive and that is like throwing oneself against a brick wall, because the dead can't respond at all ...' He had wept, he said, for his mother. 'I cried this week. Crying is the most terrible and shameful thing there is, at least to me, because I feel humiliated, and I will never cry again, whatever happens. But nothing worse than what has happened can ever happen again...'

Two letters written that summer, before his mother's death, to Douglas Jay, who was then at All Souls, give a good idea of Rees's state of mind. The first is on mauve writing paper: Shiela is Shiela Grant Duff, a schoolfriend of Peggy Garnett, who became Peggy Jay; B.J. is Maire Lynd.

Tydfil Place
Cardiff

Dear Douglas,

We are involved in ruin: I have lost your dinner jacket and also the key of All Souls which is not to be found. Your ruin is greater than mine. I'm very sorry. I don't know quite what to do: if I had forty pounds I would give it to you but as you know I haven't and I suspect you haven't either. I hope there is some way out of this disaster. I may have left it somewhere in my room and am writing to Allnutt [*Rees's scout at New College*] about it and also about the cost of your dinner jacket and I will write and tell you the result. It is very boring here, but even boredom has the advantage of being very uncomplicated and I am able to walk and to write. I hope to finish my novel this month. I would like to take advantage of your bed (this sounds, as perhaps Shiela [*Grant Duff*] would say, a little impure) but I'm afraid I can't. I have to stay here and work and be with my people as I am going to Germany after my viva, in time, I hope for the revolution. But I expect to be in London for perhaps a week before my viva so I shall see you then.

This morning I had an invitation to a garden party of B.J.'s mother; will you be there? I am glad B.J. [*Maire Lynd*] refreshed you: I take the deepest interest in her, so do not smirch my character with her as you seem to have smirched it with Peggy and Shiela who appear to believe me the most abandoned and immoral of men, and that, as you know, I am not . . . David Garnett's *The Grasshoppers Come* [*a novel about a long-distance flight in a monoplane*] excited me greatly and I thought it the best new book I had read since *A Farewell to Arms*. It is very short but seems to have all the qualities of the best writing – a plot which does not, like most modern novels, stand still, but progresses and not only progresses but is composed in such a way that even the mere events seem to happen beautifully, and that, of course, is to be found in very few books – and also his style seems to me extremely moving, largely, I think, because it is purely narrative and not discursive. I hope you will read it and write to me about it. I was greatly excited by it. At home where nothing happens an event like that takes the place of falling in love with people. Write to me sometime: I am very sorry about the key. My love to Peggy and Shiela.

Goronwy

It requires the greatest strength of mind not to be driven mad by this hot weather when one is in a town.

This letter followed:

Dear Douglas,

Here is a poem for you to read: I wonder if you will like it: write and tell me if you do or not. It was very nice of you to take the loss of the key so calmly, but indeed I was depending on your accomplished lying. You were quite right to tell B.J. I would not go to Golders Green: but I wish I were. I am beginning to get wild and bitter again as I do after some time by myself. B.J. disturbs me, she is exactly like a young girl of Turgenev's. I am very angry with myself for not knowing B.J. better when I had the opportunity, but I was rather frightened by her . . . I want very much to leave everything and everybody I knew behind me: I hate the thought of doing the All Souls and don't want to get one. If I don't leave Oxford now I shall become as genteel and unreal as everyone else there (but I don't think you are). But of course my people, like most people regard gentility and unreality as admirable things to be . . . I am angry and miserable for having fallen in love again with someone who cannot fall in love with me. I feel as if I were the only species of a genus and all the rest of the world comfortably arranged, according to their various kinds, in species where generic characters make understanding possible but exclude me.

Goronwy

Douglas Jay told me that he did not know who the person was 'who cannot fall in love with me', but the letters Rees wrote to Maire Lynd at that time indicate that it was almost certainly her. They had a very intense correspondence throughout that summer, before and after the death of Rees's mother, and he was doing his very best to appear interesting and complicated, as well as affectionate. Maire, who was reading Greats, was the daughter of writers Robert and Sylvia Lynd, and many of Rees's letters are written to her north London home in Keats Grove, Hampstead. A good example of Rees pulling out all the stops was received by Maire in July 1931 (she kept all his letters until her death in 1990). In one corner of the first page he had noted: 'Yesterday, I heard a Mozart symphony which made me feel like a heavenly being. He is the first among the sons of light.' He desperately wanted to see Maire and had sent her a poem – 'At the present time a passion for writing poems has seized me, whether good, bad or indifferent . . .' She should read George Moore – 'I worship him both as a writer and as a person' – and Proust. Maire's last letter, said Rees, was 'very delightful', but he refrained from saying anything more intimate. 'If I begin to talk about you I shall be cryptic and absurd again,' he added teasingly. But Maire was in love with someone else, though she and Rees continued to see each other for some years.

The unhappy predicament of unattainable love was, not surprisingly, the theme of Rees's first novel *The Summer Flood*, which had not yet been completed when, in the autumn of 1931, he returned to New College to spend a further year there reading history. He had spent part of the long vacation in Germany, tutoring the son of a baron in Silesia. The visit was the beginning of the long love affair Rees had with Germany, which never really ended. Germany simply became a part of him as it did for many of his contemporaries. Many years later he wrote that it was hard to explain the kind of attraction which Weimar Germany exerted on his generation at Oxford because so little of the original was left after the war. To try to recover the image to which they were so attracted would be, he said, like 'trying to restore a lost masterpiece which has been painted over by a succession of brutal and clumsy artists'. The task was rendered even more difficult because the masterpiece never really existed and the Germany of Weimar in which they believed was really only a 'country of the imagination'.

He and his contemporaries, Rees said, suffered from a number of illusions: that there was no distinction of guilt between the Allies and the Central Powers in the Great War, that both sides were equally responsible for 'that appalling tragedy' and that the terms of the Versailles Treaty were unfair, a 'pure assertion of the rights of the strong over the rights of the weak and of the victor over the vanquished'. For this reason, it was clear that Germany, more than any other country, including their own, deserved sympathy and understanding. 'It must be remembered that we were very young men, who will always respond to ideas of this kind. The young dislike power, because they do not share it; the middle-aged adore it, because it gives them some assurance that the world will continue to be as they had known it . . .' To sympathize with Germany was, he explained, 'a mark of our violent revulsion against the Great War and its consequences, and against the generation which had helped to make it and to conduct it to victory'. They were making a protest at the disgust they felt for the England of Baldwin, Lord Birkenhead and Sir William Joynson-Hicks. But it was not just a political stand: Weimar offered 'all those experiments, in literature, in the theatre, in music, in education, and not least in sexual morals, which we would have liked to attempt in our own country, but which were so patently impossible in the face of the massive and infuriating stupidity of the British middle class . . .'

Exciting reports about Germany were coming back to Oxford by word of mouth. 'Ever since the inflation young Englishmen had visited Germany in greater and greater numbers,' Rees wrote, 'and they returned to us in Oxford with wonderful travellers' tales of this land of freedom and, even better, licence; where one could be on the right side, the proletarian side, in politics, and at the same time take advantage of the fact that social disapproval has ceased to exist; where morals had been discarded as a bourgeois prejudice; where sex was permitted, indeed encouraged, to take any form it chose, however eccentric; where nightclub tables were decorated with phalli made of marzipan; where Mr Issyvoo was having a perfectly delightful time living in a slum in the Hallesches Tor; what more could a young man need to satisfy his heart's desire?' Just as everyone else was doing, Rees wanted to go and see 'the whores and the queens and the Lesbians on the Kurfürstendamm', 'tramp in the Black Forest with the Wan-

dervogel and breathe the inexpressibly sweet air of a society in decay
...' Instead he found himself out on the Silesian plains, riding with
his charge and shooting wild cats with Baron Franz von Reichendorf.

Returning with his traveller's tales to Oxford in the autumn, Rees
recalled in his memoirs that he had met his history tutor from the
previous year in the street while he was looking for rooms, and that
it was he who had suggested that Rees should sit for the fellowship
examination. However, as he refers to 'doing All Souls' in his letter
to Douglas Jay written that summer, it is clear that he had already
been planning to take the examination. Rees never kept a diary and
he always had difficulty remembering dates. Indeed, this inability to
recall a sequence of events with accuracy was to cast much suspicion
on what he had to say about a significant event many years later.

On 2 November 1931, All Souls Day – three weeks away from his
twenty-second birthday – Rees was lunching with some friends in his
rooms when a servant from the college came to inform him that he
had been elected to a fellowship and would be expected, in that
capacity, to dine at All Souls the following evening. A similar message
was conveyed to Quintin Hogg. I know little about the papers Rees
sat, but Freddie Ayer, in the first part of his autobiography, *Part of My
Life*, told of his own unsuccessful attempt to try for All Souls the
following year: 'It was the first year in which it was possible to take a
paper in philosophy. Previously the examination had been confined
to law and history, though the inclusion of general and essay papers
had allowed the examiners sometimes to give preference to candidates
of general ability over specialized lawyers and historians. The candidates were also invited to dinner, as a test of their manners, and
summoned to an interview at which they were required to translate a
short passage at sight from Latin or Greek or one of the principal
modern languages. Like most others, I chose French and performed
reasonably well, though without reaching the heights attained in the
previous year by Goronwy Rees, who had greatly impressed the
company by seeing that the word "*dragons*", which his nervous com-
petitors translated as "dragons", must in the context mean "dra-
goons".'

Rees was not the first product of the state education system to have
achieved a prize fellowship of All Souls, but he was the first Welshman
to do so. The *Western Mail* published the following paragraph under
the headline 'Welshmen at Oxford' and written by 'Our University
Correspondent':

The most distinguished performance by a Welshman in Oxford in recent years is the achievement of Mr M. G. Rees, who has just been elected to a fellowship of All Souls. This is generally regarded as the highest mark of scholarship in historical studies at Oxford. The honour had come to Mr Rees at an early age. His career at Oxford has been characterized by sustained brilliance. He has written much poetry and is at present engaged upon a novel. He will undoubtedly go far.

There was also an announcement in *The Times* on 3 November, and Rees's father, at Tydfil Place, subsequently received the following telegram: 'ALL SOULS FELLOWSHIP RATHER BEWILDERING LOVE GONY. This was followed by a short letter on a sheet of paper that had had its top half raggedly torn off:

Dear Dada and Geraint,

I was elected to the first All Souls fellowship. I'm very bewildered and don't know quite what to think about it. I go and dine there as a Fellow tonight! The other Fellow elected was Quintin Hogg. Sir Charles Oman* delivered a hostile speech against me at the election because my history papers, he said, were the worst he'd ever read and it was an impertinence to offer them at a fellowship examination! I'm moving into All Souls sometime this week. I think I'll probably come home next Monday. But I'll write again after this first dizziness has vanished. I must come home as all this is so fantastic. I'll go mad if I stay here.

I'm very surprised and pleased

My love,
Goronwy

It is very much in Rees's character that, writing nearly forty years after the event, he remarked that his election to All Souls 'in those days ... regarded as one of the greatest gifts Oxford had to bestow and a sure guarantee of success in whatever career one chose to adopt' made him feel guilty. He knew only too well how proud his father was of him and that his mother, too, had she been alive, would have regarded it as the culmination of all her ambitions. He felt guilty, he said, because he thought he detected in the award, once again, the hand of 'chance or luck', and because it identified him with a way of life which was the opposite to what he wanted. For he, too, had 'succumbed to the wave of radical political feeling which was begin-

---

* Sir Charles Oman, 1860–1946, was elected a prize Fellow of All Souls in 1883, which he described as the 'greatest piece of good fortune' that ever came his way. He became Chichele Professor of Modern History in 1905.

ning to sweep through the universities . . .' As the Depression deep-
ened, it looked as if the day of revolution might be at hand and All
Souls was not the place to be when it arrived. Like so many events in
his life, it seemed absurd to Rees that in the year of 1931, which
Arnold Toynbee called the 'Annus Terribilis' – when 'government
after government was falling under the impact of the depression' and
the 'walls of the capitalist Jericho seemed to be crumbling before one's
very eyes' – he should be 'safely and comfortably installed at the very
heart of the Establishment'.

Among its forty members, All Souls had, at that time, one archbishop, one bishop, an ex-Viceroy of India, several cabinet ministers
of the detested Conservative Party, two of the country's most brilliant
barristers and Geoffrey Dawson, editor of *The Times*. Rees occupied,
in his absence, the rooms of Sir John Simon, then Foreign Secretary.
He wrote: 'I used to go through his wardrobe and finger, and sometimes even wear in cold weather, the excellent thick striped flannel
shirts in which it abounded.' The college was so kind and generous
to him that he was quite at a loss for something to rebel against,
although everything about All Souls, he noted, 'represented the
kingdom of this world which was about to be punished for its sins,
and which, in any case, it was the duty of any good Calvinist or
socialist to reject'. But whatever his reservations about being in such
a place of privilege, Rees remained deeply attached to All Souls for
the rest of his life and, however badly he had behaved, was always
warmly welcomed back and forgiven. For the time being, the college
offered him every comfort, and all he had to do, as the most junior
and youngest Fellow, was 'to prepare the salad before dinner', which
I am sure he was not very good at and, in the common room after
dinner, as Mister Screw, 'to decant the port', at which he was probably
more accomplished.

When Warden Pember – an old Harrovian and a cricketer –
congratulated Rees on his fellowship and asked him if he had any
plans for the future, Rees replied that he had very little idea; there
seemed no point now in taking the history school in his extra year at
Oxford. A rest was recommended after which, the Warden suggested,
he should go abroad, look at some pictures and go to the opera.
According to Rees's version of the meeting, he told Warden Pember
that he wanted to visit Vienna and Berlin and to improve his German.
Although he did not mention this to the Warden, his ulterior motive
for going abroad was to see if he could be fortunate enough to get a

glimpse of 'revolutionary events' that seemed to be at hand in Germany and Austria. The emoluments of a prize Fellow were £300 a year, with free rooms, a free dinner and subsidized drinking, and Rees stepped into a way of life that was to set an unfortunate model for the future. The college statutes also obliged him to spend a certain number of nights on the premises in any one academic year. 'It was not a heavy burden,' he wrote. 'If I spent three months in Oxford I could go away for at least a year.'

It was so pleasant and agreeable at All Soul that Rees did not go abroad until much later than expected. As he explained in *A Chapter of Accidents*, he felt he had better make some preparations for a biography of Ferdinand Lassalle, friend of Marx and Engels and founder of the German Social Democratic Party, which he proposed to write while he was away. A.L. Rowse, in *All Souls in My Time*, claims responsibility for that idea, but Sir Patrick Reilly has established that Rees told the college in May 1932 that he had embarked on a study of 'The Rate of Investment, Including More Particularly the Theory First Formed by Keynes in *A Treatise on Money*'. There is no record of Rees applying for leave to stay in Germany and no reference to a biography of Lassalle. The minutes of a general meeting of that period also show that Rees, because he had no career plans, became a Statute 111 6(ii) Fellow, and was granted a further five years after his initial two at an annual salary of not less than £300. By the time Rees finally went to Germany, during the spring term of 1932, there had been developments in Oxford which were to have a profound effect on him.

# 4

A man lives not only his personal life, as an
individual, but also, consciously or unconsciously,
the life of his epoch and his contemporaries.

From *The Magic Mountain* by Thomas Mann

In his final term at New College, at a dinner party given by Douglas Jay at All Souls, Rees was introduced to Shiela Grant Duff and Peggy Garnett, who were to go up to Lady Margaret Hall the following autumn. Shiela had two distinguished grandfathers: Sir Mountstuart Grant Duff, a leading Liberal MP and Governor of Madras, on her father's side, and Sir John Lubbock, the first Lord Avebury, on her mother's side. Her father had been killed in the 1914–18 war and she had been brought up by her mother in Chelsea. She had made friends with Peggy at St Paul's Girls' School and between school and university had done the season as a debutante. Peggy was the daughter of Maxwell Garnett, Secretary to the League of Nations Union, and later married Douglas Jay who lived next door in Hampstead. She and Peggy were both in Oxford for their college interviews and Douglas had invited them to dinner at All Souls to meet his closest friends. In her memoirs, *The Parting of Ways*, Shiela recalled that she wore a powder-pink velvet dress, made out of the court dress of one of her aunts. Douglas had already told her a lot about Rees: that he was brilliant, charming and wicked, a poet, scholar and seducer. To Shiela it was a 'magic' evening and she described Rees as being 'short and dark with green eyes and black curls' and 'Byronic and beguiling'. It was at the Balliol Commem Ball later that summer, according to her account, that she and Rees both discovered how attractive they found each other. She recounted how Rees had flung his arms around her at the end of the ball and kissed her: 'I accepted it as innocence not seduction and I was right. We promised at our next meeting never to deceive each other and never to do or say anything we did not mean.'

Just over sixty years after that ball, I went to Castletownshend in County Cork to talk to Shiela, now Mrs Michael Sokolov Grant, about my father. It was grey and raining as I drove from the ferry to her house, overlooking the sea, and I wondered how she would react to the questions I wanted to ask her. Her book had come out three years after my father's death, and had, of course, revealed to me something of his life before he married my mother in 1940. It occurred to me that it was highly unlikely that Shiela and I could possibly have seen Rees in the same light. She had, I believe, loved Mr Nobody and had considered marrying him, while I had ascribed to him all kinds of qualities that I wished a father of mine to possess. I knew from reading her book that he had made her unhappy, but I was also aware that right at the end of his life, after my mother had died, they had renewed their friendship and that this had been something of an emotional experience for them both. *The Parting of Ways* provided, for me, a very detailed account of my father's activities during the thirties, about which I knew so little, and I remain deeply indebted to her.

As I got out of the car, Shiela walked towards me, studying my face, 'No, I don't recognize anything there,' she said. She did not want me to write about Rees: it was she who had said that daughters should not write about fathers. Nor did she want me to see most of the many letters of his that she has kept, because, as she said, they were love letters. She was sending them to the Bodleian Library, she told me, where they would not be available to be read for fifty years, but she would show me a few of them. As the light Irish rain fell outside, we sat and talked but were disturbed by an exceptionally beautiful pure white cat scratching with one paw at the French windows, indicating that it wished to be let indoors. I asked what its name was. 'He's called Goronwy because he is so gentle and affectionate,' she replied.

Rees was, for the next three years, what Shiela described in her book as 'hauntingly and hoveringly ... the centre of my life' and, according to Douglas Jay, it was 'understood', before long, that they would marry. She was certainly most impressed with his election to All Souls, comparing Rees with Quintin Hogg, now Lord Hailsham, who was elected the same year, an Eton and Christ Church scholar with four years of Mods and Greats and one of Law behind him, and heir to a great Conservative tradition. Douglas had written in a letter to Shiela after Rees's election, 'You must be so happy tonight and you deserve to be because you saw Goronwy's worth yourself with your own mind ... and you accepted and admired him from that moment whatever anyone might have said about him. I am happy too. I never thought a year ago I should have that exaltation over again. And yet I have, because Goronwy was elected for the same reasons as me (for though he has lots of supreme talents which I have not got, he was actually elected for the moderate ones he shares with me and the interests in the truth we both care about) and he was elected in the same circumstances [*Douglas's sister had died just before his All Souls' exam*] and for that reason I can hardly conceive of the violence of the struggle he must have gone through ... I am as happy as last year because this fellowship, for all the intrigues, is given as a prize for the most intellectual qualities we value most – a desire for truth about the most important things and a determination not to be weak or lazy or dishonest in finding it. It's a triumph for that, whether it's him or me. That's what you must love him for if you love him for anything.'

They talked a lot – and very earnestly – about love in their little circle that was to be joined, shortly, by Isaiah Berlin, who was elected to All Souls in 1932 but had already known Rees as an undergraduate. Whereas Shiela maintained that Rees thought love was an act of imagination, Douglas had other ideas: 'Love is like understanding, that grows bright gazing on many truths ...' Rees became quite carried away by his subject when he wrote to Douglas on his new All Souls writing paper: 'I think we agree about what it is that one loves: it is a person and not any particular quality or group of qualities, not even all his or her qualities. A person is like a substance, to be distinguished from its attributes, and I think we are conscious of this in being in love and so somehow know that no change of quality can affect our love, because the substance maintains its identity through all change of quality so one cannot answer that a person whose qualities change is no longer the same person and therefore no longer to be loved. Because there is identity in change and it is just that identity which one loves and so is proof against change. But also it is just that identity which cannot be expressed or ever known by universals, because it is an individual substance and therefore cannot be said or apprehended by means of qualities, which are abstract or attributive. But we do know it and love it, just as we know and love works of art. Do you agree with this? ... It is very nice of you to offer your car, but unfortunately I can't drive it ...'

Shiela added to her first impressions of Rees: 'When I met him in his last year at New College, he was adored because of his great charm and amusement and his quick mind and his kindness.' He had 'that Welsh softness ... very polite'. She had written to him at Douglas's suggestion, when his mother died: 'When Goronwy got back to Oxford and I was there, there was a bond between us.' It was difficult for him, she said, being a Celt and 'being brought up one way and then going to Oxford', but she never heard him talking against his family at any time. It was even more difficult for him, she thought, going to New College and 'having to adapt to all those Wykehamists' because 'they all wanted to be public figures and he didn't'. She felt that although perhaps he would always have had deep internal conflicts, 'they were fomented at Oxford'. Of their close relationship, she wrote: 'I learnt more of books, listened to more music, looked at more pictures with him that anyone else and also received greater gentleness, affection and consideration. But he was very sensitive and complex. Coming from a religious Welsh home ... he had to take on protective colouring at New College among the clever, worldly and self-confident Wykehamists. "I know all the harm it has done me," he wrote to me in 1934, "and that it was very bad for me." ' In a letter to Shiela shortly after they met, Rees explained: 'By now you will have discovered that I do not accept goodness and happiness easily, that I am apt to sneer at them and denigrate them, that, as you say, I make vices of my virtues and virtues of my vices. I do not think it is conceit or egomania which makes me believe that I do it because happiness and goodness are so incredibly difficult to achieve, not to be had without immense effort, and so all appearances of them should be mercilessly scrutinized before they are accepted.'

Isaiah Berlin, however, despite his lifelong affection for Rees, is now more than candid about some of my father's more extreme and erratic ways; 'sweet', 'gentle' and 'innocent' were not words that he felt could properly be applied to his friend at that time. When I visited him in his rooms at All Souls he told me: 'Charming he was, but innocent never, or at least, not by the time I met him. The charm was irresistible and he got things very easily. He was friendly, he was physically attractive, he had a beautiful voice and charming manners, and he always seduced girls with no difficulty. That's what he enjoyed doing.' Rees, he said, had moved easily in homosexual circles, but he was not a homosexual himself. Rees had told him that two men had fallen in love with him, but Isaiah was not sure whether to believe it as Goronwy had not always been very truthful. He did not think my father had ever 'consciously sought to attract men'. Maurice Bowra, who was about ten years older than Rees and then a don, becoming Warden of Wadham at the end of the thirties, had described Rees, not entirely flatteringly, as a 'normally-sexed pansy', which Isaiah felt was quite accurate. He did not paint a very pleasant or attractive picture of my father as he was at that time: 'By inclination he was not a homosexual, so he must must simply have fallen in love with Shiela.' Shiela did not seem to be very concerned about Rees's reputation. She had formed her own impression of him and she was amused rather than alarmed when she heard that there were those who already thought of him as a 'rogue' or a 'scamp'.

A letter written by Rees to Douglas Jay from Cardiff some time before Christmas 1931 gives some indication of how he was feeling about his future and about other areas of his life. In it he told Douglas that the Warden of All Souls had recommended him for a job on the *Manchester Guardian*, but that the idea of living in Manchester was 'rather appalling'. However, he added, more cheerfully: 'But new things always appeal to me as an easy way out of the past, so I think I shall go.' He was also 'horrified' by England going off the gold standard, which had taken place in September: 'The crisis rather appals me by its stupidity, as far as I can understand it. Am I wrong to think that now, after abandoning the gold standard, we have done exactly what Ramsay MacDonald [*who had formed a coalition government in August and been expelled from the Labour Party*] and Snowden [*also expelled*] said at the beginning was impossible and unthinkable? It seems to me that if leaving the gold standard is now quite safe and involves no dangers, i.e. inflation, then it did not do so at the beginning when we were all threatened with depreciation on the German example. But if this is so, then we have used about £200 million in credits in trying to protect the gold standard when all the time it was quite unnecessary...'

Rees had been to Merthyr Tydfil, he told Douglas: 'It was once a very prosperous colliery town of perhaps 70,000 people. Now every one of them is out of work and have been for a year. In the mornings all the streets are absolutely crammed with the colliers talking and smoking cigarettes, as if it were a Saturday afternoon or the evening after a Cup Tie. But most of the colliers stay in bed till tea time because there's nothing to do and they needn't eat in bed. Most of them have about five or six children. If there is ever a local election, the only candidates are Labour or Communist, anyone else would be unthinkable. One night I was there the mayor held a meeting of protest against the dole cuts, all sorts of people spoke, they sang the Red Flag and the meeting ended up in a terrific riot.'

The situation made him very angry and upset. 'How I used to think that we all knew about these things, it was no use being sentimental, and such a state of affairs though unfortunate was inevitable. It seems to me now that it is a question of degree. If reason tells us (and I don't think it does) that we must cut the dole, we can't tax any more, we must preserve the economic system, and so these people must suffer, there's nothing to be done, it seems to me we can reply that this sort of thing is so bad that nothing could possibly be worse. It is incredibly ugly and dreary, what Balzac calls "misère sans la poésie" – the worst that can happen. Also it is unjust, and I agree with the colliers who say they would rather starve as long as the rich starve with them. Do you think this nonsense? It oppresses me infinitely – I can't stop thinking about that incredible town. To talk about goodness and beauty and truth when such things exist seems to me complete hypocrisy. All this worries and saddens me, I think, more than my mother's death. That, I suppose, was inevitable, but she really was a sort of assent of goodness and beauty; all she left behind is a sort of infinite. One can live and be happy, recognizing that death is possible and certain, even though unjust and final. But Merthyr seems to me a complete negation of life. I can't really express its significance really. What one can do I don't know, but one needn't live as if it didn't exist. That's a sort of final treachery to everything one admires. Don't think me hysterical. I think what I say is really true and must be admitted . . .'

He wanted to tell Douglas, too, how indignant he felt about a leading article in *The Times*. '*The Times* is a monster. It advised us the other day on how to behave in the crisis,' he wrote. 'It told us to surrender our "continental holidays", not to change sterling into foreign currencies, and not to let taxation restrict expenditure; rather, it said, diminish savings! All this with no recognition of what working people think. When it said "you", it showed quite clearly what sort of people it knew its supporters to be. It is a sort of insult, a monstrous blindness and it sickened me. Will you read all this? Perhaps not, but tell me what you think.'

When in the spring term of 1932, Rees went to Freiburg and Vienna and to Berlin to start work on his Lassalle book, he did not seem to have applied himself very seriously to the project. There, he fell in with some actors and appeared in a nationalist film that was being made by the production company UFA. Directed by Gustav Ucicky, *Flüchtlinge* ('Refugees') tells of the harsh experiences of German settlers in the Volga in their flight from the Russians in 1928. Isaiah saw the film at a cinema in Salzburg the following year and, to

56

his 'great astonishment', realized it was Rees playing the part of a soldier from a Highland regiment 'ordering people to go this way or that'. The British Film Institute has only a preservation copy of the film so I was not able to view it, but an archive assistant read me a contemporary review which said that the acting was 'first class', though British audiences might find the Nazi propaganda 'crude'.

Rees came home in the summer to persuade Shiela to return to Germany with him, but, as recorded in her book, her mother was worried about her daughter's reputation and did not think it a good idea. Taking the matter into his own hands, Rees wrote a letter to the worried Mrs Grant Duff which Shiela did not read until after her mother's death. He was keen to reassure Shiela's mother that the 'world' that minded about young people going away together was passing away: 'Already their day is over and their spite is meaningless. These beastly gossipings all come from people who feel "they have a position to maintain" in society; the irony is, of course, that they really have none and deserve to have none . . . It really does not matter about the mental instability and uneasiness of the educated classes: anyone who, like Shiela, possesses a considerable amount of spontaneity and passion and a greater amount of courage than most people, will escape these dangers. Her difficulty is likely to be that she will not find a society in which such virtues are valued and respected and common to others.' Shiela's mother allowed her to go.

It was apparently the despised Richard Crossman who suggested that they should stay in Wickersdorf, a progressive school in the hills of Thüringen, for a reading holiday. Rees set off first and sent Shiela this description of the place: 'I have arrived here safely and here is an account of what I found. Father Cordes lives in a small house in the village. It has a verandah with a most wonderful view, with two rooms opening on to it, one of which is mine and one is to be yours. The village is very small and primitive, about twenty houses in all and the one bad road running through it is crowded with dirty brown children. We can have all our meals at the school, including breakfast, though if we want to, we can have it by ourselves on the verandah.' There were about eight people staying at the school, a teacher to give lessons, a tennis court and a swimming pool and pools in the forest. 'The country is lovely,' his letter continued, 'of hills and valleys covered with woods and huge fields of corn, some new and green and some golden ready to be cut. And one is really in the country. From the verandah one can see nothing but miles of hills and corn and trees.

There is a garden where we can lie in the grass and the walks are lovely. We should be able to do a great deal of work ... Come soon.'

In Wickersdorf, Rees worked on another novel, *A Bridge to Divide Them*, which was not to be published until 1937. In the evenings he read to Shiela from his first novel, *The Summer Flood*, which had appeared that summer while he was away. In a letter to Douglas Jay he said that he could not get on with the new book; he could not find a satisfactory new style and there was 'an embarrassment of a vague, unformed mass of material.' Shiela was 'happy and lovely ... gay and serious by turns', and rid of many of her complexes. He had rather surprised himself by being able to live quite alone for six weeks with only one other person. Rather patronizingly, he said he felt she was developing intellectually. He told Douglas: 'Her life, I think, is a natural growth in what is good. Now she reads *War and Peace* with fascination.'

*The Summer Flood* was dedicated to his father and mother. It is about an undergraduate who returns from Oxford to spend his summer vacation with his family on the Cardiganshire coast and falls in love with a cousin. They are caught together in a sudden storm on one of the St Tidwal's islands that lie within sight of Pwllheli, where Rees used to spend part of the summer at the home of his by then married sister, Muriel, together with the rest of the family. At home in Wales, my cousin Margaret remembered, 'It caused a furore ...' Not only was Rees instantly identifiable, but so were Geraint and other members of the family: and there were all the details of his physical longing for his cousin laid out for the world to read and, worse, a very emotional section on a homosexual affair. The opening sentences are lyrical and I include them here to show how my father wrote in the style of the 'sensitive young man':

When in clear weather, you look south across Cardigan Bay from any high point on the arm of the Lleyn peninsula, you may see the whole mountainous coastline of Wales extended along the waters as far as St David's Head, at the tip of Pembrokeshire. At such times there is a perfect balance between the two elements of sea and land. But when, with the setting sun, the white strip of sand binding the feet of the hills has ceased to be visible, that natural equilibrium disappears, and there emerges a combination of mountain and sea which satisfies a romantic taste alone ... It was just at that point of day when the clear and determinate beauty of the scene was surrendering to the approaching dusk that a young man walked languidly across the country, half moor and half marsh, which separates the two houses of Brynhyfryd and Penmorfa . . .

The young man, Owen Morgan, bore a remarkable resemblance to the author. 'He was of more than average stature, a little clumsy in build, and whatever interest his appearance might arouse would attach itself naturally to the large and curiously shaped head. His broad face slanted sharply to a pointed chin that gave to his chubbiness a surprisingly sensual, half faun-like expression, which was accentuated by his full lips and the fluctuating glance of his eyes. Across his forehead fell a few locks of his black curling hair . . .' Owen's expression and 'play of feature' changed from time to time: 'When the sun lit up the ruddy face, the dark hair and the sensual mouth, he would have been thought of by any passing girl as a young man remarkable only for good looks and a pleasant expression. Such moments gave way to moods when, the mouth relaxing and even pouting a little, the curls of the hair becoming more apparent, the eyes gazing down and half covered by long lashes, the young man, under the influence of meditation or desire, threw off several years of his not very advanced age, and presented an appearance of childish and even feminine beauty . . .' He had a 'clear, extremely logical, and even imaginative mind', which often went unnoticed 'amid the physical charm the young man exercised . . .'

Owen, who was at Oxford and staying at his sister's house during the vacation, was about to meet his eighteen-year-old cousin, Nest, again after two years. He was bitingly critical of her parents who were 'innocent of any knowledge of the world, beyond the limits of a narrow circle' and had taught Nest that kissing was an 'irredeemable bargain with the power of evil . . .' There are other characters who would immediately have been recognized by members of his own family. Owen's brother, Richard, was at Cambridge and wanted to be a barrister. He 'regarded himself as the supreme court of arbitration in all the disputes of family life, even those in which he himself was involved' and thought that Owen, unjustly, received far too much attention. ' "Richard's absurd," said Owen. "He's not really respectable but just very moral. He does everything he thinks he ought to. But he's so stupid that the things he thinks he ought to do happen to coincide with what most people consider right and proper. If he were a little cleverer he'd be just as moral but everybody would think him frightfully wicked." ' Richard is confused by his brother, who was reading Marx and going to be a revolutionary one week and the next week talking about how he was going to write the best novels in the world. Another character is a stuffy aunt, to whom Oxford was a 'Babylon of the modern world', the 'gilded resort of fashionable and wealthy drunkards, gamblers and rapers'.

Besides organizing a suitably romantic and dramatic setting where he could manage to kiss Nest, Owen was much given to thinking about himself and the world around him. A silver cigarette case, a gift to him from someone called Sasha at Oxford, had him recalling the past year. ' "My dear," said Sasha, turning away from the flames that lit up his beautiful head, "you must take it. I got it for you and I want you to have it. It would be beastly of you to refuse it now." ' At Oxford parties, Owen had met 'everyone from decayed men of fashion to novelists, playwrights, poets, indeed all the somewhat disreputable celebrities who, from weekend to weekend, simulating an intense and unconvincing youth, appear at Oxford in search of distraction . . .' Sasha was from a 'long line of ancestors transmitting with corrupt blood the aristocrat's privilege of arrogance'; friends were 'virtuously disgusted' at Owen's weakness and warned him that his friendship with Sasha could do nothing but harm. They had spent a year together and there were plenty of evenings like this: 'The light of the great fire – it was winter, the end of the Michaelmas Term, Owen's birthday – flickered on the walls of Sasha's room . . . In the wavering rosy glare the sporting prints of shooting and hunting on the walls . . . seemed to come to life, and horses, hounds and men to move and race again over the green turf. Sasha leant his head against the side of the chair in which Owen sat, until Owen's dangling fingertips almost touched his smooth, blue-black hair . . . There they sat, Owen in the deep chair before the cavernous fire, on the floor at his feet, his head thrown back, Sasha, his legs curled beneath him like a girl.' In the end, as, gradually, people came to speak of him with 'almost the same contempt as of Sasha', Owen saw himself as weak-willed and, although he kept the cigarette case, he gave up the relationship. 'Revulsion awoke in him against the humiliating bondage to which he had been reduced, when but a movement of the head or a turn of the body seemed a command to be obeyed whatever shame it involved . . .'

Mr Nobody also makes an appearance in *The Summer Flood*. This is Rees, at twenty-two, thinking profound thoughts about the vagaries and inconsistencies of his nature: 'So he would think that in just such a way as he had parted his hair upon the side because Sasha complained it was vulgar to part it in the middle, or as he had tried, with success indeed, to adopt the drawling vowels of the English because the swift, short accents of the Welsh jarred upon the ears of his friends, so perhaps he set his beliefs to the prevailing winds of whatever country he inhabited, assessing truth and falsehood, and good and evil, by their mere suitability to climate. From such a conclusion he was saved by a belief in his own integrity, a secret strength known only to himself, and by the memory that everywhere, in his home and at Oxford, he had been found recalcitrant and rebellious, rejecting what he might easily have accepted had convention or the desire to please been the determining factor in his life . . .' Owen found that at Oxford he longed for the simple affection of home, and at home he longed to be free at Oxford, but 'Wherever he might go, he took with him a sensibility which stamped all circumstances with his own con-fusion . . .'

In Wickersdorf, Rees was clearly wrestling with his confusion, for Shiela recorded that she was having problems with his moods. Once, as she recounted in her memoirs, she came in to find him tearing up his new novel: 'He had been reading my diary and was angry and hurt by its ridiculous childish confessions.' Rees, she concluded at that time, was 'a very complex character'. She felt that while he came to know himself a little better, he baffled many others. In August, Rees wrote to Douglas: 'It was a year today my mother died: last night I wept, wished to die, and having lived a year without her, found it impossible to face the thought of more years: and indeed as you say, her death seems more like a contraction of the good than a mere personal loss. Shiela and I have been extraordinarily happy: but we quarrel sometimes because she finds my moodiness intolerable . . .'

In July, martial law was imposed on Berlin and Brandenburg, ostensibly because of the civil disorders resulting from the activities of Nazi storm-troopers, and there was considerable unrest just before the Reichstag elections in July. Rees wanted to go and see Berlin under martial law and Shiela noted that the cafés and broad pavements of the Kurfürstendamm were 'thronged with every kind of sinister human being one could possibly imagine: slinking men in black capes and huge black sombreros; women with cropped hair and wearing shirts and ties; others, both men and women, with ghastly painted faces; cripples, beggars and, behind them all, the dreadful uniformed and booted strike forces of the political parties swaggering up and down.' They were both 'appalled' and Shiela was 'frightened'. They wished they were back in peaceful Wickersdorf.

From Germany, they went on to Vienna, where they met Oxford friends and Muriel Gardiner, an American friend of Stephen Spender's, who was studying psychoanalysis under Freud. She proposed that Shiela, Shiela's brother, Neill, and Rees should join her on a trip to Moscow. As Shiela recalled, 1932 was the year when it first became fashionable for the idealistic British Left to look with favour on Russia, a country which claimed to have solved the problems of slumps and unemployment. However, seeing the situation for herself, she came to the conclusion that working in a factory or on a collective farm, being ill in hospital or shut up in prison, seemed 'an unpleasant fate' and that in Russia people looked 'drabber and shabbier and showed more signs of suffering on their faces than anywhere else I had been'. But she came away 'still as prepared as before to defend its new civilization,' she wrote. 'Russia was our hope of peace and our protection from poverty, for were not wars and unemployment the consequence of an economic system whose motive was private gain rather than public good?'

Writing in *The Spectator* in 1936 about Sir Bernard Pares's admiring visit to Moscow after an absence of twenty years, Rees, drawing on his own experience, remarked that 'it is doubtful whether, unless for political or theoretical reasons, anyone would have come to the same conclusion two or three years ago'. The 'anyone' he referred to was, of course, himself. A visitor then, he wrote, saw the sense of need, of strain, the lack of food and clothing, and even an awareness of the great industrial plants and factories arising under the Five-Year Plan could not diminish the impression of fatigue and exhaustion on the faces of the workers of Moscow or Leningrad. He saw little of the good clothes and plentiful food of which Sir Bernard spoke; the shops seemed empty of all save unsatisfied customers; and he saw even less of the spirit of well-being and happiness which recent visitors had observed. The Five-Year Plan was almost more of an effort than the nation could bear; it could only be carried out by continuing to use the political methods that 'characterized the communism of the intervention and the civil war'. The same 'discipline and intolerance' could be seen in the defences of political terrorism made by communist propagandists, Rees said. He went on to be a little less critical of the regime: 'But it was the success of the Five-Year Plan, the material progress it achieved, which has made possible the evolution of Russia in the last five years, and that evolution has given considerable justification to the communists' claim that ideals of personal or political freedom, of justice, of culture, of peace, can only be realized when the material and economy basis for them have been properly prepared. It is the realization that these ideals have prospered with the success of the Five-Year Plan which has lately made Western observers anxious to secure the co-operation of Russia in the reconstruction of Europe, and even to suspect that Western democracies may have something to learn from the Soviet Union.'

In January 1933, Hitler became Chancellor of Germany, which was a momentous enough event, but for Rees, on a personal level, something almost as monumental was about to happen. As the year began, Douglas Jay was working on *The Times* – but was shortly to leave because he did not feel that readers were being properly informed about what was happening in Germany – and Rees had, after all, decided to try the job on the *Manchester Guardian*. There, he wrote leaders, but it clearly did not please him, for he stayed only a few months. At the end of the summer term he was back in Oxford and, according to Michael Berry, now Lord Hartwell, playing, more vehemently than ever, one of his favourite roles, the Angry Young Man: 'It was my last year at Oxford and I had hired a steamer for a commem ball and had invited 30 or 40 guests; we went up the Cherwell to Folly Bridge and back again to the ball. I invited Goronwy and sat him next to my sister Sheila, and there was a furious row. My sister was very forthright and Goronwy was very left-wing. He told her that my family had made money out of coal and all the miners were out of work and getting silicosis and that sort of thing...'

Germany was certainly not a place for holidays any longer and Isaiah Berlin suggested that Shiela and Rees should meet him in Salzburg after the end of term and that they should all visit Sub-Carpathian Ruthenia. Shiela recalled, in her book, that they heard Mozart played in Salzburg and then set off by train into the Tatra Mountains and on to Kosice, the capital of Sub-Carpathian Ruthenia, and Uzhgorod, which was the end of the line. Isaiah practised his 'basic' Slav, met some White Russians who told him of the last days of the 1917 revolution, and had long philosophical discussions with Rees, of which Shiela said she could not understand a word. Isaiah told me that Shiela and Rees 'argued with each other all the time, though they were in love, no doubt...'

At the beginning of 1934 Rees was back in Berlin, pursuing his research into the life and work of Ferdinand Lassalle, of whom, under the terms of his All Souls fellowship, he was still intending to write a biography. In the suburbs of Berlin lived Professor Hermann Oncken, the greatest living authority on Lassalle and author of the standard biography, and there was plenty more material in the Preussische Staatsbibliothek. Rees took lodgings off the Kurfürstendamm and had daydreams about his subject. In an article I found in the cardboard boxes, he writes: 'I felt the presence of Lassalle very close to me; after all he had walked these streets so often himself, dressed in the height of fashion, his head full of youthful dreams and ambitions, and impelled by a restless energy which had impressed everyone who knew him, even his bitter critic and rival, Karl Marx. I maintained with him an endless dialogue of question and answer, all directed at discovering the secret of his flamboyant personality, dandy, man of affairs, *coureur de femmes*, a frequenter of the salons of the rich, yet the most effective socialist leader of his day, whose tragi-comic death in a duel was mourned by the entire working class of Germany; but where was the flaw, the error which had doomed his great political creation, the German Social Democratic Party, to destruction?'

It was no longer fashionable in intellectual circles to be in Berlin; Hitler had been in power for a year and, according to Rees, had 'totally destroyed the culture which made Berlin as irresistibly attractive to enlightened young men, particularly English ones, as Rome to Catholics or Mecca to Muslims'. Berlin, he wrote, 'had been a place of pilgrimage, with its own Holy Places ... but now the shrines were desecrated and abandoned, their high priests and their congregations scattered to the four winds, hunted, persecuted and traduced. The more fortunate of them sat in cafés, editorial offices, publishing houses in Paris or Prague, or took ship to England or America; in their own country, they took refuge in attics and cellars or in remote hiding places in the provinces, and by their hundreds and thousands were hunted down and herded into prisons and concentration camps. It was the greatest intellectual diaspora since the fall of the Temple in Jerusalem ...'

Rees found that Berlin, once the capital of republican and democratic Germany, had become a 'city of phantoms'; it was as if the whole structure of life had crumbled away under Hitler and his stormtroopers. Everything was 'provisional and ephemeral', 'desperately balanced between disasters past and disasters yet to come ...' There was an uneasy silence and order in the streets, almost sinister, 'as if by straining one's ears one might hear the cries and screams of those who were hunted to death like rats in a cellar'. There was no point in reading German newspapers to find out what was really happening, so Rees talked to the foreign correspondents, including Frederick Voigt of the *Manchester Guardian* whom he had met already, in the Taverne café. They told him that distinguished and learned people who had been so prominent in the cultural and political life of Germany had simply disappeared. 'For the most part it was a repetitive story, of exile, arrest, imprisonment, torture, murder; they had been swallowed up in an abyss too terrible to contemplate and I sometimes felt that, if one were to keep one's sanity, it was better not to think too much about such things,' he wrote.

Rees also took every opportunity of talking to young Germans about what was happening: 'They were not, as one might have expected, liberal or left-wing opponents of the regime; they were young men of conservative, even reactionary principles, and from the best military families, to whom Prussian virtues still meant something different from National Socialism, and perhaps their strongest feeling was a sense of shame, not unmixed with snobbery, that such a man as Hitler should exercise unlimited power over them ...' Years later, on a battlefield in Normandy, he picked up a newspaper and found some of their names on the list of those who had been executed for their part in the attempted assassination of Hitler. Things were bad that winter, but they were going to get worse. There was gossip and rumour everywhere; no one could foretell the future. And so Berlin waited 'like an animal which feigns sleep yet is still alert to any sign of approaching change or danger ...' It was very cold, there was snow, the storm-troopers aimlessly tramped the streets. 'In the icy air there was a feeling strangely compounded of expectancy and fear ... It was the air of a city waiting to see the Janus head of the future, without knowing which face of it would be revealed.' He found it fascinating; he felt that it was there, more than anywhere else in the world, that the shape of the future would be decided, and even if it might be distasteful, he wanted to see what it looked like.

There was plenty to absorb Rees, but his research project, on the other hand, was not going well. He found Professor Oncken a great disappointment: 'He was the perfect type of meticulous German historian, arid and desiccated, to whom all facts were of equal value, because they could be verified. To him, history ... was whatever was preserved in the documents, and nothing else, and he regarded me with disapproval as one who would evidently never satisfy his own austere standards . . .' The professor regarded Rees's project as a kind of 'bold guerilla raid into territory which he had long ago staked out as his own'. As for any implication that there might be some relationship between Lassalle's achievement and the great drama that was now being played out in Berlin, he regarded such ideas as unworthy of historians, all the more because he was terrified of any attempt to involve him in discussion of the current political situation in Berlin. Rees used to leave the professor's comfortable shabby house, with its books and neatly ordered garden, in a mood of profound depression. Oncken, he found, 'deprived the past of any life or colour it ever had, and in his hands it became a shapeless mass of inert material whose only value or interest was that it gave the historian the opportunity to write a book about it . . .' He concluded: 'There were times when I thought that Professor Oncken, as a type of the German academic, was more worthy of study than Lassalle himself, and that, with all his faults and his virtues, he threw more light on the contemporary situation than anything one might learn from the history books. Perhaps the men who wrote them might, in the last analysis, be more interesting than what they wrote . . .'

There were problems, too, at the Staatbibliothek, because most of the books and documents Rees wanted to look at were subject to censorship and unobtainable: 'They had become a kind of political pornography.' He had been given a reference by Sir John Simon, who liked helping members of the college, however junior and obscure. Rees noted that he was an odd kind of a friend for him to have: '. . . there was probably no subject in the world on which we agreed . . . but the Nazi authorities very reasonably concluded that no friend of Sir John's could be a danger to the Third Reich and I was given the freedom of the library.' There he grappled with whatever he could obtain on his subject's political philosophy and wondered what contemporary lessons could be drawn from the antipathy between Lassalle and Marx: could it be that therein lay the germ of the bitter conflict between the socialist and communist parties in Germany, which had such fatal results; and 'could its effects be seen even now as communists and socialists alike were hunted down in the streets and cellars of Berlin?'

In the evenings Rees took German lessons from a Frau Meyer who lived in the flat above him in the same apartment building and had, before the war, been governess to the children of Herbert Asquith when he was Prime Minister. Tears came into her eyes when she spoke of England and the Asquiths 'as if they formed some island of the blessed, immune to the misfortunes of other people'. She taught him to speak German with an impeccable Prussian accent, which caused confusion to anyone listening to him. Rees explained: 'German friends, on first acquaintance, were apt to ascribe to me some reactionary Junker background . . . working-class friends regarded me as an alien in their midst . . . because they suspected I was a German from a Germany which represented everything they hated most.' In later years, au pair girls who came from Germany to look after my children seemed quite shaken after meeting my father for the first time as they were convinced that he was a German himself and were puzzled that I had not mentioned this to them. One of them had to be gently persuaded not to address him as 'Herr Professor'.

With socialist friends, Rees visited the small pockets of opposition to Hitler and soon realized that they were very few in number and were growing fewer every day. 'Those who actively opposed Hitler were not only a tiny minority; they were defeated and dispirited, living in the middle of industrial Berlin like castaways on some desert island with only their hopes and their dreams to sustain them,' he wrote. 'It was impossible to believe that they would ever feel the touch of victory . . . As the long winter drew on and gave way to spring, it became increasingly clear that, whatever happened to Hitler's regime, it would not fall as the result of any opposition from inside Germany itself, and with this realization I fell victim to a profound depression, as if for the first time I had really grasped the full horror of what had happened to Germany . . . For me the air of Berlin began to grow oppressive with the sense of defeat and England began to beckon as temptingly as it did to Frau Meyer. Socialism, I thought, had died in Germany, as Kafka's hero, K, had died in *The Trial*, "like a dog, as if the shame of it would outlive him". If there were to be any salvation for Germany it would have to come from abroad . . .'

Rees's feeling of depression came out very strongly in an eleven-page letter he wrote to Shiela from Berlin. 'Here what seemed a nightmare in London is the sober everyday reality: the betrayal and the death of every human virtue; no mercy, no pity, no peace; neither humanity nor decency nor kindness: only madness, shouted every day on the wireless and in the newspapers, spoken by ordinary people as if it were sober sanity: and sixty million people pleased and proud to be governed by a gang of murderous animals,' he told her. 'The madness, the bestiality, the crude, ugly inhumanity – can you wonder that, among this, thinking of it continually, seeing it, living by it, I long for you and everything you mean to me – *luxe, calme et volupté* – for you and for rest, for a quiet mind, for happiness, until in body and mind I am tortured by the longing for it.' Shiela hurried to Berlin to comfort Rees when she received this dramatic letter and they were very happy to be together again and to talk about their plans for the future.

From Berlin, Rees had also written to give Shiela his advice on her idea that she wanted to be a journalist. He approved, but had a warning: 'The only danger about journalism, from a personal point of view, is that journalists are apt to become bores: they are more interested in their work than any other class of people I know and think of nothing else and since their work is above everything NEWS they are apt to acquire the type of mind which is only interested in the very last minute. One is apt to get into what is, intellectually, a very unreal world of public events and incidents, it makes one a little conceited and one is apt to forget that what one is dealing with is a very thin surface of events ... You see, one's life is like this ... You read a great many newspapers, you follow all the interesting stories, you see innumerable people in the course of your work, a great deal of your time is spent in talking to people about your work: you are very interested and excited by it all: and the days slip away very quickly until at the end of a few years you find that you are incapable of thinking of anything but NEWS. So it is very important that one should try and spend as much of one's free time as possible alone, when one can read, and think, and even more, look at the world which has nothing to do with NEWS ...'

Several pages are missing from this letter but Rees ended by telling Shiela that he would like it very much if she read *Les Fleurs du Mal*, and the diaries and prose poems and essays of Baudelaire: she might like to write a essay about Baudelaire and send it to him to read. He added: 'It sounds a very foolish and priggish thing to say, but one way to make your life happy and to prevent stupidity in oneself is to think continually of those who were truly great...'

Suddenly feeling that he had had enough of 'that great sad city,' Berlin, one evening Rees packed his bags and, the following morning, took the train to Paris.

In his own writing and when telling the story, Rees was always under the impression that he had met Guy Burgess for the first time in 1932. But he made a mistake, as he frequently did with dates. After carefully checking and cross-checking with whatever relevant memoirs I could find, it would seem that the fateful meeting took place at the beginning of the summer term of 1934, on Rees's return to Oxford from Berlin. Rees was then twenty-four; Guy was two years younger. It was an encounter that was to have dire consequences and to cast a blight over the rest of my father's life. His friendship with Guy was also to inspire, in *A Chapter of Accidents*, one of his best pieces of writing.

According to Rees's account, he met Guy at a dinner party given by the American lawyer and academic, Felix Frankfurter, who became a justice of the US Supreme Court and was spending a year in Oxford as a visiting professor from Harvard, where he taught at that time. In his memoirs of the scholars and statesmen he has met and admired, *Personal Impressions*, Isaiah Berlin, who was also at the dinner, recalled this particular evening because, in his opinion, it was unusually lively and sparkling for an Oxford gathering. Among the other guests at the house provided for the Frankfurters in Parks Road were Freddie Ayer and his first wife, Renée, Rees, Maurice Bowra, and Sylvester Gates, a friend of Bowra's who had been a student of Frankfurter's at the Harvard Law School and was now at the Bar. Isaiah remarked later that, among one or two others present was, he thought, 'the famous expatriate Guy Burgess, who was then staying in Oxford...'

The evening also gave rise to an Oxford story that was related at many other dinner parties over the years. It began with a row between Sylvester Gates and Freddie Ayer about Wittgenstein. The bone they were fighting over was a sentence in Wittgenstein's *Tractatus Logico-Philosophicus*, which, roughly translated from the German, means 'About what you do not know, you should keep silent.' Sylvester maintained that Wittgenstein said it twice in the book, while Freddie insisted he had only said it once. The matter was resolved when Freddie was sent off in a taxi to look up the reference in the text in his own flat and returned with the news that he himself was wrong. The sentence was in the preface *and* in main text of the book itself; Freddie had to pay a forfeit of ten shillings. Of the evening, Isaiah wrote: 'Why was this so memorable? Only because the mixture of intellectual gaiety and general happiness generated at this and other dinner parties was too uncommon in so artificial an establishment as the University of Oxford – where self-consciousness is the inevitable concomitant of the occupations of its inhabitants – not to stand out as a peak of human feeling and of academic emancipation. Courage, candour, honesty, intelligence, love of intelligence in others, interest in ideas, lack of pretension, vitality, gaiety, a very sharp sense of the ridiculous, warmth of heart, generosity – intellectual as well as emotional – dislike for the pompous, the bogus, the self-important, the *bien-pensant*, for conformity and cowardice, especially in high places, where it is perhaps inevitable – where was another such combination to be found?'

Felix Frankfurter thought Oxford a very odd place – for some time he was unable to find a copy of the American Constitution.

Rees's version of the evening concentrated on Guy Burgess but also made an important and highly pertinent point about Maurice Bowra, who, in his cultivation of undergraduates, was the most influential don at Oxford. Guy, he recalled was staying with Maurice, whom he described as someone who 'had probably influenced me more than anyone else at Oxford'. Bowra was said to be the greatest wit of his day, a formidable talker and a homosexual, and Rees certainly fell under his spell and continued to see him for many years. I think I detected Maurice more than anyone else in Rees's rule that to be boring was almost the worst sin in the world and in his enormous enjoyment of gossip though that, of course, is a Welsh characteristic, too. I am able to smile to myself now when I think of my father's frustration when trying to instil some of the social *légèreté* and sophistication of his Oxford days into his children, as if he were a disappointed Maurice Bowra who, instead of being able to collect around him the most brilliant undergraduates, had found himself with the duds.

My father already knew something of Guy's reputation. While still an undergraduate, he had once driven over to Cambridge with a young don who was apparently in love with Burgess. When my father reminded Guy of this trip much later he discovered something that he was never to forget: Burgess's habit of keeping every single letter that was written to him. As Rees told the story, Guy said that he remembered the visit well and added that he still had all the don's letters. 'I thought that perhaps he was boasting; but after a search through the incredible disorder of his rooms he produced a neat little bundle of letters labelled with the name of the enamoured don.' Rees recalled. But Guy, and the significance of his squirrelling away of letters, comes later.

On that evening, Rees remembered, he and Guy immediately

became great friends. 'Indeed, he did not belie his reputation,' he wrote. 'He was a scholar of Trinity and it was thought that he had a brilliant academic future ahead of him. He talked a great deal about painting and to me it seemed that what he said was both original and sensitive, and, for one so young, to show an unusually wide knowledge of the subject. His conversation had the more charm because he was very good-looking in a boyish, athletic, very English way; it seemed incongruous that almost everything he said made it quite clear that he was a homosexual and a communist.'

After dinner they walked back to All Souls together and drank whisky in the deserted smoking room late into the night – the first of many such evenings spent over a bottle of Jameson's. Describing how Guy had made a pass at him, Rees added that he 'quickly and cheerfully desisted when he discovered that I was as heterosexual as he was the opposite'. Guy would have made a pass at any young man, he explained, because 'sex was both a compulsion and a game which it was almost a duty to practise'. However, according to A.L. Rowse, as he recalled this incident in *All Souls in My Time*, Rees did not cope with Guy's advance quite as smoothly or coolly as he professed. Rowse wrote: '... I set eyes on Guy Burgess only once, when Goronwy Rees brought him in for a drink after dinner. Burgess was in the smoking room only half an hour before the junior Fellow came up to complain to me – I was senior that night – that Burgess had made a pass at him. What was I supposed to do about that? I said merely: "Well, you can keep out of his way."'

They talked, according to Rees, about the relation of painting to the Marxist interpretation of history and about the busmen's strike Burgess was helping to organize in Cambridge and my father found that there was 'something which was, as it were, his very own, in everything he had to say'. Marxism, Rees wrote, was for Guy simply a way of looking at the world which seemed as natural to him as the way he breathed; he was the perfect example of the 'intellectual-homosexual-aesthetic-communist young man who was rapidly establishing himself as the classical, and fashionable, type of progressive undergraduate.'

A recently published book, *Deadly Illusions* by John Costello and Oleg Tsarev, a former Russian agent, has established from the KGB files that Guy was at this time trying to arrange to have himself recruited as a member of the still evolving Cambridge spy ring. Kim Philby, who had asked his economics supervisor, Maurice Dobb, a junior Fellow of Pembroke College and himself a communist, how he could best serve the cause, had been put in touch with a front organization in Paris and had already been spotted as a potentially valuable recruit by a London-based talent scout for the NKVD, forerunner of the KGB. Dobb had produced a list of seven Cambridge contacts as possible candidates for recruitment and Guy's was the last name on it; Philby added, however, that while Burgess was ideologically 'very strong' his character was that of an *'enfant terrible'*. It is also known that shortly after Rees first met him, Guy was sounded out by an NKVD 'illegal' agent in London. There were reservations about him, however keen he was to offer his services: he knew about Philby and he knew about Maclean and because he was an inveterate gossip his discretion could not be counted on.

Rees could not have been more forthcoming about how impressed he was by Guy at that first meeting. His contemporaries, he said, adopted communism in the thirties as an intellectual creed, but 'somehow there always remained in them an assimilated residuum of their liberal upbringing which was in conflict with the faith they professed'. In Guy, there was no such conflict; it appeared to have been resolved: 'In this respect, at least, he never changed through all the years I knew him, so that, whatever the vagaries of his conduct or his professions, I somehow took it for granted that fundamentally he always remained a communist, even if, for reasons of his own, he chose to deny it ... Marxism had entered so deeply into him that he simply could not think in any other way. This was a characteristic which I came later to recognize in professional communists whom I met in Germany and Austria, but never, so far as I am aware, in any English ones.'

Rees and Guy were so pleased to have met each other that they made tentative plans to visit the Soviet Union together during the summer vacation. In the end, Rees was unable to go, although Guy did and came back and told his new friend all about it. The year ended in a somewhat vague and uncertain way for Rees. In Berlin he had decided that instead of writing about Lassalle he was more interested in undertaking an 'intellectual history' of the young Karl Marx. But when he put forward the proposition to Warden Adams of All Souls, it was greeted with 'alarm'. The Warden, Rees recalled, 'felt that the College should not support so unorthodox a project'. What was he to do with himself? In the months to come my father was to turn away from Oxford towards the bright lights of London, where he would find life more exciting; tracking his movements during this time I was to find increasingly difficult.

# 5

And I in the meantime
Will be flirting
With this one and that one . . .

Libretto by Lorenzo da Ponte
From Mozart's *Don Giovanni*

By this stage of my father's life, very definite traits had emerged in Mr Nobody which were never to leave him. The dazzlingly brilliant start that he had made had, if imperceptibly, already begun to show signs of slipping away: while his contemporaries were setting off on the paths of their chosen careers — diplomats, politicians, academics — my father still seemed to be enjoying himself gambolling about in the green fields of freedom, like a young animal put out to pasture in the spring. It had not gone unnoticed: Shiela's mother had pronounced Rees not suitable as 'husband material' for her daughter and some of his friends, while continuing to delight in his company, were beginning to wonder where he was going. Others, by then, accustomed to his ways, simply waited to see what would happen next. In later years, when navigating choppy waters, my father used to say that something would turn up. Plenty turned up in 1935.

Shiela, who had become a journalist, had, by then, decided that marriage to Rees was 'not really a feasible possibility' at that time. He was drifting. After his brief period on the *Manchester Guardian* he had taken a job on *The Times* but had given it up within a matter of months; he had not had a positive reaction from the BBC to which he had applied; and he did not want to take a position that had been offered to him on the *Evening Standard* because, he said, he would not work for Lord Beaverbrook. In the spring of 1935, while waiting for the publisher's reaction to his second novel, he visited Shiela, who was working in Paris; then he went on to Spain. From there, he wrote to her: 'I often think you must get tired of my shiftlessness, poverty, inability to give you what you should have — house, animals, certainty, safety: I am very sorry, I want terribly to give you them, you make me so happy: but I must try to write and it isn't easy to do that and give you things . . .' In another letter he wrote of what he did want to concentrate his attentions on: he was going to learn to write again

74

from the very beginning, using no adjectives until he had learned to use nouns and verbs properly. He was not going to write about anything 'ambitious'; he was going to abandon trying to describe very complicated things until he could manage the simple task of describing a man walking down the street. He was going to be a very good writer one day, he told her. The letter was filled with love: 'You see, I am frightfully excited . . . I think really it is your saying you love me. It is like finding out one is very good after believing, on the best evidence, you are very bad . . .'

But the end of the relationship was already in sight. Shiela went on to Germany to work as a secretary in the offices of the *Daily Telegraph* in Berlin, and Rees sent her a poem, the last verse of which began with the lines: 'Come back from that country, Whose heroes are hangmen . . .' While in Germany, she saw Adam von Trott, whom she had first met at Oxford where he was a Rhodes Scholar, and when he heard that she had been planning to marry Rees, he proposed to her. She told me that she had never mentioned this to Rees, who was by now beginning to get very concerned about the prospect of war. In another letter to her, he wrote: 'I hate that England should perhaps have to fight again: but I think it is necessary. It is terrible that such things should be necessary . . . But I don't think that Europe is done yet and it will recover. Things will become easier one day: it will be lovely if they do and we are together. That is what I hope for. I think these next few years will be hard and perhaps terrible; if it were possible, I would like us to work and learn to know each other and love each other, and then when things change we shall be fit for a better world.' He had been thinking of the world, he said, in terms of Dürer's *Ritter mit Tod und Teufel*. 'The Knight is in a dark wood, with death and the devils around him, on each side: but he rides straight on, over skeletons and serpents and he is smiling. I think the world today is like that wood but that people can be like the *Ritter* if they want to and if they are, will come out of the wood, and so should you and I together. One thing that frightens me is this: that one day the world will change and become lovely and there will be no one fit for it and I should like to be . . .'

It is difficult to establish exactly Rees's political frame of mind in the mid-thirties. An entry in Shiela's notebook records that Rees had said: 'It is vitality and desire which make it impossible to be a communist . . .' And in a letter to her, part of which is lost, he wrote diffidently about communism; its methods would destroy production, lower living standards and bring about war. It was one of his more long-winded communications – the political equivalent of not being able to describe a man walking down the street: 'A communist to whom I said this would smile his superior smile and say I was: a) bourgeois, b) intellectual, c) utopian and impractical, because at the present time society rests on two classes, one which exploits the other, and the exploiting class cannot be expropriated without violence. I think they can, a) because the communist is wrong in thinking there is such a clear class division, and b) because in so far as there is an exploiting class, he is already being expropriated . . . I think that the working class is exploited because a) he does not have a just or a fair distribution of the product, and b) because he is not allowed to produce as much as he could if there were no artificial restraints on his production. But I don't think he is being exploited by a class and therefore an attack on a class is no way to solve the problem.'

In a letter, Shiela told me that she would 'argue hotly' against any idea that Rees was a communist. They had not been at all impressed with Russia when they saw it in 1932 and there was still less to admire in it when Stalin started killing his *confrères*. She was adamant; they were idealistic and innocent, they did however find something appealing about the communist slogan 'From each according to his ability: to each according to his needs'. There was not much more to it than that. Shiela did not believe Rees was 'taken in' by ideologies and neither of them was a 'joiner'. She said they were both also deeply opposed to the idea of class hatred. 'I don't think he was very interested in politics at all; he would have been the last person to join even the Labour Party, never mind the Communist Party . . .'

According to Douglas Jay, Rees could most appropriately be described as a 'social democrat' at that point in the thirties. 'Exactly how far he thought Marxism and Stalinism went too far and was anti-liberal and so on is difficult to say, but I think that, by the mid-thirties, half of him thought that,' he said. 'But I really do not think he was very realistic about these things. In a way, it is true that he wasn't very interested in politics at all. He was interested in drama and fiction . . . he wrote novels . . . and to my mind there was a Celtic element in all this. I think he saw politics as a kind of drama that you watch as if you are watching a play and you do not have to take a view of who is right or who is wrong.' Isaiah Berlin, who was to write critically about Karl Marx in his little book of the same name, published in 1939, was born in Riga; he had come to London as a boy with his parents who had been through two revolutions. As he told me, he was, of course, anti-Soviet from start to finish and, although he was a close friend of Rees, did not approve of any of his forays into politics.

In 1935 Rees joined *The Spectator* as assistant editor under Wilson Harris. Once again, A.L. Rowse takes credit for the appointment. In *All Souls in My Time*, he wrote of his role in attempting to give my father some purpose in life. Goronwy, he said, had been to Germany, where he seemed to have done little but 'have a good time with the boys, did nothing, came back and handed in his cards'. Thereupon, he, Rowse, and John Sparrow got him the *Spectator* job. 'He could now have a good time in London,' Rowse commented. 'He was a lightweight, an irresponsible ...' The magazine was, as it is now, a Conservative weekly, and a fairly unlikely billet for Rees. But it paid him a salary of £500 a year for three days' work a week, which enabled him to take a flat in London.

This move brought to an end his affair with Shiela. As she explained in her book, Adam von Trott had encouraged her to stay on in Germany and when she asked Rees if he would mind, he had replied: 'The terrible thing is that I do not ...' She did not like Guy Burgess and the increasingly important part he was playing in Rees's life and she was unhappy when Rees took a flat in Ebury Street, Victoria, just around the corner from his new friend. Shiela found Guy 'repellent' and he reminded her of how alienated she had felt at Oxford from some of Rees's friends: 'They were all brilliant and clever, but also somehow cynical and amoral ...' She had tried to accommodate them because she felt Rees needed them; he had such a receptive mind, he assimilated the books he read, the pictures he looked at, the music he heard and the conversations he took part in with more 'pleasure, intelligence and feeling' than anyone else she had ever known. Goronwy, meaning 'spring of sparkling water', was the perfect name for him; for not only did he have what a poet friend had called his 'leaping thought and lucid mind' but what Shiela described as 'clear pools' in which he stored 'all the treasures of the human spirit which fascinated him', those treasures included 'suffering as well as joy, evil as well as good'. Now they were parting and it saddened Shiela. 'For three years at Oxford, we had shared a simple childish world entirely encompassed by our affection for each other, our happiness in each other's company,' she said. But perhaps the writing had been on the wall for some time. She recalled how her old nurse, who remained with her family as a housekeeper, had once complained: 'Is Mr Rees ever going to do any work instead of always reading and writing?'

Rees was still in the course of writing his second novel, *A Bridge to Divide Them*: he was still, as he was always to do, reading; and now he had a job as well. Just as he had thrown himself into social life at Oxford, he was now throwing himself, with equal enthusiasm and vivacity, into London literary life and, apparently, having quite as much success. Although he still had his fellowship of All Souls, he spent less and less time in Oxford and, as well as quarrelling with the girl he was supposed to marry, had quarrelled with most of the friends they had in common. In his memoirs he told of how, in the summer of 1935, he had fallen in love with a girl with a 'sharp, almost microscopic, painter's eye', who made him see things that he might otherwise have missed. There are several stories about how Shiela and Rees finally parted. Shiela's version is that she had become fed up with him being 'taken up by writers and publishers, and above all by a publisher's lady and by lady writers'. She drew the line at one particular 'publisher's lady'. Rees persuaded her to go with him to a party given by the publisher in question; she did not want to go and when she left, as she recalled, she knew that she was leaving Rees for ever and that he would not call her back. He did not. I know of another version, which, of course, is not told by Shiela: she and Rees were on a bus together when Rees got off, leaving her there alone, having decided that he was not going any further, not only on that bus journey but also in terms of their relationship.

According to Rees, he would have been totally happy that year, had it not been for 'the shadow of politics which fell increasingly heavily upon anyone who took any interest in such subjects'. The Germans had occupied the Rhineland, in Germany the concentration camps were full and, in 1936, the Spanish Civil War began, in which several friends of Rees who had joined the International Brigade were killed. He and Guy talked endlessly about their sympathies for the Republic in Spain and for the Franco–Soviet pact and how they supported the Popular Front. But Rees said that while he himself used arguments based on instinct or emotion and, sometimes, a bit of reason to justify his viewpoint, Guy used 'complicated and somewhat cynical analyses of power relationships in Europe'. Rees was aware that something had changed in him. 'He seemed positively to dislike and despise the liberal and humanitarian instincts which led others to the same conclusions as himself.'

I am grateful to the literary critic, Walter Allen, for responding to my appeal in *The Spectator* for information about my father with a letter giving details of several sightings of him in the thirties. He had first met Rees, he said, as a member of a left-wing, anti-fascist society called For Intellectual Liberty. FIL was founded by Margaret Gardiner, daughter of Sir Alan Gardiner, the Egyptologist, who had been at Cambridge in the twenties and was asked, in 1936, by the French *Societé des Intellectuels Antifascistes*, to set up a sister organization in England. On the committee were E.M. Forster, Henry Moore, the physicist P.M.S. Blackett, and C.P. Snow, and Allen said he used to meet Rees, Louis MacNeice, Stephen Spender and Victor Pritchett at meetings. He also saw Rees at *The Spectator,* to which he contributed reviews. 'Rees was very well known in intellectual circles because he was at the magazine. He drank treble whiskies, which was a bold drink, and was also pretty well known for his affairs with women.'

Louis MacNeice had become a close friend of my father and remained so; we were to be neighbours after the war and during my childhood the two of them would go on drinking sprees and on outings to rugby internationals (also drinking sprees). In his auto-biography, *The Strings Are False*, which he finished in 1941, but would not allow to be published until after his death, Louis wrote about the two camps in literary London at the time: the 'old gang' who were just literary and the 'new gang' who were all left-wingers. The new gang, he explained, was 'addicted to committees' – 'committees to save democracy, to protect writers, to assist refugees, to pass, when everything else failed, a measure of protest.' The big subject was Spain and there was 'a great deal of talk . . . about realism which was now almost equated with propaganda,' he wrote. Louis had seen Rees in action – a 'typical' case of the new gang – and was scornful: 'Academically brilliant . . . a novelist . . . a playboy . . .' He was 'short and wiry, with black curly hair and that Welsh charm which takes an ell if you give it a millimetre and would have made a wonderful travelling salesman . . .' He described one evening, at a gathering of, in the main, writers opposing Fascism, at which Cecil Day-Lewis and Rees were the speakers. Day-Lewis had a 'tired Oxford accent', qualified everything and was questioning. Rees, on the other hand, when he got to his feet, 'spoke like a revivalist, flashed his eyes, quivered with emotion, led with his Left and followed with his Left, punch on punch, dogma on dogma, over and overstatement, washing in the blood of – well, nobody asked of whom, but it certainly made you stop thinking . . .' Rees had plenty to say about the proletariat: the only progressive class in society. Writers, he said, had to lay down their personalities, take their orders from the working classes and make themselves a living trumpet for them to blow through. After the meeting, Louis reported, Rees said he felt like oysters and suggested that one or two people should accompany him to Prunier's, where oysters were expensive. It was, of course, ridiculous and Louis had absolutely no time for it or Rees's infatuation with Marxism. Marx, he said, was to the poets of the thirties what Rousseau was to the poets of the Romantic Revival: 'This in spite of Marx's own warning against the romantic revolutionary ...' Intellectuals turned to communism, he thought, as 'an escape from materialism'.

It was at this time that Rees entered what my mother used to call his 'lady novelists phase'. Through Maurice Bowra, he had met Elizabeth Bowen whose husband, Alan Cameron, was Director of Education for the city of Oxford; they lived and entertained a great deal at their house in Old Headington. Maurice Bowra described Elizabeth in his memoirs as tall and well-built, with 'the manners of someone who has lived in the country and knows its habits'. She was 'handsome in an unusual way', he wrote, 'with a face that indicated both mind and character. Unlike some Irish, she did not talk for effect, but kept the conversation at a high level and gave her full attention to it. She had a slight stutter which added force to her remarks. She had the fine style of a great lady who, on rare occasions, was not shy of slapping down impertinence, but she came from a society where the decorum of the nineteenth century had been tempered by an Irish frankness. With all her sensibility and imagination, she had a masculine intelligence which was fully at home in large subjects and general ideas ... Though she was entirely at home in the modern world and deeply committed to it, she had her roots in a more spacious and more assured society.' While in Oxford she wrote a novel every year with the exception of one. Elizabeth was ten years older than Rees but had formed an attachment to him, although I am not sure of its exact nature. While my mother was always quite happy to talk about Elizabeth, whom she had met, my father became sheepish when the subject arose and would usually leave the room. Victoria Glendinning's biography of Elizabeth Bowen, published a few years before my father died, furnished a few useful details about their short-lived relationship. 'Goronwy was very clever, very unpredictable, and very attractive to women,' she wrote.

In 1935 Elizabeth and her husband, who had been appointed

Secretary to the Central Council of School Broadcasting at the BBC, moved to a house in Clarence Terrace, Regent's Park, which was the perfect setting for Elizabeth's parties. Alan Cameron would come home from the BBC to find rows of black hats, belonging to his wife's literary friends, hanging in the hall, and he invented the generic term 'Black Hats' to describe them. Rees was a Black Hat and what happened at Elizabeth's home in Ireland, Bowen's Court, in the summer of 1936, greatly enhanced his growing reputation of being a Bad Hat as well.

Meanwhile Guy Burgess, who had left Cambridge in the summer of 1935, had, in November of that year, become secretary to a pro-German Conservative MP, Captain John Macnamara, described by my father as 'so far right ... that it was quite reasonable to call him a fascist'. He was deliberately hiding his commitment to the cause and had gone 'underground'. In May 1936 Guy worked for a trial period at *The Times* but did not like the routine and, in October 1936, joined the BBC as a talks producer – an appointment with which, according to *Deadly Illusions*, his Soviet controller was more than happy. It was at about this time that my father so colourfully recalled the state of Guy's flat in Chester Square and his dissipated way of life. Rees said he saw Guy at least once a week during this period, and, in retrospect, it was as if Guy had been playing a 'gigantic hoax' on him.

The flat in Chester Square was decorated in red, white and blue, a colour scheme which Guy claimed was the only one which any reasonable man could ever live with. White walls, blue curtains, red carpet. 'But this patriotic decor was completely submerged in the indescribable debris and confusion of the party which had evidently taken place the night before', Rees recalled. Guy himself was in bed, in his blue sheets beneath his red counterpane, which was littered with Sunday newspapers. On one side of his bed stood a pile of books, including *Middlemarch*, one of his favourite novels, which Rees thought he must have read at least twenty times, Dickens's *Martin Chuzzlewit*, Lady Gwendolen Cecil's *Life of Lord Salisbury*, Morley's *Gladstone*, and John Dos Passos's *Manhattan Transfer*.

Rees filled in more aspects of the picture: 'On the other side of the bed stood two bottles of red wine, a glass, and a very large, very heavy iron saucepan filled to the brim with a kind of thick, grey gruel, compounded of porridge, kippers, bacon, garlic, onion and anything else that may have been lying about in his kitchen. This unappetizing mess he had cooked for himself the previous day, and on it he proposed to subsist until Monday morning. As he pointed out, it was economical, sustaining, and eliminated the problem of cooking for the entire weekend; as for intellectual nourishment, what more could one require than the Sunday newspapers, including the *News of the World*, and the books that were piled up beside him?'

Guy was manipulative, he flattered, he cast spells on people – women, however, were rarely very keen on him – despite his absolutely disgusting habits. As I was told many times while I pursued my search for the truth about my father, Guy's badness made him attractive. Rees noted, standing back again as if he were not one of those who had fallen under Guy's spell: 'It used to amuse me to observe Guy's power of manipulating his friends, and it was clear to me that on the whole they were chosen precisely because they were willing victims of it. Nor was there any reason to be anything more than amused by it, as by yet another addition to the general spectacle of the human comedy. It would have been absurd that there could be anything serious in the influence of one who was so obviously an anomaly in the social system, so compulsive a drinker, so completely promiscuous in his sexual life, whose fingernails were so neurotically bitten and filthy, and whose ordinary behaviour was so outrageously and child-ishly designed to *épater les bourgeois*. One might as well have taken Mme Verdurin seriously. Yet, even so, it was, to me at least, an interesting fact that Guy's influence on his friends was never relaxed; secretly, persistently, it was always there, whether they acknowledged it or not.'

He was the most persistent person Rees had ever known. If Guy wanted to see the Marx Brothers at the cinema and Rees wanted to see Greta Garbo, 'it was always the Marx Brothers whom one saw . . .' If one went for a drive in his car and wanted to go to the country while he wanted to go to the seaside, somehow one always found oneself at the seaside. If one wanted to drink white wine and he wanted to drink red (and he always did want to drink red), it was always red wine that one drank. 'He was persistent as a child is persistent who knows it will always have its own way if it is willing to behave badly enough,' said Rees, and Guy was always willing to behave badly enough. He had a 'formidable power of the will' which for the most part went unnoticed, my father felt, because of the general disorder and absurdity of his personal life.

The NKVD was also assessing Guy and their reports are included in Costello and Tsarev's book, *Deadly Illusions*. In an early, and most revealing assessment, Moscow was learning what it had taken on. Burgess, said the report, had imagination and was full of plans and initiative, but had no 'internal brakes'. He had a tendency to panic easily and was also prone to fits of despair. Although falling over himself to take on tasks, his instability prevented him from following them to their conclusion. He was upset by the most insignificant of difficulties and lied, although not maliciously, to cover up errors on his part. 'In relations with us he is honest and does everything without objections and sometimes produces an impression of a person who is too readily subdued. Though he dresses scruffily, he still likes to attract attention. This is a generally characteristic feature of his. He craves to be liked and only reluctantly acknowledges his weaknesses.'

In September of 1936 Rees was invited by Elizabeth Bowen to stay at Bowen's Court, her house in Ireland. What took place there has been well documented, and there is little to add, particularly as the three main characters in the drama are no longer alive. The guests at the house party also included Roger Senhouse, a publisher, Rosamond Lehmann the writer, whom Elizabeth had known since early Oxford days and whose fourth novel, *The Weather in the Streets*, was published that year, Isaiah Berlin, Con O'Neill, Stuart Hampshire, John Summerson whose book on Nash, architect of the Regent's Park terraces, had just appeared, Michael Gilmour, a solicitor, and Noreen Colley, Elizabeth's young cousin. Isaiah told me that Elizabeth was in a nervous state as she greeted her guests, and that Rees arrived like a 'toreador in Carmen, jangling bells and terribly excited . . .' Rosamond was famously beautiful, as Stephen Spender described in *World Within World*: tall, statuesque, with almond-shaped eyes, and a warm, impulsive manner.

That evening, after dinner, the party played games on paper, although Rees did not take part in one called Architectural Consequences because he said he could not draw. Instead he sat on the arm of Rosamond's chair. 'They did nothing, they could have, I suppose, but they did not. But certainly something was going on,' Isaiah recalled. What was going on was later described as a *coup de foudre*. The following day, everyone went to have lunch with an Irish publisher who lived in a castle nearby. Rosamond and Rees were in a car together and offered to take Isaiah back with them to Bowen's Court. 'Suddenly I heard Rosamond say to Goronwy something that I have never heard anyone say off the stage, which was "I think it is now or never ..." I did not know what they meant, but it was funny and it stuck in my mind.'

In the next stage of the drama, Noreen Colley told Isaiah that she had been put in a room with a very thin party wall and had heard things she should not have heard. 'She wanted to know if she should tell Elizabeth. I said, certainly not, not on any account,' Isaiah told me. But, much later, she did. By then Rosamond had left the house and letters in her recognizable handwriting were arriving for Rees, who had stayed on at Bowen's Court. Elizabeth was naturally very upset; she told Rees that her father had gone mad in the house and maybe he would too, if he stayed there with her. 'Elizabeth could not understand why he had done it, she was very puzzled, because in her kind of life this sort of thing was not done,' Isaiah said. I understood from Selina Hastings, Rosamond Lehmann's biographer, that Rosamond always claimed that nothing improper happened between her and Rees, and that she would never have dreamed of hurting her hostess in such a way.

However Isaiah added a postscript for my enlightenment. Whereas Victoria Glendinning maintained that Elizabeth did not mourn for long over her loss, Isaiah believes that was not the case. Some time after the Bowen's Court drama, Rees asked Isaiah if he could borrow his rooms at All Souls so that he could entertain a lady for tea. 'About a fortnight before, I had written to Elizabeth saying that things really must not go on like they were ...' he explained. 'She was still talking about the row she had had with Rees. I told her to forget him, that she was making far too much of it. In reply, she had written me a long letter, in which she was very overdramatic. She said that she had had all kinds of people to stay at Bowen's Court, even sex maniacs, but to use the house as a brothel was something she could not bear. It was mad jealousy, of course.' On his way to Cambridge on the train, Isaiah realized, with horror, that he had left Elizabeth's letter in a small room adjoining his main room at All Souls where the telephone was installed and where Rees would certainly find it. It was not until a year later, when he and Elizabeth went to lunch with Cyril Connolly, that he learned of the consequences of his carelessness. For some reason, the conversation turned to people who steam open letters; everyone around the table that day confessed to having done so. Isaiah recalled: 'Elizabeth suddenly said, stammering: "I wish great friends did not leave letters from other friends where other people that I know can look at them ..." After lunch, I gave her a lift in a taxi and

84

asked her what had happened. She said that Rees had, indeed, read her letter in my rooms at All Souls and had immediately gone to London and had a violent scene with her at her house. I apologized ten thousand times. Goronwy said nothing to me nor did she at the time of the letter. This thing went on for years ...'

Stuart Hampshire, who was elected to All Souls in the autumn of 1936, gave his own version of what happened at Bowen's Court during what became known to the house guests as 'the Weekend where a Great Deal Happened'. Five years younger than Rees, Stuart knew Maurice Bowra and Isaiah Berlin and had been at prep school with Guy Burgess. He had met Rees but did not know him well. However, he knew that Elizabeth was in love with Rees and noticed she was nervous. Rees, he said, had made 'an immediate impact' when he arrived at the house, but things began to go 'badly wrong' when he sat on the arm of Rosamond's chair while the rest of the group were playing the 'rather tiresome paper games' after dinner. It somehow 'struck a rotten note'. He told me that Rees, describing the weekend in a letter, had said, 'rather wrongly, that we were all standing around that very beautiful house like "timeless Toulouse-Lautrecs", which made me giggle. I mean ... Toulouse-Lautrec ... those great tall jowled women and Isaiah ... Rees must have lost his head when he wrote it.' He thought that Rees and Rosamond had not met before, although my father knew John Lehmann, her brother: 'It looked like a first meeting; she was very amorous.' Everyone went on to drink too much, he said, and there was a 'frightful sense of tension' until most people 'left the sinking ship'. After that, of course, everyone talked about what had happened and lots of letters were written, mostly by Elizabeth, Rees and Rosamond.

Stuart continued to see Rees at All Souls and was curious about his activities. He thought it was a 'bit odd' that Rees should be working at *The Spectator*. 'Not that it was shocking or anomalous, but it was a bit stuffy,' he said. He used to talk to Rees about literature, left-wing politics and the Nazis, the writing of Henry Yorke who was a friend of Rees's, and Kafka. 'Goronwy was very quick at picking things up. He could certainly talk interestingly about literature and he was very sensitive and observant, but he never had an intellectual outlook which gave him a mission to do something he thought important to do.' Stuart considered that Rees's social gifts far exceeded his intellectual stability. Rees, he said, was 'charming and flirtatious, particularly with men ...' People were 'dazzled' by him, and he had a facility for adapting whatever he was talking about to the person he was talking to. 'But the absence of boring plod was very conspicuous in Goronwy. The man who thinks he has got something very important to say about German history or politics or Kafka can be very tedious, but Goronwy could never be tedious enough for his own good . . .' The influence of Oxford, Stuart felt, was perhaps 'too much' for Rees, coming as he did from what Maurice Bowra used to call a 'quiet background'. 'Goronwy was picked up on the football field by John Sparrow, who told Maurice he had found a fellow with a charming giggle, who was also intellectual. That's how it happened . . . that's how Goronwy was taken up.' Stuart said he could see a natural bond between Rees and Guy; they were both good talkers, but they both seemed to lack intellectual direction. 'Goronwy wrote very well, but he never knew what he wanted to write about. He could write impressions, all of which were very good, but they were not part of some large scheme of things. Guy only got an aegrotat – it means you are ill – at Cambridge, he could never write anything down, he was entirely a talker.'

At Elizabeth Bowen's home in Headington, Rees met Robert Graves's niece, Sally, who had first come across him through Maurice Bowra and in Isaiah Berlin's rooms when she was at Somerville College. Sally, who later became Principal of Lady Margaret Hall, saw Rees socially in London and 'bumped into him' at some United Front marches and demonstrations after the start of the Spanish Civil War. 'He was very attractive and unfrightening to an undergraduate, an affectionate person, such warmth came oozing out,' she said. 'What I chiefly remember about him is the sparklingness of the eyes. He looked at you when he talked to you. I remember warming to him because he was not asking me to sit up and be clever.' In 1936 she returned from abroad and found herself at parties given by Rees in his flat in Ebury Street. At one of these, she met Guy, who was showing off a pair of American trousers with a zip fly – a novelty in those days; she could not make out whether he was on the Left or on the Right, she told Rees. He replied that Guy had described himself as a 'Conservative Marxist'. At that time, she said, Rees's politics were much the same as hers. 'We were on the right side in the Spanish Civil War, we were shocked by the same sort of things, public executions, capital punishment, you know . . . all those sort of liberal causes. It never struck me that Goronwy was a dyed-in-the-wool Marxist. We were all terribly naive and rather romantic.'

In Oxford, Maurice Bowra was reading extracts from *The Summer Flood* to amuse guests at dinner parties, and in London, Rees was throwing himself into being what Philip Toynbee described as 'the gayest of gay dogs' and what Stuart Hampshire felt he wished to be seen as, 'a breath of fresh air'. In July 1936, Rees was putting readers of *The Spectator* straight on the question of decadence and railing against Victorian stuffiness. Some professors had attacked the age as degenerate: morals were loose, manners were bad, society was unstable. 'The professors would have us believe the age degenerate because it does not observe the moral standards of 1910,' he wrote. 'To them, all deviations from these standards ... are to be condemned ... Those who have been lucky or unlucky enough to live when Victorian morality has broken down, who find it natural that it should have broken down, can have no nostalgia for the days of Victoria. Indeed, to have that morality restored would be intolerable ...' Was he thinking of Wales? He deplored the idea of restoring what one professor had called 'the vanished domination of the Victorian middle-class ...' Perhaps what was being seen were the germs of a 'freer and humaner way of life', he suggested. 'For example, what in 1910 may have been seen as a lack of respect for fathers may now be evidence of a happier relationship between fathers and their children, and what some deplore as the sexual freedom of the age may give greater prospects of human happiness and goodness than the tyranny of a rigid and conventional morality.'

It was a review of a book by James Hanley, *Grey Children: A Study of Humbug and Misery in South Wales* – a report from the distressed areas – that Rees wrote for *The Spectator* in November 1937 that apparently inspired Guy to tell my father that he was working for the Comintern. Rees recounted in his memoirs that he considered it a 'rather emotional and sentimental' book, but Guy was full of praise for the review, which was entitled 'In the Valley'. 'He ... generally made me feel that I was a writer of great originality and power ...' Rees explained. Hanley was, indeed, writing about a subject close to my father's heart – the suffering of the unemployed – but his book exasperated Rees. Mr Hanley, he wrote, had conveyed an impression of 'overwhelming misery'; it was a 'misery of a special and peculiar kind ... and to many people it implies a final condemnation of the society which has produced it ...' South Wales was being evacuated, which, he considered, was a curious answer to the problem. 'If you tell men and women, already inclined by temperament and tradition to revolutionary opinions, that their sufferings are caused by an impersonal economic system, you leave them but one choice. Lenin could not do better.'

Hanley's book, he said, was valuable because of the picture it gave of the 'enormous complex of suffering which is bred by unemployment ... Its foundation is extreme poverty, underfeeding and vile housing; and upon this rises an elaborate superstructure, the humiliation and degradation of enforced idleness, the slow ebbing of vitality, the softening muscles, the frayed nerves, the irritated sensibility of those who are underfed, are not allowed to work and cannot afford pleasure, the subjection to the official, the clerk, the Unemployment Regulations that justify enquiries into every detail of private life, the breaking up of homes and families, the loss of sons and daughters by emigration, the withering away of an admirable society, the interminable days spent lounging on street corners, in the park, in the hills, in the rain of South Wales, or lying in bed to make food less necessary.'

All this had to be endured alongside people's desire to be useful members of society, watching their own decay, in 'dark, narrow cottages' with shared outdoor lavatories. The fault of the book, Rees commented, was that Mr Hanley had aroused pity for these people, portraying them as isolated, whereas, in his own view, 'their lives and their sufferings are so closely related to the working of modern society that they are a condemnation of it ...' Mr Hanley should have gone further than the Welsh valleys, he said. For a complete picture, he should 'show beside the hovels and cottages of the distressed area the great parks and mansions and fortunes which like them are founded on coal, but unlike them still flourish...'

No wonder Guy Burgess was so impressed. He made his overture one evening, sitting in Rees's flat with the customary bottle of whisky between them. His 'exaggerated respect', Rees remarked, made him feel, dimly, that Guy was making a fool of him and he felt irritated. He did not think it was that good a review. But Guy told him that he considered it showed that Rees had 'the heart of the matter' in him. The heart of the matter? According to Rees's account, Guy's eyes looked 'oddly empty and expressionless' as if he were 'considering some immensely important decision' with a seriousness and gravity that was so unusual that Rees began to feel quite uneasy. And then he said: 'I am a Comintern agent and have been ever since I came down from Cambridge.' Rees, naturally, was very surprised and said he did not believe him. When Guy insisted that it was the truth, Rees asked him why he had felt the need to reveal this. Guy then said that he wanted Rees to help him, to which my father replied, 'I don't know. What can I possibly do to help you?' As the conversation progressed, Guy informed him that only a few people knew about his position and if Rees asked no more questions he would give him the name of one person who knew what he was doing. That person was Anthony Blunt.

Of course, when Rees's second volume of memoirs, *A Chapter of Accidents*, was published in 1972, he could not mention Blunt's name, but he described Guy's collaborator as someone who 'could not have carried more weight with me', whom he both 'liked and respected greatly' and 'with whom I would gladly have joined in any enterprise'. I have always felt very doubtful about Rees's response on being told that Blunt was involved; he never liked him. Guy told Rees, 'You must never speak to him about it. I shouldn't have mentioned his name to you. It's essential, in this kind of work, that as few people as possible should know who is involved. You must promise never to mention the subject to him.' According to my father, he gave his promise and Guy did not speak again that evening either about his secret work or about the part which he appeared to assume that Rees would play in it.

The following morning, he awoke and went back over this conversation with Guy and 'tried to acclimatize myself to the extraordinary fact that a friend of mine was an agent of the Comintern'. He was not particularly shocked, he said, but it would take him too long to explain why; that would entail writing the history of an entire generation and the 'appalling political tragedy' of the thirties. In fact, he admired Guy, for he had sacrificed his personal life for what he believed in, unlike himself, who was a 'political dilettante'. The only trouble was that he could not quite believe what Guy had told him. He had only Guy's word, which was 'notoriously untrustworthy and unreliable'. It was hard to see him as a hero; easy to see him as a *fantaisiste*. In any event, if this were true, why had Guy chosen to reveal 'this highly compromising piece of knowledge' to him? He did not think he could be of the slightest help to Guy and it seemed much more likely that this was just another of Guy's 'elaborate manoeuvres for exercising power over his friends'. Rees confessed that, if that were the case, it had been quite a shrewd idea, for '. . . it had precisely the romantic quality to which I was most vulnerable'.

The more Rees thought about it, the more he felt as if he were trying to solve one of those Chinese puzzles in which one box opens, only to reveal another, and there is no solution. He had never accepted any of Guy's statements as 'plain, unqualified truth' and he was not going to take Guy's word for it that he was working for the Comintern. The whole thing was 'too preposterous', but, with the ambivalence that Rees somehow always managed to bring to this affair, he added, 'Yet somehow, at the same time, I also believed he had been telling the truth.'

I have read these words over and over again, as I know those for whom they have even greater significance have done, to see whether, between the lines, there is not a clue that the outcome of this conversation with Guy had been other than the one my father described. But Rees, in turn, seems to have presented me with a Chinese puzzle. There is nothing concrete there. One is left guessing. Had he, or had he not, made a commitment to Guy? Was it more than a misunderstanding? Had they drunk too much? I found myself returning to this riddle again and again and feeling more and more uncomfortable, for I was questioning the truth of my father's version of events.

I had, of course, been told by those who knew Rees at the time that they sensed he had taken a significant step of some kind, though this is something he always firmly denied. On the very few occasions that I ever dared to ask him directly whether he had been a spy, stumbling and stuttering so that I should not actually have to enunciate the terrible word, his response was always, 'I did nothing.'

I wanted more than anything else to believe my father's account, yet, in describing the incident in *A Chapter of Accidents*, he does, almost deliberately, leave the reader in suspense. But what does emerge from the text as a certainty is that although Rees promised that he would tell no one what Guy had revealed to him, he broke that promise almost straight away.

In the early 1980s Rosamond Lehmann told Simon Freeman who, with Barrie Penrose, wrote *Conspiracy of Silence: The Secret Life of Anthony Blunt*, that Rees came to see her after this conversation with Guy in a 'state of tremendous agitation'. Her husband, Wogan Philipps, was away in Spain driving an ambulance. 'Goronwy told me that Guy was a Comintern agent and that he had been asked to join him,' Rosamond recalled. 'I did not think it was such a shocking announcement. All the young men were going off to fight for the International Brigades in Spain and I thought that this was just Guy's way of helping . . . Anyway, I asked Goronwy if he was going to help Guy. He just huffed and puffed.' The book, published six years after my father's death, contained a number of accusations against Rees. According to the authors, 'Many others in the Burgess-Blunt-Rees circle remain convinced that Rees's story is a concoction of half-truths and downright lies. Like MI5 they decided that Rees had been willing to help Burgess, passing on gossip from the conversations of politicians dining at Oxford college high tables and, during the war, when Rees worked for military intelligence, handing over genuine secrets.'

Several of Rees's friend and acquaintances told me they thought it was possible that he had 'helped' Guy but they had no evidence to prove this. Stuart Hampshire said he could well imagine it had been so. 'Rees did not behave in any way to make one think he was, as a lot of my friends turned out to be, overtly communist,' he said. 'He was not, obviously, the real thing.' However, Guy was known to be a recruiter, he said. Even at prep school, he recalled, Guy was 'disgusting', with a kind of 'slobbery quality', but he thought Rees was 'sort of captivated by him . . .' The puzzle was that Rees did not have access to any interesting information. Stuart tried to reassure me. 'People were not being shot all over Europe as a result of what Goronwy might have told Guy.' There was a 'great alcoholic haze' over both of them, he said. Rees had no interest whatsoever in the homosexual side of Guy's life, but Stuart thought he might have found some 'glamour' in the fact that Guy appeared to know everyone and everything.

Stuart Hampshire attempted to reconstruct for me what might have happened in the relationship between Guy and my father. Although Guy was so often described as 'amusing', in Stuart's view he was very destructive and malicious, with a tremendous capacity to flatter. 'He had this trick, which some Americans have, of giving you the impression that somehow you are a world historical figure and it matters tremendously what you do,' he said. 'Maybe Goronwy fell for it. There will have been a great deal of flattery. He would tell Goronwy, who was very preoccupied with Nazis, as we all were, that there was a way he could do something and that he should be serious about his life instead of just being a general sort of man about literary matters. There will have been some rather good Marxist patter, rather good on objectivity and solitary thinkers.'

In 1937 Rees's second novel, *A Bridge to Divide Them*, was published by Faber. Although the affair with Elizabeth Bowen was over and his life was now with Rosamond Lehmann, the dedication is to EB. It is an odd book, and very unlike *The Summer Flood*, in which Rees wrote from his own experience. I think I can detect Elizabeth's influence in the style – plenty of dialogue, short sentences of observation and a strong feeling of place – but it is really rather dull. The 'bridge that divides them' is being built across an estuary in South Wales, joining two towns. On one side are a well-off, influential family, owners of tennis courts and employers of servants, with well-kept gardens and terraces overlooking the estuary; on the other side are Annie and Johnny Jones, who have left the mining village where they first met and are very poor because Johnny does not want to work down the pit any longer. A friendship develops between Johnny and a young woman from the privileged family on the other side of the bridge, but whatever was about to develop between them never does because he dies in an explosion on a ship. A reviewer in *The Times* found that the sense of expectancy with which he had taken up Rees's new novel was 'unhappily not fulfilled'. There was none of the 'the elusive sense of beauty or the springiness of youth that distinguished his first book'. The critic felt that Rees had tackled a subject too small for the medium of a novel. 'A short story would have done justice to it,' he wrote. 'The characters misfire; the word "elusive" applied to his first book seems to have encouraged Mr Rees in nebulousness. His second suffers from the modern fascination with futility and inexpressiveness. It may be very effective to bring out a theme pianissimo: but there must be a theme. That is what Mr Rees lacks.'

*A Bridge to Divide Them* did not provide as much fun as his first novel for his friends at Oxford, who were arguing about appeasement. Stanley Baldwin had retired in May 1937, and Neville Chamberlain, the Chancellor of the Exchequer, had become prime minister, designating peace in Europe as his goal. Maurice Bowra observed in his memoirs that there was a 'strong feeling' for appeasement at All Souls, and that the younger Fellows of the college argued against Geoffrey Dawson, the editor of *The Times*, and his friends. Bowra was not an appeaser; what particularly embittered him was the 'cold-blooded indifference' the appeasers showed towards the barbarities of the Nazis. They were gentle and humane men, he said, but they 'refused to look the facts in the face and invented disreputable sophistries to avoid them'. Undergraduates, however, saw the question differently; they felt that the emergence of the Nazi Party was 'but another testimony to the callous indifference and incompetence of their elders, and they clamoured for some larger cause which could set much more than Germany right'.

Rees wrote of the years between 1937 and 1939 as a time when 'many men were troubled with bad dreams' that were 'haunted by two nightmare figures, Adolf Hitler and Neville Chamberlain'. In the Soviet Union, the terror created by Stalin was at its height. Robert Conquest, in his book *The Great Terror*, estimated that in January 1937 there were five million people in camps and prisons and over the next year a further seven million were arrested. As I ploughed through book after book on the period, I cringed as I came to the realization that my father, in his 'secret life', was one of those of whom Orwell said, 'The sin of nearly all left-wingers is that they have wanted to be anti-fascist without being anti-totalitarian.' I was made aware, as never before, of the enormous change that overcame him somewhere on his journey through life. For the Rees I knew, as I was growing up, was a ferocious Cold Warrior, and many of the views he held then are firmly embedded in my consciousness. He told me never to believe in ideologies, which pretend to have all the answers; I should think for myself. And he would not tolerate any anti-Americanism in our house. In his view, we would never have won the war without the United States.

Although Rees gave the date as the summer of 1937, it was during the previous summer that he and Guy – and Rosamond – went to Paris for a weekend rally organized for the Popular Front by the International Association of Writers for the Defence of Culture, one of the many front organizations set up by the German communist, Willi Münzenberg. He was the foremost operator of the Comintern, whose gift for persuasion made fellow-travelling fashionable and who, Rees was later to say, had been the most effective Soviet agent of influence in the thirties.

One evening Rees, who was on the executive committee of the British section, and Guy dined in the Bois de Boulogne with the American writer Theodore Dreiser, who spoke at the conference, and Louis Aragon, who was one of the leaders of the French delegation. Rees was bowled over by Aragon, who, he said, was brilliant, cultivated and socially chic 'as only a French communist intellectual can be'. Aragon had been converted to communism by way of surrealism, and he looked on communism as the 'natural heir' of the avant-garde movements in which he had played a part. He was less interested in changing the world than in shocking it, a view which Rees may well have shared. Guy allied himself with Dreiser, 'slightly uncouth, slow-moving, slow-speaking', an 'unreconstructed Middle Western populist' beneath his Marxism. Rees recorded that Dreiser and Guy were irritated by Aragon's 'intellectual acrobatics': 'Like two Anglo-Saxon puritans they regarded him as frivolous and affected and superficial: they thought him too clever by half.' But revenge was exacted when Aragon mistakenly entered into a disquisition on English literature, in which his taste was no more sure than that of any other Frenchman. 'Then they flung themselves upon him with great Anglo-Saxon swings and uppercuts which he as nimbly avoided, until at length he was borne down by the sheer weight of their attack and Guy was given the opportunity to launch into his favourite dissertation on George Eliot as the greatest of English novelists, which was new to them though far from new to me; yet in its way it was so good that I was always glad to listen to it again.'

Stephen Spender, with whom my father translated Georg Büchner's *Danton's Death*, published in 1939, told me that it must have been about this time that Rees had mentioned to him, as they were walking together in Suffolk, that his ambition was to be the English Aragon. 'Goronwy did not say he was a communist, but, of course, Aragon was. I remember that walk and it rather struck me that it did mean that he wanted to be an *éminence grise* of some sort.' It was just like Goronwy, he said. 'There he was, doing and being nothing very special, yet talking about wanting to be somebody as important as Louis Aragon.' But Stephen was familiar with Rees's ways. 'I really don't think Goronwy could be bound by anything. There was a sort of anarchism about him, which is why I never regarded him as quite responsible for the things he did which people took objection to. He was irresponsible and he was frivolous.'

Rees soon had other matters on his mind, for Elizabeth Bowen had taken her revenge on him for having abandoned her for Rosamond in her novel of 1938, *The Death of the Heart*. I have been told that at first he was amused and even a little flattered to find himself portrayed in it, going so far as to tell Rosamond that it was brilliant. But he then became angry and wrote to Elizabeth, threatening to sue for libel. In the novel Elizabeth introduced another of her little worlds of middle-class emotional tides and undercurrents, this time in a house in a Regent's Park terrace which bears a remarkable similarity to her own.

94

*The Death of a Heart* is a story about betrayal; more specifically it is about the dreadful behaviour of a young man called Eddie. Anna and Thomas Quayne, a partner in an advertising agency, are temporarily in charge of Thomas's orphaned half-sister, Portia, brought up abroad in cheap *pensions* and rented villas, while she takes classes at a small private school in Cavendish Square. In London, Portia meets a number of interesting people, including the impecunious Eddie, who was a friend of a cousin of Anna's at Oxford and has been employed by Thomas's firm – at Anna's insistence. Of course, Eddie turns out to be an absolute bounder; he is Rees. The first thing one learns about him is that he suffers from 'cosmic black moods', which are the 'things he was principally noted for'. The following passage is even more revealing: 'Everyone seemed to get a kick out of his relations with Eddie; he was like a bright little cracker that, pulled hard enough, goes off with a loud bang. He had been the brilliant child of an obscure home and came up to Oxford ready to have his head turned. There he was taken up, played up, played about with, taken down, let down, finally sent down for one idiotic act. His appearance was charming: he had a proletarian, animal, quick grace. His manner, after a year of trying to get the pitch, had become bold, vivid and intimate. He had become a quite frank *arriviste* – at the same time, the one thing no one, so far, knew about Eddie was quite how he felt about selling himself...'

Eddie was 'as clever as a monkey', with a 'young debauched face', a 'high forehead, springy bronze hair, energetic eyebrows and rather too mobile mouth'. He could sometimes look 'strikingly innocent'. At first he has eyes only for Anna, who is briefly taken with his 'farouche grace', but goes too far when he tries to kiss her. Matchett, the housekeeper, does not like him; he is forever 'popping in and out' of the house like a 'weasel' and he has no manners and no class.

Portia, however, who dreams of love, welcomes Eddie's attentions. There is a scene at Madame Tussaud's where Eddie, over tea and crumpets, talks to Portia about how complicated he is. Everyone hates his brain, he says, because it is the one thing he does not sell: 'I sometimes hate it myself. I wouldn't be with these pigs if I hadn't first been so clever ...' Eddie then entertains her in his room filled with books and offers her what Portia describes as 'very nice cold foods off cardboard dishes' and gives a little performance of how he has 'ladies' to tea in the afternoon. Portia tells how Eddie pretended to throw his hat off on the divan and 'pat his hair up in front of the glass', before walking round the room, looking at things, and 'sort of swaying himself'. Eddie curled up in a chair 'like a lady' and smiled at Portia in a 'mysterious way'. She explains, 'Then he showed me all sorts of things he does himself, like picking up the lady's fox fur and making a cat of it. I said, what else do you do, and he said, as little as I can get away with, darling. I said, why ever did he ask them to tea, and he said it was cheaper than giving them lunch out, but more tiring in the long run.'

At this stage of the novel, it is already clear that Eddie is going to hurt Portia, and he does so by flirting with another girl under her nose. He becomes more and more impossible and Elizabeth Bowen includes a cruel view of his shabby rented room, with a vase of dead flowers, a lumpy divan and foreign books 'overcrowded, thrust with brutality into the deal shelves . . .' Had Eddie been richer, she wrote, 'his interior probably would have had the classy red Gallic darkness of a man-about-town's in a Bourget novel − draperies, cut-glass lamps, teetering bronzes, mirrors, a pianola, a seductive day-bed and waxy demi-monde flowers in jardinières. Like the taste of many people whose extraction is humble, what taste he had lagged some decades back in time, and had an exciting, antimoral colour . . .'

Things became increasingly miserable for her until, finally, Eddie tells her that in her trustfulness she is driving him mad. Mr Nobody flashes into the plot when Eddie says, 'I cannot feel what you feel: I'm shut up in myself . . . I don't want you; I've got no place for you; I only want what you give . . . What you want is the whole of me − isn't it, *isn't it?* − and the whole me isn't there for anybody. In that full sense you want me I don't exist . . .' When Portia asks him whether he means he feels that he could be happy without her, he replies that that is precisely the situation. The last glimpse of him is when he takes a bottle out of a cupboard, pours himself a drink, and gives 'one of those defiant laughs with which one sometimes buoys up one's solitude . . .'

Victoria Glendinning, in her biography of Elizabeth Bowen, took the view that Eddie was not at all an unsympathetic portrait. 'What, really, was there for Goronwy to take such violent exception to?' she asked. 'If she used Goronwy, it was to magnificent effect . . .'

A few years after Rees died, Peter Quennell wrote about him and Elizabeth Bowen in his collection of contemporary portraits, *Customs and Characters*. Rees, he said, had 'all the talent of his dark and devious race' and had studied the 'Byronic spoiler's art'. He told a story of how Rees, when expecting his older 'ladies' to visit him, would place a vase of almost dead flowers on a sitting-room shelf, intending to 'rouse their passions' by 'exciting their protective instincts'. The ladies would immediately rush out and quickly return to receive the *coup de grâce* with the 'freshest and finest armfuls of blossoms they could buy from a Mayfair florist . . .'

Peter Quennell seemed to collect stories about Rees. According to him, my father spent part of one 'festive' night telling Quennell's female companion about Baudelaire's *Lettres à sa mère*. The next day, to her great astonishment, the volume reached her through the post, but it contained no kind of message. Quennell was suspicious. He lifted up the book and held it upside down; out dropped a small cardboard square, inscribed with only a telephone number, which Rees had slipped between the pages. This appears to have been a handy device. Barbara Skelton, in her autobiography, *Tears Before Bedtime*, mentioned that she had once met Rees at the Café Royal and he had slipped an invitation to lunch between the pages of her book.

When Quennell's book was published in 1982, the *London Standard* (as it called itself then) gave it to Rosamond to review. Eight years before her death, she was remarkably kind about my father: 'Goronwy Rees is another character brought vividly to life: that seductive semi-cad, romantic opportunist, brilliantly gifted, lovable and loved, spoiled child, dangerous to know. Although the episodes here described are comical, they give one a mournful frisson.'

In September 1938, at the Munich Conference, Chamberlain gave in to Hitler's demands for the German-speaking Sudetenland of Czechoslovakia; war was only a year away. At All Souls, they were debating and discussing; in London, Rees was preparing himself to do something that was to astound his friends.

# 6

Damn your writing,
Mind your fighting.

Collected by A.P. Wavell for *Other Men's Flowers*

Damn the appeasers ... If they were not going to fight the Germans, Rees was. On 20 April 1939 he went to Handel Street in Bloomsbury, near the offices of *The Spectator*, and joined the Royal Artillery Territorial Army. He was posted to the 90th Field Regiment and given the number 903013. He had taken himself by surprise as well as his friends. He thought it was 'one of the most unlikely acts I could ever commit, like climbing Everest or joining a leper colony ...' But the step also had for him, he said, the kind of attraction, criminal and seductive, 'which the *acte gratuit* had for Lafcadio in *Les Caves du Vatican*'. As for his friends, he remarked later, it was the criminal nature of the act which struck them most strongly; its seductiveness they could not understand. But, Rees argued, he had spent two years trying to persuade people that it was imperative to resist the advance of National Socialism, by fighting if necessary, and since the time seemed to have arrived, he thought he ought to accept the consequences. Guy, he recalled, regarded it as a 'foolish and romantic gesture', even treachery, to fight for a government as detestable as Mr Chamberlain's. Indeed, given his outpourings on the 'working class' and the 'proletariat', and well aware that war was a state of affairs from which the masses had the most to lose and the least to gain, my father did feel guilty about joining an army that served a government led by Chamberlain. Fighting for the Conservative Government, he said, felt like going to fight for the Devil.

On Wednesday evenings, as he walked round to the Drill Hall in Handel Street, to be shouted at by a Sergeant Bulford, he comforted himself by whistling the tune of a Welsh children's hymn he had learned at Sunday school:

> I am a little soldier
> Who learns to draw the sword
> To battle for my Saviour
> Till death brings my reward.

98

It was at this point in my quest, thinking of my father in his uniform, that I paused and tried to take stock of all I had learned so far of what my parents had tried to keep from me. As I have already said, my mother always gave me the impression that it was better for me that I did not know about the 'other' life my father had led before he met her. Now, looking back, I can see that it was really better for them both that I did not know. Yet there was always, in my mother's desire to keep the truth from us, an element of protectiveness, both for my father and for us, the children. Her sister, Mary, having listened, patiently as always, to my regrets about the past, once said to me: 'She could not have told you, Jenny. She could not.' What I had found out about my father in the years leading to the outbreak of war was not pleasant, though I felt I was approaching a situation where I might be able, if not to forgive him, then at least to understand him. The worst feeling about not knowing the whole story was that it made me feel so feeble and so vulnerable, in a sense, to suggestion. How *could* I not know my father? Arming myself with knowledge and information would surely give me the strength I needed to confront the truth of his life. That, at least, seemed simple. But, in fact, I was finding that nothing was simple.

I had discovered enough to cast considerable doubt on the accept-able story of Mr Nobody: the clever, innocent young man from a modest Welsh family going up to Oxford, where he is spoiled by the attentions of those who find him charming and attractive, travelling to Germany and witnessing the horrors of Nazism, taking a political stand and being buffeted about by the cruel winds of the thirties. There was clearly more to it than that, though.

It occurred to me, as I looked at this particular part of my father's life, that it was here that I was most likely to find the key to the mutterings and insinuations of those who knew him and, indeed, the allegations and accusations that followed him to end of his life. It was surely here, at this point of the trail, that I could somehow establish whether my father was lying or whether Anthony Blunt and Ros-amond had been lying when they levelled their accusations against him. In a way, his 'other' life had come to an end here, in the late thirties, when his sense of anger about appeasement and his passionate anti-Nazism were at their most fiery. He may have thought he had managed to reject and shed a great deal of his background but he never lost his sense of Calvinist rectitude about issues that were important to him. I clung on to the idea that there were very good reasons why Blunt and Rosamond should lie in the face of their incrimination of Rees, there were the comforting facts that no one had ever come up with any proof of complicity nor had his name been given by any Soviet defector. However, I knew my search would have to be very specific, and that, inevitably, I was going to have face up to asking the question I dreaded: 'Was my father a spy?' Indeed, as I was to find, even this would not give me the clear, finite answer I yearned for. I could not know, and had no way of checking, how much people were telling me and how much they were holding back. Perhaps, I thought, no one wanted to carry the responsibility of being the person to tell me the truth, if the truth were available.

I was all too aware that many of those who knew Rees in the thirties had enjoyed gossiping and telling entertaining anecdotes about him ever since. What, by now, was fact and what was fiction? To find out would mean questioning the very heart of my father's account of his relationship with Guy and the possibility that he had lied about his complicity in what has become known as the Cambridge spy ring. Not for the first time and not for the last time, I felt like Alice falling down the rabbit-hole.

As, in my researches, I moved on from what I suspected were the dangerous years of 1938 and 1939 to the years of the war, my mind kept going back over what I had been told. There were, for instance, the few sentences Isaiah Berlin had mumbled to me, in his deep, resonant voice, when we spoke in his rooms at All Souls. 'This part is murky,' he said. 'Rosamond told me that Rees had told her that he'd been a secret agent ... but that he had done nothing ... that's all I can report to you.'

But what could Rees have known, I asked Isaiah?

He went on: 'I know what he could have done, he could have repeated to Burgess gossip in All Souls ... among eminent people, that's all. All Souls was full of important people ... the people who governed England ... and they talked freely. If there was any gossip, he might have reported it to Burgess. He might have done it as a communist, or he might have done it as an agent or a friend ...'

Important people ... Rees, as he said, hated Chamberlain, who had been Prime Minister since May 1937. On his accession, he had moved Sir John Simon to be Chancellor of the Exchequer, where, according to the *Dictionary of National Biography*, he 'was part of the inner Cabinet concerned with the formation and execution of both domestic and foreign policy'. In February 1938 Chamberlain made

Lord Halifax his Foreign Secretary. So, if one added up the key appeasers there they were at All Souls: Simon, Halifax and Geoffrey Dawson, editor of *The Times*. However, Halifax, I learned, rarely visited the college, apart from attending the annual Gaudy and for the election of new Fellows. In his excellent biography of Lord Halifax, *The Holy Fox*, Andrew Roberts noted: 'It is absurd to suggest that the leading All Souls Fellows involved in appeasement – Halifax, Dawson and Simon – were influenced in their thinking to any significant extent by the arguments they heard at the College high table ...' He had spoken to Patrick Reilly, who thought it truer to say that they had influenced All Souls more than All Souls had influenced them. A.L. Rowse wrote in *All Souls in My Time*: 'The college has a clear record on Appeasement. It happened that a few of its leading figures in the public eye were wrong: Halifax and Simon ... and, above all, Dawson ...'

Certainly Guy would have been interested in anything said privately in the college by any of these people so that he could transmit the information to his controller, but as Rees and he talked to each other all the time about everything imaginable, why would my father have to enter into some kind of collaborative arrangement with him? It did not make sense.

Noël Annan, who had been at Cambridge, told me his suspicions about Rees at that time; he thought it was 'likely' that Rees was one of Guy's 'sources'. Rees, he said, 'could have provided clever analyses of trends in English politics. He followed politics with great interest. He knew his thirties politics inside out and abroad as well ...' But what did Guy have to tell the Russians? The plan, of course, as Noël explained, was to get people into Establishment positions, so they could lay their hands on revealing documents. As clever spymasters, they were prepared to wait for results from the Cambridge ring. 'They said, these are young men and they are going to come to the top,' Noël told me. 'Give them the time and meanwhile we will take whatever we can and we will encourage them ...'

Rees, Noël Annan told me, had nothing to give them because he was not in any position of importance. 'But what he could have done was to do what, of course, Guy did, and give Guy impressions of right-wing Conservative politicians.' What the Russians were very interested in, at that time, was how serious the British were about standing up to Hitler. Rees's line, Noël thought, would have been that the British were not serious at all, they would sell the Russians 'down the river', which is what Stalin appeared to believe. He continued: 'They sold out at Munich, they sold out all along the line, why should we trust them? So, it's that kind of background information they wanted . . . it was never anything secret . . . not done in a spirit of treachery, done in a spirit of helping the one power that he thought stood for the working class and their interests.'

Stuart Hampshire thought it 'probable' that Rees was recruited by Guy because he had become 'captivated' by him, but one had to put everything in proportion. Philby was serious, Anthony Blunt was serious, but Guy was a boaster, he loved to brag about how much he knew. 'He saw himself as this romantic mole figure talking to important people like the Berrys and Eden and the rest of them . . . Goronwy came every weekend to All Souls and there would be the other fellows like John Simon and Geoffrey Dawson,' said Stuart. He thought Rosamond could be believed when she said that Rees had told her what Guy had revealed to him. Rees, he said, had become very 'preoccupied' with the Nazis, as had everyone at All Souls, so if he did get involved with Guy it was 'surprising, perhaps, but intelligible, though not amazing or incredible like some of the people who have been said to be spies, because he was not in touch with anything interesting at all.'

In the Territorial Army my father found plenty to interest him. According to Rees, the regiment had been reduced to 'utter disorganization' because, that spring, there were so many new recruits. They could be divided into two camps: the young crowd from the City, who worked for banks, insurance companies and solicitors and talked about cricket, and a rougher, possibly more lively, group from the East End, labourers, barrow boys, dock-workers and bell-founders, who spoke a different language. It was perhaps inevitable that Rees should have made his friends in the latter camp: he has written, beautifully, of Foxy Barker, a costermonger's son who worked in a hatter's in Jermyn Street, and of Whitey, a former boxer from Whitechapel, with a broken nose and deaf in one ear, who acted as guide and adviser to him during those early days of military life.

It is difficult to imagine that my father showed the slightest talent for the working of guns, large or small, or that he was at all useful in any of the tasks, however basic, such as peeling potatoes, that were set him. For someone who did not like rules, he had moved into a world dominated by them. By putting on a uniform, he seemed, in one flourish, to have embraced all the conventions for which he once had such disdain, but, for all the monotony he complained about, military life seemed to suit him. The leaf in the wind had been picked up by a breeze and blown on and there was to be no going back.

The writer in Rees, the perpetual outsider looking in, discovered endless material for social observation and Mr Nobody found that being in uniform conferred a kind of anonymity on him which gave him freedom. Besides, while sometimes being tedious and boring, it was mostly very exciting. Whitey taught him how to survive and he seemed to have done an excellent job. At camp that summer, the new recruits were bashed into shape. Rees wrote: 'It did not matter that the regiment was hopelessly badly trained, organized or equipped for any military operation. It did not matter that the training camp was, for the purpose of acquiring military efficiency, an enormous waste of time and effort and money. What did matter, it seemed, was that recruits to the Territorial Army should be broken as quickly and thoroughly as possible into the habits of military life; that they should learn to accept boredom, monotony, inefficiency and waste as the fundamental conditions of life in the army; and that they should also learn to regard themselves as amply compensated for learning such lessons by the opportunity to drink themselves silly whenever the occasion offered and their means afforded. It was like being blooded for the hunt; it was the way to acquire morale . . .'

Whitey, wisely, kept him away from the rowdy evening drinking sessions. Rees said he felt more like a camp follower than a soldier, existing on the fringe of the regiment, like the vagrants who attached themselves to Elizabethan armies. Whitey, who was detailed to the cookhouse with my father, also taught him to steer clear of anyone in authority. Rees learned to take cover as soon as he saw an officer or an NCO approaching and to respond to any questions addressed at him either with silence or to reply, 'smartly and blankly', with 'Don't know, sir.' Dumbness and blankness worked very well, he found. 'One could be sure that irritation at one's stupidity would overcome any desire to secure an answer . . .' Very soon he did not have to make any effort to keep out of the way; people were only too glad to avoid noticing him. Whitey's lessons served him well, Rees thought.

A few days after the end of the summer camp, in late August 1939, Ribbentrop signed the Soviet–German Non-Aggression Pact in Moscow. Rees always swore that this was the point at which he, like many others, gave up his communist sympathies and ceased to be a theoretical Marxist though he was 'not far from becoming an unconscious Marxist instead'. That he parted company with the cause at this point seemed to have been accepted by most of those who knew him. Guy Burgess and Anthony Blunt were on holiday together in the South of France and came home as soon as the news broke. Blunt told the late Robert Cecil, the former diplomat and academic who had written a book about Donald Maclean and interviewed Blunt in 1981, that out of the three of them the person who was most upset by the Pact was my father.

Rees admitted in *A Chapter of Accidents* that he realized something very important had happened because Guy had left his car – 'one of the possessions he valued most in the world' – at Calais and had crossed from France by the night boat. 'He was in a state of considerable excitement and exhaustion; but I thought I also noticed something about him which I had never seen before,' he wrote. Guy was frightened, strained and apprehensive in his behaviour towards Rees; it was unusual. But when Rees denounced the treachery of the Soviet Union and said that the Russians had now made war inevitable, Guy 'merely shrugged his shoulders and said calmly that after Munich the Soviet Union was perfectly justified in putting its own security first'. Indeed, if they had not done so, they would have 'betrayed the interests of the working class both in the Soviet Union and throughout the world'. Rees told Guy that neither he nor the Soviets really understood what Hitler was like and that one might as well entrust the interests of the working class to a rattlesnake as to him. According to Rees's account, Guy asked him what he intended to do. Rees replied, 'To do? I don't suppose I've any choice. I'll be called up.' Guy then said: 'And what about me? And the Comintern?' to which Rees answered: 'I never want to have anything to do with the Comintern for the rest of my life. Or with you, if you really are one of their agents.' He assured Guy that he would never again raise the matter.

When Anthony Blunt discussed this event with Robert Cecil in 1981, he told Cecil that Rees was 'one of us' until the Pact was signed. One interpretation of Rees's version of his conversation with Guy, as I have just related it, is that it might refer to some kind of past commitment on his part to collaborate with Burgess and Blunt. But Rees never admitted to that. Of this time, Rosamond Lehmann recalled: 'After the Nazi–Soviet Pact life went on. I asked Goronwy how it would affect Guy. He said Guy had dropped his position as a Comintern agent. But they went on seeing each other a great deal.

Guy got drunker and drunker as time went on. He and Goronwy used to argue all the time.'

Almost immediately after the signing of the Pact, 90th Field Regiment was mobilized and sent to the London docks 'to maintain order in case of civil disturbance' and, on 2 September, the day after Germany invaded Poland, Rees became a full-time soldier. When I was small he used to tell me a story about how he had been woken up at night in the warehouse in which they were billeted by rats running across his chest. On 3 September, the day that war was declared, Walter Allen, who was living in Bloomsbury, was on his way to a restaurant for dinner when he was 'accosted' by a solder. 'It was Goronwy, who, to my surprise, was a private in the Territorial Army and had just been called up,' he recalled.

From his new address, Regimental HQ, 90th Field Regiment RA, Handel Street, London WC1, Rees, about to be given thirty-six hours leave, wrote to his brother, Geraint, who was to join the Welsh Guards: 'I feel very isolated here, can't see my friends and have worked like fury; I have been recommended for promotion to Lance Bombardier! John Sparrow has joined the Oxford and Bucks Light Infantry as a private. The war depresses me extremely: I feel it's a waste of my and other people's lives even if we're not killed. Our leave is preliminary to a month's intensive training before we go abroad, I think to France. I have just been on guard all night and am very tired . . . Very much love, Gony.'

To his father and his sister in Cardiff, he wrote the following letter from the same address:

Dearest Dada and all,

I'm so sorry I haven't written before, but we don't have much chance, though things have been much easier lately. There's only about 15 of us at Handel Street now, the rest of them are at the docks. Our duties are to go on guard here and keep the place clean; and we're able to keep ourselves clean, too, as we have some shower baths, and get an evening off about three times a week, and I can go to my flat and see friends who are in London. But it's very monotonous and uninteresting; my diversion has been to try and read a book about Karl Marx which my friend Isaiah Berlin has just written and sent to me . . . I hope Geraint's commission will come through soon and he will get away. I'm negotiating with my office and hope they won't leave me quite flat and if they repent I hope I will be able to contribute something to the new establishment at Tydfil Place. I hope you aren't worrying too much, especially about me, I get on quite well and the people around me are very interesting. My application for a commission should now be before the War Office. I hope they don't take too long considering it. I think we shall move from here soon to go into training somewhere in the country, it should be quite interesting though hard work ... Everyone in London seems confident we shall win the war easily and quickly: I hope it is true and believe it may be. Write to me soon and send me all your news: I'll write when I know we are going away.

With all my love to all,
Gony

Very soon, Rees was told by the adjutant that a letter had come from the War Office stating that he had been nominated for a commission in the Welsh Guards and arrangements were being made to transfer him to the next officers' training course – just after Christmas – at the Royal Military College, Sandhurst. Rees's Ebury Street landlord, Major Dudley Ward, was Regimental Adjutant, Welsh Guards.

Rees described how this was viewed by his adjutant, who was a regular soldier: 'It offended his instincts that the Welsh Guards should resort to recruiting its officers from the untrained rabble, more like francs tireurs than soldiers, which formed the rank and file of the 90th Field Regiment ... He could not restrain himself from dispatching an orderly to identify the gunner whom the Welsh Guards had so eccentrically claimed as their own, with an order that I should report to him immediately in his office. It was if he wished to see with his own eyes how low the army had sunk.' Rees had to be woken up for the interview; it was the first time, he claimed, that he had spoken directly to an officer, due to Whitey's tuition. 'Until then, I had successfully followed Whitey's guiding principle that officers were persons to be avoided at all costs ...' The adjutant looked at the letter in front of him and asked Rees if he had been nominated for a commission in the Welsh Guards. Until now Rees had been able to adopt the 'Don't know, sir' formula which he and Whitey accepted as the perfect reply – safe, non-committal and conveying just the right degree of stupidity – to any question addressed by anyone of higher rank. This time, it happened to be true. According to my father, a 'spasm of despair' crossed the adjutant's face. 'He was a good man and a good soldier and it was the future of the army he was thinking of ...' He asked Rees if there had been some mistake. Rees replied with the statutory 'Don't know, sir', and left the room. Behind him, he recalled, he heard the adjutant cry out, furiously, as if in pain, 'Good God, what's happened to the Brigade!'

I discovered that one of Rees's references for a commission came from Sir Ernest Swinton, the Chichele Professor of Military History at Oxford and a very popular Fellow of All Souls, who had helped to develop the tank during the 1914–18 war. He sent this letter to my father from All Souls:

Dear Rees,

I have today written a certificate as to your fitness for a commission, and I hope you get it. With the Guards you will have your bellyful of action! One word – which I have no right to say to you as a Fellow of the College, but have as an officer – tighten up a bit – be punctual and on the spot. You've got all the brains and guts and leadership necessary, so do not give the impression of slackness and casualness!

Good luck! I am glad you have joined up.

> Yours sincerely, in haste,
> E.D. Swinton

In late September Rees was posted to 161st Officer Cadet Training Unit and wrote to his father from Sandhurst thanking him for a watch. Having received very few letters from my father myself, I was surprised to see how childish and detached these communications to his father were, although, obviously, there was a great deal that he could not explain about himself and his activities.

Dearest Dada,

Thank you very much for the watch, which is just what I wanted and will be of the greatest help. We have been working very hard but it is coming a little easier now that I'm more used to my surroundings and I don't feel quite as hunted as I did at first. On Sunday we had a half holiday (everything here is like returning to school) and I went to Oxford and came back here in the evening. It's a great pleasure to get out of here occasionally. Otherwise there has been very little to tell you; life is very monotonous here with none of the human interest of being in the ranks . . .

> With all my love,
> Gony

In March 1940 Rees was appointed to a commission as second lieutenant in the Royal Welch Fusiliers a most literary regiment in which had served, among others, Siegfried Sassoon and Robert Graves. The regiment marches with a goat at its head and its soldiers are easily identified by the 'flash', the five black silk ribbons worn on the back of the tunic collar. This is a relic from the days when soldiers wore powdered wigs with pigtails, which, to prevent their regimental red tunics from getting dirty, were wrapped in 'queue bags' tied up with black ribbons. The 'flash' is elegant and distinctive and many people noted how smartly turned out Rees always was in his RWF uniform.

According to the battalion's war diary, on 10 May 1940, the day Germany invaded Belgium and Holland, Rees was posted to 8th Battalion from the RWF Infantry Training Centre at Wrexham. By now he was thirty; the average age of the battalion in October of that year was twenty-three. He was soon sent off on an intelligence course, but before he went wrote another of his informative letters to his father and sister from camp at Avonmouth near Bristol, suggesting that he might be stationed at a derelict house called Neville Hall, belonging to the Marquess of Abergavenny. He told them that he was being kept out of bed three times a week by night duties and he was glad to be getting away from the 'very monotonous and uninteresting duties we have to perform here . . .'

Who knows whether it was boredom, the literary tradition of the regiment, or deeply-felt indignation, but in the early summer of 1940 Rees was inspired to write to the new monthly review, *Horizon* – whose May issue had proposed that war is the 'enemy of creative activity' – accusing the editor, Cyril Connolly, of being very superior about the ordinary soldier. Rees's 'Letter From a Soldier', published in the July issue, opened: 'You say that "War is the enemy of creative activity and writers and painters are right and wise to ignore it." I quote this phrase because, as I think you will agree, it expresses very clearly your attitude to the war, and summarizes the conclusion of an argument which, in different forms, has appeared in almost all your monthly Comments in *Horizon*. May I say why I disagree, though a mind numbed by soldiering is hardly capable of formulating an idea or phrasing a sentence . . .'

What Connolly was saying to artists, according to Rees, was: 'Let the British and French soldiers protect you, but ignore them while they die for you and wait till they have killed the ogre that threatens . . .' He found this objectionable. He was not asking writers to take up arms, but he did not think it was right that they should ignore the war. The soldier, he asserted, 'has the right, in return for his blood and his life and his despair, to ask that those most qualified, by their sensibility, by their more lucid perception of values, by their release from belligerence, should comprehend, analyse, illuminate, commemorate, his sacrifice and his suffering and the horror to which he is condemned, to understand and reveal that even in war he is a human being and not a brute too ignoble for the artist's notice; most of all he has the right to ask this because the values which he, poor devil, dimly feels he is being called upon to defend are those without which the artist cannot live . . .'

While a million soldiers die, Rees said, the artist will live and create – and apparently he is to accept the fruit of this sacrifice as a free gift and acknowledge no responsibility to the giver. Connolly's proposition that the soldier should die so that the artist should live clearly infuriated Rees. 'No voice will break the terrible silence of the soldier, while he cannot break it himself; he has no voice, he has only a rifle,' he wrote, with passion. 'If this should happen, do not be surprised if the artist is without honour; for God's sake never complain, as I have seen *Horizon*, that the artist does not receive his due from society. Why should he? for on his part he acknowledges none . . .'

It all made a great talking point. Rees's letter was reproduced in *Horizon* together with the following paragraph: 'We consider this article of sufficient importance to take the place of "Comment" in this number. The Editorial Reply is on page 532.'

In the Reply, Connolly did not concede much ground. *Horizon* had not taken the war seriously enough, he wrote, but the fact remained that war *is* the enemy of creative activity, because the 'military virtues are in conflict with the creative and because it is impossible in wartime for most people to concentrate on the values of literature and art. The point which *Horizon* has made is that though this war is being fought for culture, the fighting of it will not create that culture . . .' In the next issue, Connolly struck back at those who considered that *Horizon* should give more space to the war. He ran an essay on military tactics written by a retired major general who was a leading authority on tanks.

In *A Chapter of Accidents*, Rees noted that Guy, who was then working for the BBC, wrote to tell him that he had liked the article and 'envied' him for being a soldier. Rees could not quite understand why and remarked that there was nothing to stop Guy being one, too, if he wanted. But, at that time, he said, the view prevailed that it was somehow undignified for an intellectual to be a soldier. Going into the Civil Service, the Office of Information or the BBC, and keeping away from the brutality of war was seen as serving one's country 'usefully and intelligently', while there was something 'immoral and absurd' about being a soldier.

Rees's letters home that I found with my grandfather's diaries are all undated, and so it is difficult to follow the sequence of events that so dramatically overtook him during the next few months. However, some time during the late summer or autumn of 1940 he was sent up to the Wirral, from where, attached to 38 Division, he was posted to Parkgate, overlooking the estuary of the Dee, and, in the distance, the mountains of North Wales. I am sure I can remember from my childhood that the tide came up over the sands to the edge of the little road leading alongside the bank of the estuary, but today there are nothing but reeds as far as the eye can see. There, Rees met my mother, who may still have been only nineteen, for her birthday was in August. She was ten years younger than he. Rees used to tell me that when he saw her riding a bicycle he decided she was the most beautiful girl he had ever seen. My mother's youngest sister, Susie, who was then ten, claimed that she had found him first and had engaged him in conversation over a garden wall. It was a whirlwind romance and Rosamond Lehmann, who considered that Rees was still hers, was aghast when she heard they were to be married before the end of the year. She and Elizabeth Bowen and Guy all wrote to Rees to tell him that this was a disastrous idea for someone as fickle and irresponsible as he was.

My mother was the eldest of four children; her siblings all had red hair, though she was fair, and, in the words of her sister, Mary, who was three years younger, very 'dashing'. Known as Margie, she was named after a direct forebear – on her mother's side – called Margaret Ewing, who, at sixteen, had come south with Bonnie Prince Charlie's entourage in the '45 Rebellion. She was very young; she was not a lady novelist, or a radical nor a bluestocking. Not long out of school, Margie played golf, smoked, painted her fingernails, drove a car, wore daring bathing suits and had a large circle of beaux, which was then somewhat depleted as most of the young men in the vicinity had been called up. At the time my father met her, she was driving an ambulance for the war effort. One way and another, she cut quite a dash in Parkgate, which, although only a few miles from the dingy backstreets of Birkenhead, was where the affluent professional and middle classes of Liverpool had large comfortable houses with tennis courts and servants.

Her father, T.T. Morris, known to his family as Bingo and to his business friends and colleagues as Tommy, was an underwriter and became the general manager of the Liverpool, London and Globe insurance company. He came from a well-known Lancashire family: several Morrises had been Lord Mayors of Liverpool and Bingo's father had managed the Rose Bridge colliery in Wigan, which belonged to his uncle. My mother's mother, Peggy, was a Barton, and her grandfather owned the iron and steel works at Carnforth in north Lancashire. Peggy had been born in Birmingham, Alabama, where her father had steel interests and, as a child, I remember her singing a lullaby to me that began: 'Go to sleep my little picaninny, Mamma's little Alabammy coon ...' Bingo had a splendid singing voice, too, and one of his favourite songs, which he liked to deliver as he shaved in the mornings with his badger-hair shaving brush, went something like this: 'My gal's a high-born lady, she's not black just a little bit shady ...' Edward Fitzgerald, who translated *The Rubaiyat of Omar Khayyam*, was unhappily married to a Barton – her father, Bernard Barton, the Quaker poet, was a member of the original National Committee for the Abolition of the Slave Trade with William Wilberforce. Another Barton invented the horizontal flax wheel in Carlisle in 1766.

My mother and her sisters went to a school called Huyton College, in the Liverpool suburbs, where Barbara Pym was also a pupil. I was sent there, too, and all my teachers were rather like characters in Pym novels. Many of them had lost their fiancés in the First World War and had subsequently dedicated their lives to educating girls to become useful and serious members of society. Discipline was very strict and we spent a lot of time charging around hockey and lacrosse pitches. Although the Huyton philosophy was exactly the same, as was the uniform, in my mother's day, she did not, I think, quite conform to the Huyton standards of success. My aunt, Mary, who went to Oxford from Huyton and later taught English at Bedales, told me that my mother was 'naughty' at school, but very popular. 'Margie was slightly disapproved of by the staff,' she said. 'She was not academically bright at all, though very intelligent, but very good at all sport. I think she was typical of her generation. She was very pretty in the style of the time and was one of the first girls in Parkgate to paint her nails.' She was also wonderfully practical and innovative. Out of almost nothing, my mother could effortlessly produce a delicious meal; she could bake, she could ice cakes, she could make perfect meringues; with her sewing machine, she could turn curtains into an evening dress, a blanket into a coat, and rustle up a loose cover for a sofa in a matter of hours. These gifts, along with a passion for driving rather fast and fixing engine faults in motor cars, she had inherited from her mother,

Peggy. I am told that when Bingo first met my grandmother, she had her head underneath the bonnet of a car. My mother was also a marvellous gardener and many times succeeded in transforming back yards filled with weeds and old scrap metal into sweet-smelling and verdant bowers. Her talents were to be given plenty of opportunity for expression during her married life and without them it is hard to imagine how we would ever have survived.

I drove up to Parkgate to look again at the place where my parents met, and found the air of affluence still intact. The Morrises' black-and-white timbered house, Desborough, where I was born in March 1942, is still there, overlooking the cricket pitch, but a small development of new houses has taken over what used to be the large garden. The house itself is now divided into three, and opposite, across an unmade road, I found the house where Rees might have met Margie at the tennis party given by a family with five daughters, who were very popular locally. My aunt Mary told me: 'The beginning of the war was pretty exciting, you know. All the young men we knew in Parkgate had gone off to be pilots and when they flew overhead they dipped and wiggled their planes for girls like Margie to see.' But Margie was not interested in pilots any more.

In August 1940 Rees had been appointed to Intelligence and it was from Matlock in Derbyshire, where he was on a course, that he broke the unexpected news to his family:

Dearest Dada and Enid,
I've been meaning to write for some time, I've had some news to tell you only I haven't been quite certain what to say. When I was at Parkgate I fell in love with the Morrises' daughter and now if I can I want to get married. I hope this isn't too much of a surprise for you, nor an unpleasant one. Her name is Margie, her age is 20, she is very young and I am exceedingly happy with her. If I could I should get married tomorrow in spite of the war and everything else; unfortunately I haven't any money and a Lt's pay isn't anything to marry on, so we thought that we would wait until I was a captain, which may not be very long. My division has now moved to Aldershot and I shall join them after this course, and if it were possible to get married Margie would come and join me there, as I should be allowed to live out. It seems very unfortunate that all this has happened in the middle of a war, but on the other hand I should probably never have found her but for the war, so it seems to cancel out. She has spoken to her parents and they seem to be quite willing. I want you to meet her very much, it doesn't seem to be very easy at present, but I may be able to get some leave after returning to Aldershot and if I do I will bring her home. I'm sure you will like her

and I hope this will bring you as much happiness as it does to me.

Meanwhile, I have to work very hard on my course but it's very interesting and almost enjoyable. We live in a huge dark gloomy Hydro but the country is lovely and normally we spend every morning out of doors on exercises, which I enjoy very much. I've found several old friends here, including one who was a don at New College and now on the directing staff here . . .

I don't think you can be any more surprised than I am at my news, I only hope you will like her as much as I do. But until you see her at least congratulate me on my luck and send me your best wishes, it's sad we can't both come and see you as we should like to.

With all my love,<br>Gony.

Please don't say anything to anyone else.


The next letter home from the Hydro told of a visit to Parkgate to inform Bingo and my grandmother of his intentions. Rees wrote: 'I went to stay with Margie this weekend and with a great effort managed to speak to her parents, who were extremely kind and appeared to be very pleased. Her father told her he would give her an allowance of £150 a year and I think we ought to be able to live on that and my pay, so we thought we would get married as soon as we could and thought that Christmas might be a good time. I'm sorry to spring all this on you so suddenly; but I don't think I shall be in this country very long, in all probability my division will be ready to go abroad after the winter and both she and I would like to be married for a little time before I go. So you will have to perform a wedding ceremony, if you will, for yet another of your children . . .'

The hardest part of his course seemed to be over, he said. 'They seem to be quite pleased with me, which is surprising as my head is in such a whirl that I find it difficult to concentrate and am apt to fall asleep in the middle of lectures . . . I never thought I should come to this, it will cause a considerable change in my mode of life.'

In November, Bingo wrote to Rees's father to say how happy everyone at Desborough was with the engagement: 'We have seen so much of Goronwy during the summer and he has become so much a welcome member of our family life that we had nothing but gladness in our hearts when he asked Margie to become his wife. They have obviously given themselves wholeheartedly to one another and we are confident they will be as happy together as we would all desire. Though young, Margie is a very level-headed practical little person and we are as sure that she will make Goronwy a good wife as we are confident of his loyalty and devotion to her on their way through life together ... I can appreciate your pride in him for he has already attained much that could only have been attained by sterling qualities and high endeavour. We feel we have every reason to rejoice that a kindly fate has brought him into our lives ...'

My mother's letter, written on the same day in her large, confident handwriting, was very formal and simple. 'Dear Mr Rees, I was so glad to hear from you and to know you feel so happy that Goronwy and I are to be married' was about as much as she could manage. Once they were married the following month, she gave up calling him Goronwy. He was always Rees to her. And, as she dropped his Welsh name, another part of his past dropped away.

In a letter of November 1940 to Dig, the wife of his novelist friend Henry Yorke, part of which is missing, Rees revealed more: '... her name is Margie Morris and I fell in love with her. She is very young and not at all clever and rather tough and I adore her. It isn't possible to describe someone one is in love with so I won't try but I hope you and Henry will meet her sometime and will like her, you must. I only hope I am as lucky as Henry has been, you and he are the only people I know who are an encouragement to get married. I'm rather alarmed at what I've done, so please write. Also it has caused terrible trouble with Rosamond, who tells me I'm behaving like a lunatic, but there isn't anything else I could or wanted to do. You see how really undependable I am, it rather alarms me but now I feel I shan't have any need to be undependable any more. So you see I have been in rather a daze for the last few weeks and have found it rather difficult to attend to the war or to my military duties – once I forgot them altogether with very bad results ... with all my love, Goronwy.'

Before the wedding there was a flurry of worried letters home from Rees, who was made up to captain in November. He had not had been able to buy a ring, he explained, or find somewhere for them to live in Aldershot. 'I'm beginning to be quite busy and have to give lectures and run courses but it's very hard to keep one's mind on war and the Army in the state I'm in,' he wrote in one letter. He and my mother had been to see his father and sister, Enid, in Cardiff. After the visit he wrote home: 'We had to go via Bristol and from the train you could see the fires and ruins left after the air raid that night ... I enjoyed the weekend tremendously and so did Margie, she was rather frightened when she came but soon recovered ...' There was a last-minute request: 'By the way, if I may mention such a subject, please don't go and spend a lot of money on a wedding present. There's nothing Margie and I could use or need at the present moment, and it isn't a time to run into expenses. Later on things would be different. But I am in dire need of money and a *small* cheque would be the most useful thing for us. I hope you won't mind my saying this . . .' Rees managed to buy a wedding ring but lost it, along with all the cash he possessed, while on manoeuvres on Salisbury Plain; Bingo had to buy another ring and lend him the money for their honeymoon.

They were married at Neston, just up the road from Parkgate, shortly before Christmas 1940, and a letter written on New Year's Eve, by Rees to his father, contained a graphic account of their first few days of married life, when they found themselves in the bombing of London. His description of their time together could be said to set the pace and the tone for the whole of their marriage – for my mother was just as excitable as my father and shared the same ability to bring drama to the most ordinary of situations.

38 Div HQ<br>Home Forces

Dearest Dada and all,

I'm sorry I haven't written before. I think I have been enjoying myself too much. Margie and I had a lovely honeymoon, I couldn't have been happier. The first four days we were on the farm at Underbarrow, very comfortable and with unlimited supplies of butter and eggs and poultry, and very quiet with no trace of the war except that the first night of all we could see miles away the gunfire over Liverpool and we felt anxious about you. The weather was wonderful, it was warm and sunny each day and we walked for a little and went for drives in the country which is very beautiful. The day before Christmas we went to Blackpool where we stayed in an astonishing private hotel full of middle-aged families having a jolly Xmas. They looked at Margie and me with great suspicion and were so fascinating we could hardly bear to go out of the house. But we did manage to visit the Aquarium and see a play with Diana Wynyard and Rex Harrison, which was quite amusing, and to go to the Tower, where there must have been thousands of people dancing. Then we went to Parkgate for the night and the next day set out for Aldershot, loaded with luggage, turkeys, rugs, coat, and a puppy [*my mother's Pekinese, Fly*].

We came through London and arrived safely at Aldershot, where a series of disasters overtook us. The first serious one was when we arrived at the rooms I had taken and found the woman had already let them to someone else; so at eight o'clock we found ourselves stranded in the blackout with all our luggage and nowhere to go. We drove round and round Aldershot, visiting one dreary house and hotel after another, without any success, and I was very nearly in despair until finally our taxi man, who had become a firm friend, timidly suggested a lodging house he knew of which was to take us in – and an astonishing place it was – a lodging house for troops but incredibly clean, kept by a Mr Porter with a French wife and a French servant, all of whom chattered incessantly; our bedroom had a French window out on to a yard filled with geese and Muscovy ducks; when we woke in the morning and heard all the French chatter and the ducks quacking and looking in at the window it was hard to believe one was in England and in Aldershot. We liked the place so much we nearly stayed there, especially as it only cost four shillings a night for bed and breakfast. The next day I had to go to the office and Margie tramped around Aldershot and finally found some very good rooms in a large house where we have a very comfortable sitting-room, and a bedroom, it's really nicer than the place I took, so we are very happy.

The next great disaster took place on Sunday. We needed some bedlinen and towels so we went up to Ebury Street and had tea with the Dudley Wards, who are still there though all the windows have been blown in. We went to Waterloo and about 6.30 were in the train waiting to leave the station when first there were terrific gun flares which we watched with interest but without much concern; then glass began to fly about as bombs came through the roof of the station and finally about six or seven incendiary bombs dropped on the platform immediately outside our carriage door. By now everyone was bolting for shelter. We had two large suitcases of things and lugged these after them into the shelter where we stayed until one o'clock among the thousands of troops and some of the strangest people I've ever seen, including some who inhabit the cellar so permanently that they've converted part of it into private flats for themselves by means of blankets hung on lines, and decorated their homes for Xmas with streamers and coloured paper bells and mistletoe, and they stand at their doors chatting to each other exactly as if they were in a slum street and about 11 o'clock the young men of the family stroll in with their hands in their pockets after an evening out. Sometimes we heard an enormous thump . . . and the walls of the underground shelter would sway slightly. We sat on our suitcases and once or twice went up to see what was going on: the roof was blazing away in parts and falling in onto the trains which were also on fire, and the glass roof where it wasn't burning was lit with a rosy glow as if all the sky was on fire. When we got back a water main had burst and was flooding part of the shelter . . . and when at 1.0 o'clock the all clear went I had to carry Margie through the water. By that time we felt as if we had lived in a shelter all our lives and all the people round us were our close friends.

When we did get out, it was rather a terrifying sight. It was as light as day, and in the street was a crater about 30 feet deep and a broken water main simply gushing water in a torrent and down the street under a bridge all we could see was a roaring mass of flame like the inside of a furnace. We were still dragging our suitcases which we'd managed to preserve, and picked our way through floods of water and ruins of houses and walked about half a mile until by incredible luck we managed to find a taxi whose driver advised us to go to the Strand Palace Hotel. We drove over Westminster Bridge where we saw one of the most extraordinary sights you can imagine. All the buildings along the river were lit up by the fire, and the river was a wonderful rosy red with its reflection and it looked as if the entire city was on fire, a huge dome of fire with masses of thick white smoke and in the middle of it all you could see St Paul's standing out as if it were floodlit. It was one of the most beautiful and terrifying sights you can imagine: Moscow must have looked like that when it was burned. When we got to the Strand it seemed incredible to find people sitting quietly drinking and talking as if nothing were happening; outside you could hear machine gun fire which was our fighters drawing the Germans off. We were very exhausted and extremely dirty, we drank some tea and finally collapsed into bed feeling very happy to be alive and the next day we staggered out to Clapham Junction and managed to get a train to Aldershot. So that was how we spent the night of the great fire. Londoners are extraordinary people: I never saw anyone show any sign of fear or panic or even complain, and the firemen and the ARP wardens are really incredible, nothing seems to disturb them.

Margie and I were both so fascinated by everything that we almost enjoyed it all; but it does make you feel sick at heart to see London in ruins, it looks old and shabby and decrepit and abandoned like a deserted city, but I doubt it ever looked so beautiful as it did during the fire. You can imagine that when we reached Aldershot we felt as if we never wanted to go out again or do anything except sit at home in peace.

We are lucky to be so comfortable. I'm able to see Margie sometimes at lunchtime and nearly every evening, except tonight, which is New Year's Eve, when I am on duty, and can sleep there on Saturday and Sunday. I feel extremely lucky to have her with me, it even makes the Army almost bearable and we're very happy . . .

With all my love,
Gony

Rees had been re-elected to All Souls for a further seven years, but because of the war he was able to be present at only five general meetings of the college out of twenty-one. However, whenever he could he continued to return to Oxford where he still had plenty of friends, all keen to keep up with what he was doing.

Noël Annan remembered meeting Rees for the first time in Oxford some time during the war and they were to get to know each other much better when they worked together in the Control Commission in Germany in 1945. Noël thought that he was probably staying the weekend with Maurice Bowra when the meeting took place. 'At about noon one day, Maurice said to me, "Well, come on, off to All Souls. I think it's about time you met Goronwy Rees ..."' He asked Maurice to tell him about Rees. 'I have forgotten exactly what he said, but I am sure it was something about being amusing, satirical, ironical and all the rest of it,' he said. When they got to Rees's rooms, he was shaving and wearing a pair of pyjama bottoms; Maurice was delighted to see him so attired. According to Noël, Maurice made a 'great thing' of turning to him and saying, 'You see, look at his back, it is scarred from the pitface, scarred with coal from the pitface ...' It was the joke about the barefoot boy from the valleys again. 'I remember Goronwy's smile, there was that shy, curious smile spread all over his face, which meant I think this is quite funny but I am not entirely sure I like it,' Noël recalled. Everyone had, of course, been talking about Rees's marriage and of Rosamond, with whom Noël had friends in common. He said he could well imagine Rosamond being malicious about Rees. 'I think he got fed up with her possessiveness. She was a most possessive lover,' he told me.

Stuart Hampshire believed that Rees's marriage to my mother had come as a 'frightful blow' to Rosamond. According to my aunt Mary, Rees had a 'problem' with Rosamond. She recalled that when Rees had wanted to end the relationship, she would not leave him. 'She was getting older, and the aspects of her that he once found so attractive and appealing about her had begun to displease and tire him. She would not leave him alone when he and Margie were married. This was very difficult and very upsetting for Margie. She once told me that Rosamond had rung her to say that Goronwy had spent the night with her and she had found his pyjamas. She wondered if Margie would like them back.' Rees appeared to lack the strength or the will to make a clean break with Rosamond; it made my mother very upset. Mary's feeling was that Rees just 'could not bear to give Rosamond the push ...'

Guy, of course, ever generous with his advice, had warned Rees against getting married and, according to my father, had sent a 'long, affectionate and almost paternal letter about the dangers which both

I and my wife were about to incur'. My mother was, Rees remarked in his memoirs, someone who would not have known what one was talking about if one had mentioned the word 'Comintern'. (Later she was to become quite an expert not only on the Comintern but on espionage in general.) Guy thought Rees was unstable, volatile, undependable, fickle, much addicted to women, unable to support himself let alone a wife or a family, egotistical and pleasure-loving, 'and he hoped I had not deceived my wife into thinking otherwise'. He added that 'it was extremely unwise of me to think of getting married at all and even more foolish and rash of my wife to marry me . . . In spite of this, if I were really determined to take such a desperate step, he was delighted if we were happy and we should all three meet at the first possible opportunity.' My father showed Guy's letter to my mother, and, he wrote, 'She cried a little, but was quickly reassured when I told her that Guy was doing, as he thought, his best, by trying to pluck me out of marriage like a brand from the burning; no doubt he thought it would be in both our interests. Even so I could see that she thought it a very odd letter from a very odd person, and suddenly I had a very sharp sense of how very strange a creature Guy must seem when seen through the eyes of someone who had not become as inured to his eccentricities as I had . . .'

According to his account, Rees did not see much of Guy until later in the war when, on leave, he visited the flat in Bentinck Street, belonging to Victor Rothschild, that Guy was sharing with Anthony Blunt who was then with MI5. As we now know, Guy and Blunt were both working for the Russians and were upsetting their control officers because, by living together, they were breaking the rule that agents should not be seen with one another.

At the time Guy was proffering warnings, Rees was 'occupied with too many other things' to concern himself with his friend's activities. Already the question of other women was putting a strain on his marriage and my grandparents did not like their daughter being upset. The stress which war brings to all relationships, the age difference between Rees and my mother, which later meant nothing at all, and the entirely different ways of life they had each been accustomed to, created extra tensions.

After ten years of pleasing only himself, my father did not seem able to accept gracefully that his bachelor days were over; he never did. He was frequently unfaithful to my mother, though there was never any doubt at all in anyone's mind that he loved her very much.

My mother's unhappiness at his philandering was not something she ever confided to me and usually he was very discreet about his affairs. But I remember once, shortly before my own marriage, my mother told me that the way to be happy was to try and think of the man in one's life in the same way as one thought of a favourite cat. 'You see, with a cat, you like to see it go out in the garden and enjoy itself and then you are very pleased to see it again when it comes in,' she said. Whether she ever managed to master that approach I cannot say, but to the very end, she and my father took the greatest pleasure in each other's company. He was totally dependent on her. But when they met, he had already had ten years of doing whatever he liked and pleasing only himself and he was not going to be held back. As a result, there were awful rows at Parkgate.

My grandparents were an odd mixture of being very conventional and yet with flourishes of eccentricity that were not entirely unusual among people of their class. My grandfather, Bingo, read the *Daily Telegraph* and was much revered in the Liverpool business world for his wisdom and his integrity; as a young man he had worked for his firm in New York and this had helped to broaden his outlook. He had a large repertoire of music-hall songs that he enjoyed singing and liked to tell stories that began, 'When I was a little girl ...'; he was also a brilliant creator of outdoor treasure hunts, which had hunters searching in the trunks of trees and under stones for his clues, each of which was a poem. But Bingo loathed socialists, so, although he was very tolerant of Rees, there was always that bone of contention between them. My grandmother was a formidable and strong-willed woman, whom I adored because, like so many war babies, I was more or less brought up by her. She and Rees fought like cat and dog, and there was one instance when he threw a plate of pudding at her, though I do not remember it. She did not like Parkgate, or having to entertain Bingo's large circle of business colleagues. What she wanted to do was to live in the country and raise Dexter cattle, which her family had done when she was a child, and it was only when Bingo retired that she was able to realize this cherished wish. She was at her happiest surrounded by plants and animals and there were hardly any points on which she and Rees shared the same point of view.

My grandparents were conventional in the sense that they liked people to behave correctly and to be courteous and respectful of what they themselves considered to be the virtues and values of decent people. Later my father was to have a deep affection for Bingo and a great deal of respect for my grandmother, but at that time he saw them in the much the same light as he saw his own family: they were people who wanted to put him in chains and restrain him; and they expected him to conform and be that most dreadful of things, respectable. The trouble was that he was married to their daughter. Margie, he soon learned, came with her own bundle of problems. High-spirited and still very young, she wanted to giggle and fool around as she had been used to doing with the Parkgate boys; Rees wanted to sit and read, as he had always done and as he would always do.

All this was going to take some time to work out and, in the meantime, there was a war on.

# 7

War changes all things, materially and morally,
and we ourselves change with them.

From A Chapter of Accidents

In January 1941 the newly-married Captain Rees was appointed General Staff Officer, Intelligence Training Centre, and my parents went to live in Cambridge where my father lectured on the interrogation of German prisoners. Freddie Ayer, then in the Welsh Guards, was on one of his courses. In his autobiography, *Part of My Life*, he told how he had rung Rees in London before meeting him in Cambridge and my mother, whom he did not know, answered the telephone. Freddie spelled out his name for her and remembered saying: 'Its A for Apple, Y for Youth, E for Excitement and R for Revenge', but my mother remembered it otherwise. She was sure he had said A for Arrogance and R for Romance, but Freddie was absolutely certain that his version was correct.

Whenever my mother and father could be together, they were, but my mother spent a great deal of time at home in Parkgate. That summer she became pregnant (for me and my sister, Lucy, home was, until the end of the war, with our grandparents). At the beginning of 1942, Rees was posted as a GSO 2 (Intelligence) to GHQ Home Forces in London, and stayed with Henry Yorke, a close friend but whom he rarely saw because Henry worked on night duty with the fire brigade. Towards the end of 1941, he sent news of developments to his family in Cardiff:

Dearest Dada and Enid,

I'm very sorry I haven't written for such a long time. I have been very busy as I am now in charge of the course since Gerald Wellesley has gone out to the Middle East. It means quite a lot of extra work and more responsibility but it's more interesting and in time may mean a majority, which would be very welcome. But it hasn't come as yet. At the end of the last course I had to go and visit a prisoner of war cage, which was very interesting, and staying in London with a friend called Henry Yorke. Margie went to stay with her aunt in Chipping Camden and I joined her there and we enjoyed ourselves very much. Last weekend Shiela [*Grant Duff*] came to stay with us and seemed to be very well and happy; she is now head of the

Czech section of the BBC European Service. Margie and I hired a car the weekend before last and drove to Oxford where I attended our All Souls Day Gaudy. It seemed quite unchanged, there were 45 fellows there, including the Archbishop and Simon and Greene and we fed on grouse brought down by the gun of the ex-editor of *The Times* [*Geoffrey Dawson*]. Margie stayed with Roy Harrod [*the economist*] and his wife, and we saw her sister, who is very happy at Oxford, and went to lunch with Maurice Bowra in his Warden's Lodgings at Wadham. It was a very enjoyable evening.

The baby is growing rapidly and now kicks. Margie is going home on December 20 and I shall join her for Christmas and return here on the 27th and I'm afraid will then have to take up a bachelor existence once gain. The baby is expected towards the end of February and if it is possible I will try to take a few days off between now and Xmas and Margie and I will try to come and see you in Cardiff; but these days I have to try and economise.

I went to dine with the Master of Trinity last week and am going to dine at Trinity again this week with an old friend called Professor Hardy, who used to be professor of Mathematics.

We have hired a nurse to look after Margie when the baby comes. The Morrises have been very kind about it all and are paying nearly all the expenses which is a very great help. Write to us soon and send us all your news. We are very well and happy here.

Very much love from us both,<br>Gony

Before long Rees was moved again, this time to HQ South-Eastern Command in Reigate to join General Montgomery's staff at the end of March 1942. He was warned in advance that Monty was a 'terror', but Rees was to develop a lasting affection and high regard for him and would never hear a word spoken against him. In *A Bundle of Sensations* he described how he first came face to face with the great man: 'One saw a narrow foxy face, long nosed, sharp and intelligent and tenacious, with very bright and clear blue eyes, and a small, light, spare body.' The effect was not at all imposing, he felt, except for his eyes and 'an indefinable look in his face of extreme cleverness and sagacity, like a very alert Parson Jack Russell terrier'. What impressed Rees was his 'air of extraordinary quietness and calm, as if nothing in the world would disturb his peace of mind'. He spoke quietly and his manner was quiet, too. It gave Rees the sense that, with Monty, everything was in order, like a good housewife whose domestic arrangements are always ready for any conceivable emergency'. And, contrary to the experience he had had of many senior officers, my father found Monty 'extremely polite, so that one almost forgot his rank, and this could have been dangerous, except that not for one moment could one forget that one was in the presence of a very remarkable person'. So struck was Rees by this calmness that, on their first meeting, his initial feelings of panic and alarm quickly died away. As he was asked to sit in a window seat with his back to the garden, he was able to examine Montgomery's face in the evening light; observed that it was moulded 'with the kind of fineness one sees in some animals that are very finely bred and trained for the particular purpose they have to follow'.

Montgomery wished him to act as his personal representative to Admiral Mountbatten's headquarters, where the planning of the Dieppe raid was taking place. For the next few weeks Rees was obsessed by details of the consistency of the shingle of the beach at Dieppe and how the tanks were going to land, and he reported regularly back to Montgomery at Reigate, seeing him, always with great pleasure, usually in the evening after dinner, which was his favourite time for meetings. Sometimes Rees saw him even later in the day: 'Then, if it were not too late, he would receive me in bed, looking exceedingly clean, like a schoolboy after his bath, in his flannelette pyjamas, his Bible open beside him on his night table, himself propped up on his pillows, his foxy face as alert as ever, showing no trace of tiredness. I had the feeling that the moment I had gone the eyelids would close like a shutter and he would immediately be asleep. When he was awake, he was thinking, clearly, rationally, lucidly; when he was asleep, he really slept. I felt sure there were no dreams. And why should there be? After all there was nothing to worry about...'

But Operation JUBILEE, mounted in August, was not to be a success. When training had come to an end, on the eve of the Dieppe raid, Rees was issued with large numbers of forged French banknotes in large denominations, to be distributed to a small party of Sudeten–German socialists in British uniforms who were to be attached to the operation in order to carry out, as he put it, 'some suicidal mission'. The banknotes were delivered to him, mysteriously, by a sergeant 'of no known regiment', in a sealed parcel under the clock at Victoria Station. He was, in the end, unable to distribute the money to the men, and as their names appeared on no official records, he never knew what happened to them and their mission. In July, plans for the raid were finalized and Rees found himself in Portsmouth, boarding the Hunt-class destroyer, *Garth*. The ship's task was to cover the flank of the assault force during the sea-crossing, and later to engage, and if possible silence or neutralize, one of the gun batteries which were known to be located on the high cliffs on the eastern side of Dieppe. That night he was given the commander's cabin to sleep in, where, he wrote, he awoke to find it an effort to remember what he was doing there. 'It was hard to grasp that Operation JUBILEE had begun ... at that moment I remembered being told that a destroyer is so thin-skinned that a revolver shot will pierce its armour; it seemed strange that men should be exposed to so many dangers in so frail a vessel, as if they were to venture to sea in an egg-shell.'

He went up on deck, quite unprepared for what was to come. He had the 'sudden impression of travelling blindly at great speed into a darkness that was filled with the noise of wind and water'. *Garth*, he wrote, 'like a hunting dog, was making great sweeps on the flanks of the assault force, casting to right and left in the darkness as if at any moment she might smell out an enemy and pick it up in her teeth and worry it to death'. In the darkness it felt as if the ship was entirely alone. On the maps and charts of the operation, the assault force, each ship and craft carefully in position, had looked like a solid and compact body, 'as if we were going to cross the Channel in a pack ...' Now, there seemed nothing but grey water surrounding him as the destroyer rushed forward 'like some highly strung neurotic animal that had broken away from the herd'.

After ploughing off her course to rescue a pilot who had been shot down, the destroyer was hit by a bomb, though she was still able to engage the guns on the cliffs as she was detailed to do. Then she was hit a second time, with considerable casualties and damage, and meanwhile Dieppe appeared not to have been captured. Rees reported: 'There should have been the noise of demolitions as each unit destroyed its particular objectives. And they should have been regrouping to hold the town against counter-attack and carry out the orderly withdrawal which formed the closing phase of the operation ...' But nothing of this was to be seen or heard. In desperation, the Royal Marines were being despatched at the last minute in a 'hopeless' attempt to drive the assault home. Rees noted, regretfully: 'It seemed a waste of life to do so when the landing had so clearly failed ...' He was not only disappointed, but critical of what he had seen; the Headquarters ship, on which it was intended that he should have sailed, had not been able to maintain proper communications with the troops on shore. The operation had gone horribly wrong and

Rees, with his new military eye, observed ruefully: 'There had been no opportunity of applying the doctrine of flexibility so dear to the Staff College – always reinforce strength, never reinforce weakness.'

*Garth*, with a somewhat stunned Rees aboard, limped home, with orders to pick up as many survivors as possible. 'The men we took aboard . . . looked as if they had learned some terrible lesson that was still too vivid to them for them to express it clearly either to themselves or to anyone else; but that was because they had learned it so thoroughly. "Never glad, confident morning again"; many were badly wounded, all were suffering from shock and exhaustion. They had the grey, lifeless faces of men whose vitality had been drained out of them,' he wrote. They were bitter and resentful; they had been flung into a battle far more horrible that anything for which they had been prepared. They swore and blasphemed at leaders they felt had betrayed and deceived them. Rees remembered: 'I thought that this is what a beaten army looks like, for no army is beaten until it has lost faith and confidence in those who command it. These men had, at that moment, and it would be a long time before they recovered them again.' Operation JUBILEE was over.

Shortly after he returned from France, he wrote the following letter to his family in Cardiff:

> HQ
> SE Army
> Home Forces
>
> Dearest Dada and all,
>
> You may have heard from Geraint that I went to Dieppe last Wednesday and you can imagine it was a very exciting day in my life. I didn't really think, about 9 o'clock on Wednesday, that I should ever see England again. Fortunately I returned whole and unharmed; I was very lucky. In spite of the danger it was a very welcome outing from my Command and it seems very dull to be back. I had the pleasure of commanding four 6-inch guns at one period of the operation! If you see a Pathé news film of the raid you may see me on board a destroyer and rather oddly dressed. Margie was very excited to hear I had gone. She is now working in the little factory in Neston where her sister was working. I hope to see her on Thursday as I am going to Cambridge to give a lecture on the raid, and shall be there for two days and Margie will come and join me. I'm looking forward to it very much. I hope you are all well . . . Look after yourselves and write soon.
>
> Very much love,
> Gony

I had been born five months before Dieppe, on 16 March 1942, at my grandparents' house, Desborough, in Parkgate. On my birth certificate, my father's occupation is given as 'Major, Royal Welch Fusiliers (Journalist)'. He had been made up to acting Major only a few days beforehand. I was christened Margaret Jane – Margaret after my mother and my grandmother – but have never been called anything else but Jenny. When I asked my mother why this was, she said that the vicar would not christen me Jenny as it was not a Christian name. My father had chosen it; Jenny is the name of a prostitute in Brecht's *Die Dreigroschenoper*, so I still carry about with me something of Rees's days in Berlin in the thirties. I have no early memories of my father at all until he returned to us at the end of 1945, and I do not remember my mother either. I recall, dimly, the shapes of rooms, the smells and impressions of the gardens of my grandparents' various houses and spending many happy hours with a donkey that belonged to my aunt Susie, who, only eleven years my senior, was like an elder sister. My parents were frequently separated: when my mother could join my father she would drop everything and go; when she could not, she had to stay at home.

In August 1943 Rees was appointed GSO II, Planning Staff (Operations), 21 Army Group, which meant that for some time he would be preoccupied once again with the details of beach gradients, tide and moon tables, underwater obstacles and all the other secret information needed to mount an invasion of the French coast. In Parkgate, my mother was by now expecting my sister, Lucy. Some time that autumn Rees wrote from HQ, 21 Army Group, London W1, to his father and sister in Cardiff to say that he had been to Liverpool to see my mother and myself, whom he described as 'very nice indeed'. 'She is full of character and has developed an overwhelming passion for what she calls boo-boos, by which she means books. Her greatest pleasure is to sit on one's knee and turn the pages of the Children's Encyclopaedia, and is willing to do so for hours on end.' My sister, whom he obviously expected to be a boy, was 'fast on his way' and was to arrive some time around Christmas Day, 'which is rather inconsiderate'. He said he had been very busy and had just come back from a few days at sea on a combined exercise which was 'very interesting and very enjoyable as we had lovely weather and it was like a very pleasant sea cruise.'

My sister, Lucy, was born on 21 December 1943, at a house that my grandparents had taken in Noctorum, near Birkenhead. She, too, was named after a character in a Brecht play. On his own in London my father had been able to revert to his old bachelor habits and spent a great deal of time at his former favourite haunts such as the Café Royal and the Gargoyle Club. He saw quite a bit of Guy Burgess and the comings and goings at the flat in Bentinck Street. 'The work of the planning staff, which for reasons of security was restricted to a minimum, was hard, the hours were long, and an evening at Guy's flat was like some fantastic entertainment devised specifically to take one's mind off one's labours, though I doubt very much if Field Marshal Montgomery would have greatly approved of it,' he wrote. 'Watching, as if in a theatre, the extraordinary spectacle of life as lived by Guy, I felt rather like some tired business man who had taken an evening off to visit a strip-tease club.'

At that time, Guy was bringing home boys, young men, soldiers, sailors and airmen whom he had picked up in the streets. Proust, Rees remarked, said that war provokes an almost tropical flowering of sexual activity behind the lines which is the counterpart of the work of carnage which takes place at the Front. As a result, spending an evening at Guy's flat was like watching a French farce, into which had been injected all the elements of a political drama: 'Bedroom doors opened and shut; strange faces appeared and disappeared down the stairs where they passed some new visitor on his way up; civil servants, politicians, visitors to London, friends and colleagues of Guy's, popped in and out of bed and then continued some absorbing discussion of political intrigue, the progress of the war and the future possibilities of the peace.'

He found himself wondering about Guy's activities, and tried to apply some of the lessons he had learned in military intelligence to the puzzle of what Guy might or might not have been doing. Rees explained in his memoirs that military intelligence was a 'peculiar, and frequently under-rated branch of war which induces, in its best practitioners, an almost animal sensitivity to the risks which it involves, not to themselves, but to others ... A good military officer knows that if there is any failure or error on his part he will be responsible for the deaths of others. This can be an advantage or a disadvantage compared with other kinds of intelligence operations: in military intelligence you know, usually fairly quickly, whether the information you have collected and disseminated is correct, for the evidence is before you in the shape of bodies spreadeagled on beaches or on wire, or, quite simply, mangled beyond recognition'.

The advantage of the military intelligence officer is that his work, like a scientist's, is subject to empirical proof, Rees wrote. The disadvantage is that where he is proved to have been wrong the evidence is provided by 'the flesh of men who have been unnecessarily sacrificed' and that he has to carry on his conscience. But however hard he tried to apply to Guy the lessons he thought he had learned as a military intelligence officer, he found they were irrelevant, for the principle of objective verification could not be used. Rees did not know what to think about Guy. 'From time to time I used to wonder whether he had been telling me the truth when he said he was a Comintern agent, and if he were continuing his activities, the flat would have made an admirable operational base, simply because its exaggerated element of farce would prevent anyone from ever taking it seriously ... But, however much I searched my mind, I could never get any further than totally unverifiable suspicion and speculation and these, I think rightly, I dismissed ...'

It looked as if Guy was being just what he pretended he was: 'a rather eccentric member of the British intellectual ruling class, who was using the war to advance his own career.' It seemed, to Rees, a very long time ago since Guy had asked him to help him in his work as an agent and there were all kinds of reasons to dismiss the idea that Guy was still operating as such. In any event, by the summer of 1943, he had left the BBC's Talks Department, where he had worked for three years, and had taken a temporary job in the News Department at the Foreign Office. Rees reflected, with some relief, 'If the Foreign Office had no doubts about him, why should I?'

It would have been about this time that Peter Quennell ran into Rees at the Café Royal, 'wearing a smart uniform', and suggested he might like to join him and his future wife. As Quennell told the story, he had to leave the table for a few minutes. While he was away, Rees told Quennell's companion that he was about to leave England as a member of a commando raid upon the Norman coast; it was a deadly secret and he knew he could trust her. If he returned – and he might well not – could he bring her some pebbles gathered from a French beach? Better still, would she promise to keep his glove, and allow him to pick it up, at any address she chose, once he was back in London? Quennell considered Rees's 'romantic overture' to be worthy of the Vicomte de Valmont, the master seducer of Choderlos de Laclos's *Les Liaisons Dangereuses*. When I wrote to him about this rather nasty sketch of my father in his book, *Customs and Characters*, he replied that he remembered Rees for his 'philandering ways and perhaps too-ready use of his personal charm' and wished he had known him better. I had the impression that Quennell, who died while I was writing this book, was still trying to work him out. Like so many other people, Michael Berry encountered Rees shortly before D-Day. 'I saw him just before the invasion of Normandy at Monty's HQ, a tented camp just outside Portsmouth – he was the life and soul of the mess,' he said.

According to Rees, he had, by this time, dismissed any real suspicions of Guy. Burgess was taking no trouble to conceal his sympathy for the Soviet Union, which Rees felt was an indication that he could no longer be an agent, and Anthony Blunt, who was then in MI5, was still living with Guy in the flat in Bentinck Street. Of Blunt, Rees wrote: 'I had every reason to believe in his integrity and his intelligence, and at that time he certainly knew more about Guy than I did. He was in a far better position to know about Guy than I was, and if he saw no reason to worry, why should I?'

Rees even played with the idea, so he related in his memoirs, of what would have happened if he had shown Burgess the final draft of the operation orders for OVERLORD that were, one spring day in 1944, handed to him to take to each commander-in-chief for signature. He did not use an official car, but, carrying the documents in his briefcase, caught a taxi outside his HQ. Rees recounted: 'Each commander-in-chief predictably behaved in character. My own, on the authority of his Chief-of-Staff, had already appended his signature. The Naval Commander, Admiral Ramsay, knowing exactly what the Royal Navy had to do and how he proposed to do it, politely asked me where to sign and added his name. The Air Commander, Air Marshal Leigh Mallory, examined every sentence of the long document with the minuteness of a scholar and pedant, and to each of them suggested long-term alterations of phrasing, of style, of punctuation.' Rees had to tell Mallory that, after eighteen months of preparation and with the men, the ships and the planes now ready to move to their battle stations, no further changes were possible and 'somewhat surlily, slowly, painfully' he signed his name. It had been a long and tiring morning and it was when Rees sat in his taxi being driven from one headquarters to another that he 'could not help wondering what the effect would have been on Guy if I had suddenly ordered it to his flat and placed OVERLORD in his hands. Would he then, perhaps, have told me what he was up to?'

After the invasion, Rees was appointed an instructor at the Control Commission School, which was preparing for the occupation of Germany by a military government. The British element of the Control Commission was formed in London in the autumn of 1944, although the European Advisory Commission had been meeting since 1943. Douglas Jay, who was then at the Board of Trade, had not seen Rees at all during the war, but recalled that on 7 May 1945 he had by chance met him, in his uniform, outside the Athenaeum. As always my father, who liked to be in the *avant-garde* of gossip, had a titbit to pass on. 'Goronwy told me that the Armistice was to be signed the day after tomorrow and we stood and talked,' said Douglas.

On 5 June 1945, the Allied Control Commission effectively took over the running of Germany and a week later, Rees, by then a lieutenant colonel, was posted to the Commission's political division to become senior intelligence officer to the staff of Sir William Strang (later Lord Strang), the Political Adviser to the Commander-in-Chief, Field Marshal Montgomery. Noël Annan, who was to join him later, explained to me that the Political Division was virtually the Foreign Office division; it was responsible for the diplomatic side of the Control Commission, that is to say, relations with the Russians, the French and the Americans, and operated rather like an embassy. Working on the consular side, it was the job of Rees, and later Noël to report on the state of affairs in Germany. Rees's perfect German of course came in useful, as did his extensive knowledge of pre-war Germany. He knew, said Noël, which people had been Nazis.

Noël had heard a great deal about Rees and had kept up with the news of his amatory adventures during the war because they had many friends in common, but he did not really get to know him until they started working together. He remembered Rees being always 'very smartly turned-out in his RWF uniform, with the flash, and he wrote marvellous despatches'. For a while they had desks in the same room and Noël recalled, 'He would sit there, studying and reading whatever might be occupying him at that moment. He was terrifically good company and we had a riotously funny time.' Although he knew little about Rees's political past, Noël said that he almost certainly knew he had been left-wing: 'But, then, who wasn't?' Well, Noël for one. My father, he said, had had a 'good war', but it was not something he talked about. 'He was somebody who talked on the whole very much more about the present, I mean what he was doing in the present. We talked a lot about universities and people we knew; he had a wonderful gift for painting a thumbnail sketch of somebody . . .' Rees, he added, was always very considerate to servants and drivers.

Many of the Control Commission papers may be read at the Public Record Office at Kew so I was able to gain some idea of what my father did in the course of his work. Towards the end of his life, I suggested to him that he would be the perfect person to write a book about the denazification of Germany after the war. He said it was not a very interesting subject. But he told, in *A Bundle of Sensations*, of how the Political Adviser, Sir William Strang, who later became Permanent Under-Secretary at the Foreign Office, 'had once played a sinister role in my political mythology as that obscure Foreign Office official, Mr William Strang, who had been despatched by Mr Chamberlain to Moscow to obstruct any possibility of an Anglo–Soviet military agreement. I had assumed that he would correspond with the unattractive part for which I had cast him in history.' However, Rees was in for a pleasant surprise. Sir William, son of a farmer and educated at a grammar school and King's College, London, was not a bit like he had expected him to be. 'He was entirely free of those mannerisms of speech and behaviour which are acquired at a public school and the older universities; he was modest and shy and diffident, irked by the grandeur imposed on him by his ambassadorial rank, and had a touching faith in my capacity as a soldier to overcome any obstacles which might meet us on our journey,' Rees wrote. Sir William had an immense capacity for work, he corrected the drafts and despatches with 'a meticulousness that was very near to pedantry'. He was more like a scholar than a man of affairs, and Rees found this 'immensely refreshing' after five years in the army – 'where even scholars very quickly began to impersonate men of action'.

When, in June 1945, Rees arrived in the small spa of Bad Oenhausen on the north German plain – HQ of the 21st Army Group – he found that the town had not suffered any damage during the war. 'It was as if the Germans, having conquered Britain, had decided to govern it from Llandrindod Wells,' he wrote. But things were not running very smoothly. The London office of the Control Commission had received a disgruntled message from the office of the Political Adviser complaining that no car was available, and there were no cooks and no batmen: 'It is monstrous to be stuck here with no conveyance when the Commission has been preparing its job for NINE months . . .' One of Rees's first tasks was to requisition a house in Lübbecke, a little town a few miles away from the spa, for the Political Adviser. The only house large enough belonged to a businessman and was, he decided, 'a classical monument to the kind of bad taste that flourished under the National Socialists, in which new and old were mingled without any discrimination and architect and interior decorator had worked harmoniously together with an unerring eye for whatever was most vulgar and ostentatious'. Plate-glass windows stretched from floor to ceiling; chairs were hideous and uncomfortable; the 'dim, dark, pretentious' library had very few books except 'a selection of those heavily-bound, pseudo-scientific works of pornography which seem an essential part of the furniture of any educated German businessman's house'. No house could have been less suited to the tastes of the Political Adviser, who, he wrote, was 'the simplest and least ostentatious of men and at home lived in a modest little suburban villa called *Tree Tops*...'

The office – in which Rees was responsible for political reporting – covered an intriguing variety of duties and, sitting at my desk in the Reading Room at Kew going through the contents of the brown files, I found myself staring into space with pictures in my mind of what Germany was like at the end of the war. It was the summer of 1993, and evening after evening the nation watched the frightening chaos of Bosnia on television, with the pitiful images of displaced people and refugees, their homes destroyed, setting out on the long road for who knew where with all that was left of their belongings. My father would have been surrounded with much the same situation, but on a far larger scale. Just before he left Germany in November 1945, he was to write a graphic description of the tour he made with Sir William, but in the meantime the office of the Political Adviser was dealing with all kinds of administrative problems.

One was the matter of the Dutch horses, described, in the records, as a 'tangled and rather unsatisfactory tale' to which the Political Adviser had to address himself. I gathered from the file that when the German 25th Army was evacuated from the Netherlands, a good deal of its horse transport was Dutch. No one knew how many horses had been bought or how many had simply been taken, but the Canadians allowed the Germans to retain enough animals to carry out their move, on the understanding that those belonging to the Dutch would subsequently be returned. However, there appeared to be no reference to any such undertaking in the terms of surrender. Some 4300 horses had been handed back before the Germans left, but the Germans had used a further 5200, only some of which were their own, on their homeward trek. 'It has been reported that some of the horses which the Germans were allowed to take out of the Netherlands to pull their transport are not going to be returned. If this is indeed so, there will be serious political repercussions and small wonder. It is unthinkable that such a state of affairs could be allowed to exist and I sincerely hope that those authorities responsible for this will consider their decision, otherwise the Dutch will have cause to lose faith in the integrity of the Allies.'

There was also correspondence about Dutch cattle; the Dutch were making forays over the German border to round up cattle that had been taken from them by the Wehrmacht. The Supreme Headquarters Allied Expeditionary Force (SHAEF) mission to the Netherlands felt that the cattle should be returned, but the military government in Germany was of the opinion that they should not be given back from 'an agricultural point of view'. This had to be sorted out as well. Sir William's office was also a letter-box for passing on messages to special people in the British zone. The Roman Catholic Archbishop of Westminster wanted greetings sent to three new German cardinals, and a Mrs Bill, formerly a children's nurse in the household of HM Queen Mary, asked if a letter could be delivered to a Herr Kogürch in Hanover, who was the son of the Princess Royal's former maid. There was traffic, too, in the other direction. The Chinese community in Berlin, for example, wanted a letter delivered to the Chinese Ambassador in London.

The office was closely involved with the question of what to do about Nazi music, such as the stirring battle and marching songs that the Germans had hoped would be their accompaniment to victory. A note in the 'Music – Military and Nazi' file states that the purposes of the occupation were to convince the Germans that they had suffered total military defeat and to ensure that German militarism and National Socialism did not continue to operate underground or in any other guise. The national anthem had been banned 'for the time being'. A preliminary list of seventy-three Nazi tunes had been drawn up and there were another forty-one with 'objectionable titles'; one contained derogatory references to Mr Churchill and Mr Eden and there were some very distasteful songs: one, called 'Das England-Lied', had as its first line, 'Wir fahren gegen Engeland', meaning 'We march against England', and another opened with 'Brown are the shirts and red the blood ...' The list also included a 'bellicose and extremely patriotic' song called 'Die Wacht am Rhein' (The Watch on the Rhine), which was written in 1840 when Prussian nationalistic spirit was 'being inflamed by excitement-provoking songs'. A note added that Bismarck claimed it was as good as having another Army Corps on the Rhine. The Control Commission's London office informed SHAEF that 'in the early stages it seems likely that the Germans will be too cowed to play any – let alone music they know is likely to annoy us'. Later they could be permitted to play any music of a non-Nazi and otherwise inoffensive character. The onus of deciding would be put 'fairly and squarely' on the Germans. After all, said the note, 'they know much better than we do what music is likely to cause riots ...' If the proprietor of a *Biergarten* discovered that five minutes of the 'Horst Wessel Lied' got him closed down for a month, 'he would be unlikely to try it on again ...'

I found several reports corrected by my father, in his small, neat handwriting. In August 1945 he was present at an all-party demonstration to commemorate the victims of National Socialism at the Tempelhofer Stadium in Berlin, attended by between 50,000 and 70,000 people. 'Making every allowance for German enthusiasm for public demonstrations of any kind (including National Socialist ones) and the common desire of all Germans to free themselves of guilt by associating themselves with the guiltless, one could nevertheless hardly fail to be impressed by the atmosphere of grief and depression which pervaded the assembly, especially if one's last memory of the stadium was of a Nazi torchlight procession, accompanied by the most military of music,' he observed. In a political summary, dated 7 September, he described a victory parade held by the Allied forces in Berlin to celebrate the end of the war. The most impressive feature, Rees reported, was Marshal Zhukov, who took the salute; in his Prussian blue uniform, his burly chest blazing with decorations from his belt to his epaulettes, he 'threw the other commanders completely into the shade'. The Russian infantry who led the parade were equally impressive; they were followed by the French, British and American infantry. The leading armour was supplied by the British; their tanks 'beautifully aligned and turned out'. The French followed in armoured cars and half-truck vehicles; then the Americans, with light tanks only; lastly the Russians who paraded about a hundred of their 75-ton Josef Stalin tanks, each mounting a 120-mm gun. The Russians, he noted, had evidently seized the opportunity of the parade to give an impressive display of their military power. 'They threw in their heaviest armour, including Marshal Zhukov, and one wonders what impression it made on the 8 visiting American congressmen, who, in snap brim hats, chewing gum and smoking cigars, looked as invincibly civilian as the Marshal looked warlike.'

Another job for the office was to establish the whereabouts of certain wanted Germans who had disappeared without trace as the war came to an end. In one note in a file, my father was given special mention for having spotted a paragraph in a German newspaper about Baron Constantin von Neurath, the former Foreign Minister, who was wanted for questioning by the Americans as a war criminal. The report which had been sent by a correspondent in Paris, said that the Baron, who had been interned with fifty other German diplomats at Meersburg, on Lake Constance, had been transferred to Nüremberg. He was safely in Allied hands. Others were more fortunate. In August, according to another note in the file, a professor and three doctors, who had been placed in an American prison camp in May, had 'owing to a misunderstanding' been 'unfortunately released'.

My father's *chef d'oeuvre* from this period is a fifteen-page report written after he accompanied Sir William Strang on a five-day tour of the British Zone in July 1945. Sending off the report to Anthony Eden, the Foreign Secretary, Sir William explained, 'Colonel Rees kept a diary of the tour and I cannot do better than enclose it as it stands. The reader will, I hope, find that Colonel Rees's chronicle conveys the keen interest with which he and I heard the stories of our pioneer military government teams in Germany, and our sympathy with the single-minded devotion which they are bringing to their unprecedented task.'

Sir William gave his own resumé of the general aspect of the country he had journeyed through: 'A smiling countryside, beautifully farmed with bountiful crops growing to the roadsides and hedgerows: villages and small towns off the main roads quite intact; towns and villages at important communication points badly smashed ...' The larger centres like Münster or Osnabrück were half or three-quarters devastated; industrial cities like Dortmund almost totally in ruins, except for the outer fringes. The Germans themselves were generally in fairly good shape, healthier-looking, despite rationing, better-dressed and showing less sign of strain than expected, even in the worst-hit areas. In Dortmund, however, where some of the factories were working and some shops and banks now open, there were signs of malnutrition, and administrative staffs were beginning to show the effects of over-work, and through shortage of food, bad temper and tiredness. It was fortunate, he said, that the occupation had started in early summer; there were months to go before the onset of winter.

Sir William told Anthony Eden and the British government that he did not consider that the Germans in the British Zone had the 'appearance of a broken people'. He felt their suffering was still to come and warned that unless the mines of the Ruhr and the Saar could produce enough coal, and enough grain could be imported, there was likely to be 'widespread malnutrition and something near starvation in many places, with the possibility of disorder and a general breakdown'. The British corps commanders he had visited were very proud of their men; they were 'in good heart and showing the usual British good humour, practical ingenuity and common sense in tackling the new and strange jobs they have to do'. As for the Germans, well, he had been introduced to the Burgomeister of Hamburg – 'a man of culture, widely travelled and possessed of a strong sense of public duty' – who was a 'good' German. He had told Sir William that he recognized that Germany had to pay the penalty of its 'folly', rather than its guilt, but must not be tried too hard by the Allies. In general Sir William had been told that, administratively and psychologically, the Germans were making a more rapid recovery than had been expected. He felt they needed 'more to exercise their minds' – such as news and comment in their newspapers, more open schools, theatres and cinemas and opportunities to socialize – to distract them from their economic anxieties.

Rees's diary, sent to Anthony Eden, is filled with facts and figures gathered on the car journey: the British 49th Division was looking after 200,000 displaced persons at Arnsberg; there were 60,000 local children in the same area waiting for their primary schools to open; because of their political pasts, a quarter of the teachers were considered 'unacceptable' to return to school. The report is also filled with his own personal flourishes and observations. At Arnsberg, where a colonel and 120 officers at 917 Military Government Detachment were administering a population of two and a half million, he saw the strain imposed by the problem of the DPs, or displaced persons. Russians and Poles were roaming the country at will, raiding isolated farms or houses for food, valuables or women. Every night there was at least one case of rape, murder or assault with violence. The DPs were also killing cattle; in one area 3500 milking cows had been slaughtered since the occupation.

Visiting a camp of Russian DPs and ex-POWs, Rees found they

were living in over-crowded and inadequate quarters. They stared, he said, at the visiting officers with 'inquisitive, friendly and yet extremely tough countenances, lying on their palliasses embowered in the flowers and foliage which they bring back from the countryside to construct each for himself a tiny green cage, which presumably reminds him of his pastoral home ...' It was 'extraordinary', he wrote, to see these 'half-savage, half-animal, yet curiously attractive creatures' who, in a former barracks, had created for themselves the atmosphere of a peasant festival or a horticultural show.' One British officer told the visitors that their 'uncouth and savage' behaviour had dispelled any possible sympathy which the soldiers in charge of them may have felt for the cause of communism.

In Hanover, visiting I Corps, Rees learned of the concerns of local people, calling themselves anti-Fascists, who wanted a more vigorous denazification. It was felt that too many Nazis had stayed on as 'experts' in the administration and they were a hindrance rather than a help to the revival of economic and social life. Keeping them on in their posts had induced feelings of frustration and lack of confidence, and consequently apathy, in the popular mind, which, Rees reported, was filled with genuine hatred for Nazi bosses in all walks of life. This fear of the Nazis in high places was preventing collaboration with the Allies.

Reporting on the morale of the Germans, Rees found that they were by no means exhausted by their struggles and their defeat. From those to whom Sir William's party had spoken, he had gathered the general impression that they were less defeatist and more self-reliant than the French and less war-weary than the British. They were anxious and eager for the opportunity to rebuild their country; there were 'powerful energies' to be released in Germany which could be turned to a healthy and useful purpose. There were 'remarkable' examples of the transformation of towns, which, two weeks before, were almost entirely devastated. 'This recuperative power, undiminished energy and will to work, impresses everyone in contact with the Germans,' Rees wrote. 'They remain, even in their ruins, a formidable and immensely productive people.'

But, of course, there were many difficulties ahead. Sir William and Rees encountered great anxiety about the forthcoming winter, when there was fear of famine and concern about fuel. In Arnsberg, the average daily food ration was between 800 and 1000 calories – a minimum of 1200 was thought to be adequate – and local people had heard that the ration in the Russian zone was 4000. Rees felt these comparisons would soon lose their edge as a result of the behaviour of the Russian DPs and of Germans returning from the Russian zone, bringing unflattering accounts of conditions in the USSR.

At Essen, they visited the Ruhr Coal Control, which consisted of thirty-five British army officers running the entire coal production of the Ruhr, without the help of a single shorthand-typist. About 170 mines, out of a total of 200, were operating, producing about 50,000 tons of coal a day, or a tenth of the normal rate. The RCC was based in the Villa Hugel, just outside the city, which Rees described as 'a vast and luxurious house which is a monument to the bad taste of the German industrial barons' and should be preserved as a mausoleum of the German armament kings. They then proceeded to Dortmund.

Rees found that the drive through the 'devastated Ruhr is a depressing experience and Dortmund itself is a horrifying example of the destruction which can be achieved by air power . . .' Yet, on the roads and in the cobbled streets, he could see Germans with their few household goods returning to the empty shells of their former homes where they were living like 'troglodytes' among the bricks and rubble, and 'strolling, apparently without resentment, among the ruins of their town'. The local detachment commander, a Lieutenant-Colonel Wilson, told the visitors that more and more people were returning to the city centre because, in spite of the destruction and desolation, banks, shops and small tradesmen were carrying on business in vaults, cellars and the ruins of warehouses.

In Dortmund, the military government's chief worries were food, DPs, and 'the general decay of morality and law and order consequent on the examples set by the DPs'. Looting and plundering were commonplace and there was an active black market. 'This increase in lawlessness is accompanied by loss of respect for, and confidence in, military government, especially among the Church authorities and there is a tendency to think that at least the Nazis maintained law and order,' Rees commented.

Their next call was Münster, where they found that the military government had established an 'excellent mess' in one of the few undamaged buildings. Of the journey, Rees wrote: 'It was a relief to leave the Ruhr, but escaping from Dortmund became a nightmare of broken bridges, road blocks and deviations. At last we emerged on the fine straight road to Münster, which runs through rich fields of wheat and barley – a refreshing change from the devastated Ruhr. But the end of the road brought us to a ruined city. Only the tower and ragged shell of the Cathedral remain ...' There were 1600 breaches in the sewage system. The people of Münster were not entirely happy with the military government; in the surrounding countryside the locals had banded together to defend themselves against marauding Russian DPs and there were concerns that the British were not serious about denazification. Rees noted: 'Another cause of lack of faith in military government is the popular belief that they are not in earnest regarding denazification and that we regard the Nazis as a reserve force against bolshevism ...' One reason for this belief was that the people, being used to ruthless Nazi methods of suppressing opposition, 'did not understand our slow and patient procedure of obtaining evidence and proof before prosecution and regard this as a sign of weakness or evasion', he noted.

At Nienburg, they met Lieutenant-General Brian Horrocks, commanding 30 Corps (Province of Hanover), where there were 214,000 Polish DPs and the Polish Armoured Division. General Horrocks suggested that if there were free elections in Poland both the DPs and the soldiers would choose to go home. He discussed his worries and concerns for an hour before dinner, according to Rees's report, and talked about morale. 'He said that he regarded our occupation as a school of citizenship both for the Germans and for ourselves, and that he attached the utmost importance to using military government as a means to returning our troops to England as better and more useful citizens.' General Horrocks said the morale of the British troops was high at that moment, the report continued, because they felt that after six years of destruction they were now engaged in a constructive task. He told the visitors that he was not happy with the policy of non-fraternization and felt that some modification was desirable; as it stood, it was preventing British forces from re-educating the Germans by their example, their outlook and their general attitude. 'He emphasized that there is no greater unconscious propagandist of democratic values than the British soldier, if he is allowed to follow his natural desire for society and conversation,' Rees noted. But there was also a risk that the policy could rebound on the Allies; the Germans were beginning to turn sour and the 'very receptive, plastic and co-operative state of mind' that was encountered when the occupation began was in danger of slipping away.

This meeting left Rees in bullish mood. He said how 'extraordinarily invigorating and inspiring' it was to hear General Horrocks's views, which he thought were representative of the British Army as a whole, and to find the Commander and staff of a corps which had fought the Germans from Alamein to the Rhine now 'entering on new tasks with a determination to achieve the best, not merely for ourselves, or for the Germans, but for Europe as a whole ...' General Horrocks's words, he thought, reflected the 'very remarkable spirit which animates the whole of military government and which accounts for the very remarkable degree of success which, in my opinion, it has achieved'.

In Hamburg, which had been heavily bombed, the trams and electric trains were running again and there was even a circus in town. Rees saw a group of Germans looking into a showground, where they could see British troops enjoying themselves. He wondered what a German would make of the sight of 'two gallant and somewhat elderly British RSMs, plastered with decorations, slowly and proudly rotating before his eyes on the painted horses of a merry-go-round'. At Hamburg Radio, a lieutenant-colonel proudly showed them a studio where a German musical director, a German conductor and a British control officer were listening with great pleasure to the first recording of a Mahler symphony by a newly assembled orchestra which, on the previous Sunday, had performed works by Berlioz, Mendelssohn and Tchaikovsky that had not been heard in Germany for years.

In *A Bundle of Sensations* Rees admitted that he was 'astonished' when the Political Adviser told him that his report was to be sent to the Foreign Secretary as it stood. 'I had the pleasure of seeing it circulated on Foreign Office green paper; it was certainly the first time anything I had written had had such a distinguished and restricted circulation since I had written examination papers at All Souls,' he wrote.

Shortly after the end of the tour, in Berlin, Rees met Stephen Spender, who recorded in his journal: 'Lunched with Goronwy Rees (a colonel). After lunch we motored through the country and then to headquarters. We passed many fantastically beautiful villages. Gabled, painted houses, almost lost among creepers and vines. The German villagers out on Sunday walks. Neatly dressed old women in starched dark-looking clothes, one or two men in black suits and top hats. A few of these I met said "Guten Tag" and were polite in a subdued veiled kind of way. Goronwy very much his old gossipy talkative self, despite his colonel's uniform.'

When I saw Stephen Spender in the summer of 1993, he told me that he remembered talking to Rees about the Germans and how rare it was to meet one who admitted to being a Nazi. Sometimes they would say, 'But how could we have known we weren't going to win?' in a 'dazed' way. Rees had told him that the Germans he had met equated the concentration camps with the bombing of Dresden and Hamburg and felt that the guilt for atrocities perpetrated by one side was cancelled out by those on the other. Rees, he said, was very 'spontaneous' at the meeting; he seemed very happy in the army and he looked very nice in his uniform. 'That meant a lot to people like Goronwy and Freddie', he said. Stephen thought that for people like Rees, who were prone to being in debt, the army was, to some extent, ideal. 'Everything is paid for and everything is looked after, you are given time to be with your family and you are given pocket money of sixpence a week, which you can go and buy sweets with,' he said.

Later that summer, the office left Lübbecke for Berlin, where the Political Adviser was established in a large house in the Grünewald. Rees wandered around the city where he had spent so much time in the thirties, and revisited the places he knew. 'Wherever I walked, I saw, behind the long avenues of shattered façades and mountains of rubble which were all that was left of the city, the faces of friends now dead with whom I had once been intensely happy there,' he wrote. He visited his old rooms off the Kurfürstendamm and found the house gutted and abandoned, except for a 'senile incoherent old crone' living in the cellar, in whom he could not recognize his prosperous and garrulous Jewish landlady. She could give him no news of his German teacher and her family who had lived on the floor above him, except that, like everyone else, they had disappeared in the collapse of Germany. He found himself perhaps even more oppressed by the 'physical landscape of destruction' than by the fate which had overtaken his friends. The streets which had once, for him, been alive and enchanted with every kind of 'childish hope and illusion' now showed nothing but the 'endless perspective of ruin and destruction, grey and mournful and empty except for the human chains of shabby and tired women passing from hand to hand the broken bricks of what had once been their homes'. He was filled with sadness: 'In the hot August sunshine, a kind of golden haze formed by the dust which rose from the mountains of débris overhung the city; and the heat brought out the sweet and sickly smell of the corpses still buried under the ruins and gave every street the stench of putrescence and decay.'

He was glad when he was asked to stock the Political Adviser's wine cellar, even though this called for some ingenuity as Sir William was a civilian and could not therefore rustle up troops or military transport. Rees, 'by intrigue and persuasion', was able to borrow a five-ton lorry, a machine gun and a corporal and private of the Scots Guards, who were to act as driver and bodyguard. He was not sure where to look for wine because stocks had been plundered and had disappeared. He found some champagne in the French Zone and claret and burgundy in the wine markets at Les Halles in Paris, but lost his two guardsmen. He discovered them later in the fashionable restaurant, Maxim's, being entertained by a grateful French business-man whom they had helped during the early days of the liberation. Then, with the truck loaded, they set off back to Berlin. From the lorry, which kept breaking down, Rees took in the view of 'ravaged Europe': everyone seemed to be endlessly and continuously on the move, though transport was practically unobtainable and 'entire popu-lations crossed and recrossed each other, as they tried to return to homes that no longer existed, or to leave homes that had been destroyed for anywhere in the world where conditions might con-ceivably be better and could not possibly be worse'. Rees recalled that they 'limped' into villages that seemed to be totally abandoned, the windows shuttered, the shops closed, where it was impossible to find food or drink or a bed for the night or assistance with the lorry.

The road which led back into Germany ran through a devastated area 'from which life had been withdrawn through sheer lack of anything that could give it sustenance'. Rees had the 'uncanny' feeling that for months he had been wandering in a kind of 'universal No-Man's-Land' and had seen an entire civilization wither away before his eyes. As they approached Berlin, through those 'endless miles of ruin and destruction', he began to think of what lay ahead: the smell of corpses rotting under the rubble and the rats which crept out, sleek, shining and well-fed, from the ruins which lined the road from his house to the Control Commission offices. Even at night he was not free of disturbing images. 'And when . . . we camped beside the road, machine gun mounted against possible marauders, I dreamed vague frightening dreams of the death of a society and woke with the sour taste of victory in my mouth,' he wrote.

At the end of November 1945, my father was released from the army and came home. He hung up his uniform in the cupboard of my parents' bedroom in a house in Cavendish Avenue, St John's

Wood, which my mother had found and where we were all to live together as a family for the first time. I remember so well the musty smell of his uniform and creeping up the stairs, whenever there was a quiet moment, to admire his shiny buttons adorned with the feathers of the Prince of Wales. A new life for us all was beginning . . .

# 8

‘I quite agree with you,’ said the Duchess;
‘and the moral of that is — “Be what you would
seem to be” — or if you’d like it put more simply —
“Never imagine yourself not to be otherwise than
what it might appear to others that what you
were or might have been was not otherwise than
what you had been would have appeared to them
to be otherwise.” ’

*Alice’s Adventures in Wonderland*
by Lewis Carroll

Our house in Cavendish Avenue was a white stuccoed villa on the corner of Wellington Place, and that part of St John’s Wood, though far more affluent now, was very quiet just after the war. What my sister and I looked forward to, with a great sense of excitement, were the Test matches, for if we leaned over our garden wall we could see the crowds gathering at the North End gate of Lord’s cricket ground and the mounted policemen who were there to see that nothing untoward happened. From our bedroom window, right at the top of the house, you could just about see the Nursery End and, on summer evenings, when we were sent to bed early, we could not sleep because of the sound of cricket balls being hit and the appropriate response from the spectators. Sometimes we were not able to go up to bed because our room had been taken over by parties of my parents’ friends who thought it was fun to stand at the window looking out over Lord’s, glass in hand.

Many of my other memories are of food, doubtless because it was, of course, still rationed. We had a milkman who made his delivery rounds with a horse, in which Lucy and I took a great interest, and, like thousands of other children of that time, I remember being given my first banana. Eggs seemed to play a very important part in our lives; I have a memory of the day we went shopping with my mother in St John’s Wood High Street and how she burst into floods of tears when she dropped some precious eggs on the pavement. One of our breakfast rituals was a staged mini-drama in which my sister and I used to eat our boiled eggs at great speed so that we should have finished them by the time my father came down to join us at the table. My mother would turn one of the empty eggshells upside down and place it in my father's egg cup. We would sit tightly in our chairs with our eyes pinned on him as he would pick up a teaspoon and declare: 'Oh, how wonderful, there is a boiled egg for me today. I love them,' Then, with childish *Schadenfreude*, we would scream with laughter as my father's expression changed to feigned shock and disappointment when his teaspoon cracked the shell to reveal no delicious boiled egg. We greatly enjoyed having him with us.

Those post-war years were very happy ones for Rees and my mother. Louis MacNeice, the poet, and his wife, Hedli, lived next door and they were as dramatically inclined as my parents. If there was not something happening at our house, then something would surely be happening at theirs. Louis and Rees used to go to the internationals at Twickenham together, which, naturally, involved a great deal of drinking and my sister and I waged an amicable feud with the MacNeice children, Dan and Corinna, who was always known as Bimba, which involved waving sticks over the garden wall. My parents went out and entertained a great deal; they had a large circle of friends and acquaintances and my mother's talent in the kitchen and my father's generous helpings of drink always made their evenings and their parties go with a swing. My sister and I were looked after by a long string of nannies and foreign mother's helps, with gaps being filled by my aunts Mary and Susie. I remember two of them very well; a Scotswoman, with a lump on her head, who was always having to go upstairs to rest, and a French girl called Simone, who wore very high-heeled shoes with platform soles. Our 'helps' lived in a little room under the roof, which nearly always reeked of cigarette smoke, and Lucy and I used to sneak in to look at the constantly changing gallery of family photographs that were propped up on the dressing-table. When we had had our bath and were in bed, my mother, dressed up and ready to go out, would come and say goodnight: as our day ended, the social side of my parents' was often just beginning.

In the morning, when we woke, we would sometimes find some small treat left on the end of our beds by my mother, after one of their evenings out at a nightclub or a party: a chocolate wrapped in silver paper, a paper hat or a streamer. If they were entertaining at home, we would creep down to the lower landing and peer through the banister railings at the people below, laughing and talking, waving cigarettes and with glasses in their hands. If Guy came, which he frequently did, there would always be a great deal of activity in the kitchen which was in the basement. He fancied himself at flipping over soufflé omelettes in the pan, but often the manoeuvre went wrong, when there would be the smell of burning and the sound of shrieks from my mother and in the morning I would find her removing the results of his less successful attempts from the kitchen wall.

In 1946 my father had become a director of H. Pontifex and Son, a firm of general engineers and coppersmiths that belonged to the family of his novelist friend, Henry Yorke, and so began one of the odder periods of his life. His mornings were spent at Pontifex's offices in George Street, Marylebone, and in the afternoons he went to 54 Broadway, next door to St James's Park tube station, the offices of SIS (or MI6,) where he worked for the Political Section which did not run British agents abroad but assessed and evaluated information gathered by them. Freddie Ayer also worked with Rees at what my mother came to refer to as 'The Office', but his afternoon activities were kept as secret as possible. However, Malcolm Muggeridge, who once described Guy as 'malodorous and sinister', noted, in his diary for 5 September 1949: 'Went to MI6 in the afternoon and, to his considerable embarrassment, saw Goronwy Rees going in . . .' I never heard my father talk of this work and, although he always liked to have something interesting and different to talk about, to his credit he was very discreet about it.

In February, Churchill had made his Iron Curtain speech in Fulton, Missouri: 'From Stettin in the Baltic to Trieste in the Adriatic, an iron curtain has descended across the Continent . . .' All the great capitals of central and eastern Europe were in what he was obliged to call the Soviet sphere and subject, in one form or another, to a very high and, in, many cases, increasing measure of control from Moscow. The preoccupation of Rees's office was the spread of communism and he worked closely with David Footman, who was one of MI6's leading Soviet experts and was such a frequent visitor to our house that he almost became a part of our family. David Footman, whose biography of Ferdinand Lassalle, *The Primrose Path*, was published in 1946, had been introduced by Guy to Rees during the war. David once wrote of the way Guy spoke of Rees before they met: ' "He's frightfully nice", Guy warned me, "but sometimes does awful things . . ." What he had done to shock Burgess is something I never discovered.'

At the beginning of 1948, the number of children in our family had doubled with the arrival of my twin brothers, Thomas and Daniel, who were born at my maternal grandparents' new establishment, a large Georgian house called The Elms in the village of Twyford, near Winchester. My grandfather, Bingo, had retired from his company, and my grandmother was at last able to fulfil her ambition of leading a proper country life, surrounded by animals. As we made the journey by car with my parents to and from Twyford, passing the many army camps across Salisbury Plain, we learned to wave to soldiers to thank them for winning the war for us. This was to be the beginning of my own 'other' life; for, until my mid-teens when my grandmother died, I was, more often than not, sent, with Lucy and my brothers, to spend holidays with my grandparents and my aunt Susie who lived with them and who was to become, successively, a librarian, a barrister and a National Hunt trainer. In one half of my life, I was surrounded by books and writers and people who wanted to discuss 'The Decline of the West' or 'The Rise and Fall of the Third Reich' and drink until the small hours of the morning, while in the other half most of my companions were horses, ponies, pigs, geese, chickens and dogs, I joined the Pony Club, hunted, and learned about wild flowers, badgers, newts and how to milk a cow and walk a hound puppy. I never knew quite where I 'belonged', and relations were not always happy between my grandparents and my parents. If moving from one of my lives to the other caused me unhappiness, as it often did, I used to comfort myself with the thought that I had, in every sense, the best of both worlds.

My father rarely ventured into the rural half of my life, and I was always very uneasy when he did. He said he hated horses and that one of the most boring things in the world was listening to people talking about them. But there was one occasion, I remember – and it must have been a mistake on his part – when he found himself in the middle of a field with my grandmother, some terriers, and a number of children whom she had take out to follow hounds in a Land Rover. It was pouring with rain, and the smell of warm, wet dogs hung heavily over all of us as we sat there, squashed up in the back of the vehicle waiting for something to happen. There were no foxes and nothing was going on; it was increasingly gloomy and cold. My grandmother, who never liked to admit defeat, finally gave in and suggested that perhaps it might be a good idea if we all went home and played Monopoly. My father was heard to say, in the most cutting and weary of voices: 'We might as well . . . we are playing monotony now.'

By the time my brothers were born, I had started school. My father and I set out together in the mornings to walk down past Lord's cricket ground and the backs of the Nash terraces in Regent's Park to the top of Baker Street where he left me, in my grey uniform, at the Francis Holland School. On the way there, he would point out to me the block of flats where Freddie Ayer had once lived with his widowed mother. Some mornings in winter there were 'smogs', and my father and I would leave the warmth of our house and soon find ourselves in the middle of a dense, dark, damp, cold and smelly fog, hardly able to see where we were going. From Baker Street, Rees went on to the Pontifex offices, where he and Henry would spend the morning together, until it was time for him to move on to 54 Broadway for his afternoon's work.

Slightly older than Rees and very different from him, Henry was the younger son of a Gloucestershire landowner, Vincent, who had bought Pontifex and of whom he was in great awe. His mother, Maud, was a Wyndham, and had been brought up at Petworth House. Henry was at Eton and then Magdalen College, Oxford, but was sent down after two years with a half-blue for billiards. He did not get on with his tutor, C.S. Lewis. Rees had met him at Oxford, and in *A Chapter of Accidents* he described how Henry spent his days as an undergraduate. The pattern never varied. At eleven o'clock in the morning he was woken by his scout with an orange and a glass of brandy, which was his breakfast. After shaving, bathing and dressing, he strolled to the Carlton Club, where he lunched, each day, on a grilled steak and a bottle of claret. The afternoon was spent at the cinema and between five and six o'clock he played billiards with the professional at the University Billiards Club. Then he would return to the college to prepare for an evening dining with friends and consuming large quantities of alcohol before retiring to bed at midnight. At eleven the following morning, his scout appeared with an orange and a glass of brandy, and the daily routine was repeated.

Henry's first novel, *Blindness*, was published in 1926 – using his *non de plume* Henry Green – while he was still a schoolboy and his second, *Living*, which was about factory workers, appeared in 1929, the year he married Dig. Throughout the thirties Henry and Dig had been the brightest of Bright Young Things and, perhaps because of all the social distractions, it took him about eight years to write his third

novel, *Party Going*, which came out in 1939. When he could not find
a publisher for the book, Rees made him show it to John Lehmann,
brother of Rosamond, who persuaded Virginia and Leonard Woolf
to publish it at the Hogarth Press. It is, as Henry's son, Sebastian, said
in his excellent memoir of his father, which appears at the end of
*Surviving*, a selection of Green's uncollected writings published in
1992, easy to assume that he had 'little interest in business and only
"worked" at Pontifex to give himself a comfortable income so that
he could write'. In fact, Sebastian remarked, Henry did take his
business dealings seriously, despite appointing Rees, 'a great crony
and a wild character'. According to him: 'At times the drinks must
have flowed and their talk ranged far beyond the finer points of jig
and tool design.'

That was almost certainly the case. When I put my advertisement
in *The Spectator* requesting information about my father, I received a
letter from Mark Wyndham, who is Henry's cousin and also worked
with Rees at Pontifex after leaving the army in 1949. I remembered
him from photographs I have of my mother dancing with a very
good-looking man at Pontifex Christmas parties. One morning I
drove down to a village near Petersfield, Hampshire, to talk to him
about Rees and found that he was still very good-looking and kept
six Welsh black sheep in his paddock, which I knew my father would
have liked to see.

Pontifex were brewers' engineers and chemical plant manufacturers,
or in other words, coppersmiths and brassfounders. Their main customers were brewers; the works, in Birmingham, produced huge
copper brewing vats and bottling machinery. When Pontifex made
brass taps and other plumbing accessories, they had a showroom in
George Street; by the time my father joined the firm that had been
leased to another company, but the offices above had been retained.

Mark Wyndham told me that Rees did not take much part in the
day-to-day running of the business, but Henry liked him to be there
because he had a 'much bigger brain than any of us'. Of my father,
he said: 'I didn't know he was any good with money – especially
when you think of the struggles he had later – but somehow he came
up with the brilliant idea of selling off the freehold of our premises in
George Street and staying on as tenants, which gave up a large sum of
money with which we bought a little family business in Leeds, called
Braithwaite, which was doing the same sort of thing as Pontifex.' I
asked him what Henry and Rees actually *did*. 'Well, Goronwy was

there in the mornings only and then he went to his secret work in the afternoon,' he said. At one time, Rees handled the advertising and he later dealt with the 'tricky job' of allocating the newly-made machinery. It was in such demand that there had to be a priority list.

With Henry being such a creature of habit, the working day at Pontifex naturally followed a strict routine. Henry would go to the pub at about half past eleven and Rees would follow later. First, they frequented Hennessey's in Marylebone High Street and when they got bored with that they moved on to the Lincoln, which was behind Durrants Hotel. 'My capacity was awfully small, so I could have only half a pint of beer, but Henry always had two pints to begin with,' Mark recalled. 'Then he would move on to gin, and sit there like a Buddha and make up stories about all the regulars who came in every day. He would observe them closely ...' When Rees arrived, they would 'chatter away', mostly about people they knew. They might have spoken of Guy, but according to Mark, Henry was not very interested in him. Henry did not like talking about books, but they did talk about their mutual friend, Arthur Koestler, and then 'quite frivolously', he said, they would begin discussing all the people in Pontifex, 'all the typists and accountants and people like that ... they loved the Christmas staff party which we used to hold in a hotel in the West End.'

Rees was paid handsomely at Pontifex, Mark thought. 'Henry did find his brain very useful in the business, because he, Henry, did not like being there and made every excuse for not making any changes, saying his father would not approve,' he said. 'Goronwy did sometimes persuade him to make some changes and Henry liked having him there very much. He was devoted to Goronwy, but I was very much under the impression that the main reason why he was there was to cover up what he did in the afternoon. I thought that from the world's point of view if anyone asked him what he did he could say that he worked for Pontifex.'

Guy was very much around in those days, but my father's attitude towards him had changed somewhat. In 1947, after leaving the News Department of the Foreign Office, he became private secretary to Hector McNeil, Minister of State at the Foreign Office. His drunkenness and unreliable behaviour continued and, most enthusiastically, he moved to the Foreign Office's Information Research Department, which had been set up to counteract the endless outpourings of the Soviet propaganda machine. As we now know, he was able to inform his controllers about the work of the department. But it did not last long: in November 1948 he was moved to the Far Eastern department of the Foreign Office. My father recorded in his memoirs that Guy became very fond of my mother – though I know she had her doubts about Guy – and liked the domesticity of our house in St John's Wood. He was my brother Thomas's godfather. 'He used to compare me to the head of that contented little petit-bourgeois family which made Flaubert exclaim when he visited them: "*Ils sont dans le vrai!*"' Rees wrote.

According to my father, Guy had more or less ceased to discuss politics with him. There were several reasons for this, he explained. The objective of the great anti-Fascist crusade of the 1930s had been achieved, although in a way, and under circumstances, which no one could have foreseen; it almost seemed to have been won in spite of, and not because of, the crusaders. The victory, he noted, had removed the prime motive for that intense concentration on political issues which dominated intellectual life in the years before the war. A large part of the ambitions of the Left had been satisfied by the Labour Party winning the general election of 1945 and the introduction of the welfare state. For the intellectual Left, for the moment at least, there was no great cause to fight for.

It was the famous case of Alger Hiss, Rees wrote, which did most to divide him and Guy. 'He dismissed the legal arguments against Hiss's conviction as mere pedantry; they showed, he said, how far all lawyers, and especially English ones, lacked any sense of political realities. Hiss was certainly guilty; he was precisely the sort of person who was capable of carrying out the systematic programme of espionage of which Whittaker Chambers, so improbably as it seemed, had accused him; and only a communist could be capable of such a feat ...' But according to Guy, it was Hiss, not Chambers, who deserved the admiration; and indeed he repeated with great relish all the unsavoury rumours which were being used to discredit Chambers in the United States at that time. The Hiss case fascinated Guy; he saw it as a battle between good and evil in which all the good was on the side of Hiss and all the evil on the side of Chambers. Rees was just as fascinated, but he saw it in precisely the opposite terms from Guy, for by that time he had come to regard communism, or rather, the Soviet Union in the age of Stalin, as 'no less an evil, and perhaps an even greater danger, than the Germany of Adolf Hitler'. His and Guy's divergence of feeling and opinion about Hiss, he explained, reflected

The Rees family in Aberystwyth in 1911. Rees, aged two, is on the extreme right, sitting on his mother's knee. Muriel and Enid are either side of their father; Geraint is in the foreground. Below left: the Reverend R.J. Rees. Below right: Rees, on the right, aged nine, with his brother, Geraint, in the summer of 1919.

Top left: Rees at New College. Top right: Rees in 1930, when he was in his second year at New College, with his brother Geraint. Left: Rees, with struggling kitten, and Shiela Grant Duff. Above: Rees (second left) at Schönbrunn, Vienna, with (from left to right) Duff Dunbar, Martin Cooper and Neill Grant Duff.

Rees at May Day rally in Hyde Park, 1935.

Elizabeth Bowen.

Rosamond Lehmann.

Guy Burgess playing the piano at a friend's house in Moscow. Below: Anthony Blunt, and (inset) Falcon House, Sonning-on-Thames, where Blunt visited Rees in 1951 to try to persuade him not to go to MI5.

Rees and Margie on their wedding day, December 1940. Below: among those in the group are, next to Margie, her mother Peggy, with her sister Mary. In the back row, on the right is Margie's father, Bingo.

The house in Cavendish Avenue, St John's Wood, where the Rees family lived after the war; and below right, Rees with the twins, Daniel (right) and Thomas, in the garden. Below left: Margie, the author (right) and her sister Lucy in their Francis Holland uniforms, with Daniel and Thomas in the pram.

Rees (back row, right) and Margie (seated, left) at a Pontifex party. Henry Yorke is standing next to Mark Wyndham (left). Henry's wife, Dig, is second from the right.

Margie dancing with Mark Wyndham at a Pontifex party.

Aberystwyth. Above left: Rees (in doorway) of a new building at the Welsh plant breeding station opened by the Queen in 1955. Above right: Margie, Daniel and the Jack Russell terrier, Jones, outside Plas Penglais. Below left: Margie at a college function. Below right: Rees dancing with a student, Jennifer Bentley-Jones.

Happy days: Rees and Margie on holiday in Cornwall, summer 1953.

At home in Highgate. Above right: Margie and Rees with a friend, Al Kaplan, in Tuscany.

The blue-grey house in Moscow, where the author met Oleg Tsarev (right).

Margie, towards the end of her life, with Rees and Kitty at Strand-on-the-Green. Below: Rees on Jura.

a deeper disagreement which made any form of political discussion increasingly difficult. It was impossible to talk about politics without discussing, in one context or another, the subjects of communism and the Soviet Union and Guy was 'resolutely determined' to avoid discussing either of these matters.

By now my father appeared to have moved into a completely different political sphere; in January 1945 he had been nominated as a second prospective candidate for Lloyd George's seat, Caernarvon Boroughs, by the Pwllheli Liberal Association but this had, somehow, fizzled out. The war seemed to have calmed him down a little and he was now the father of four. Our house was filled, at that time, with a very wide-ranging collection of my parents' friends, both new and old; the Oxford connection was still very strong, Rees had made friends at MI6, he had his drinking circle made up of people like Louis MacNeice, Dylan Thomas, and cronies from the BBC, and there were plenty of writers and others he had known from his days at *The Spectator* and from the war years. Then there was a slightly smarter set, with Henry Yorke being one of the key characters.

Guy was then, according to my father's account, taking drugs as well as drinking heavily. 'Combined with a large and steady intake of alcohol, this consumption of drugs, narcotics, sedatives, stimulants, barbiturates, sleeping pills, or *anything*, it seemed, so long as it would modify whatever he happened to be feeling at any particular moment, produced an extraordinary and incalculable alteration of mood, so that one could not possibly tell what condition he would be in from one moment to the next.' But most often, sooner or later, he would lapse into one of the moods of 'morose silence' to which he was susceptible. While Rees deplored the 'extraordinary regime' to which Guy subjected himself, he was also astonished at the 'physical vitality' which enabled him to survive it. Anyone else, he felt, would have been dead long ago.

When those who were fond of Guy discussed him, they concluded, my father said, that he was profoundly unhappy, almost certainly because of his homosexuality. But Rees had other theories; that Guy might still be a spy and that the strain of playing the part had become too much – this he rejected – or that he was suffering because he had renounced communism. He explained: 'We know very well that such breaks with the past are not accomplished easily; on the ex-communist they inflict profound psychological scars, and painful mental and spiritual lesions, which, in many cases, prevent him from successfully accomplishing the transition from one world to another. Was it not reasonable to suppose that this would be quite sufficient to account for the distressing condition of mind into which Guy had lapsed?'

Rees suspended judgment until, one day, he remarked to Guy that he seemed to have lost interest in politics and was irritated and annoyed when Guy gave him no reply. He knew that Guy's political interests, whether misdirected or not, were the most important part of him and that if they died, the most valuable part of Guy would die with them; it was as if by abandoning them he was betraying himself. He went on trying to provoke Guy into answering and even said, untruthfully, that he had written an account of Guy's confession to him that he was a Comintern agent and had deposited it with a lawyer. Guy suddenly showed every symptom of 'extreme agitation', Rees recalled. 'He begged me to destroy the document and said that if it were ever made public, it would not only put an end to his career at the Foreign Office, but prevent him from following any other.' Rees was sure he had seen 'real and genuine' fear in Guy's face; for a moment, it had been as if he was looking at someone he had never seen before. But he had not succeeded in allaying his suspicions; rather, they had been strengthened to the point at which one conclusion seemed unavoidable.

But my father decided to do nothing; later I was to become all too accustomed to his belief that if in doubt you should do nothing. 'The certainty that one of one's greatest friends had been, and may still be, a spy is a considerable shock, even though one has considered such a possibility for a long time,' he wrote. 'Moreover, it leaves one with a very unpleasant problem on one's hands; what, if anything, is one going to do about it?' He said he found it hard to condemn Guy and gave his reasons. 'Before 1939, if like thousands of young men one was passionately opposed to the policies of the British Government, and believed that they could only end in war, one was as likely to admire as condemn anyone who had enlisted as an agent of the Comintern; especially because in those days the Comintern still enjoyed a prestige which did not necessarily attach to the Soviet Union. After the Soviet–German pact it became difficult, if not impossible, for anyone except a committed and convinced communist to maintain such an attitude, and after the war it became even more impossible to do so with each year that passed. Even so, it was still difficult to condemn anyone for having held and acted upon political convictions which one had in fact shared; in Guy's case, it seemed to me, it was only possible to condemn his behaviour if, in the very changed circumstances of 1945 and after, he had persisted in underground activities which might have been excusable, and even praiseworthy, during the period of the Spanish Civil War and of Munich . . .'

In any event, Guy had been, and still was, very close to people who 'occupied extremely responsible positions in the British security services'; they knew Guy better than he did and were, so my father said, in a far better position to judge Guy's activities than he was.

Guy and my father continued to argue and they both drank heavily as they did so. A frequent observer of events at Cavendish Avenue during that period was my aunt Mary, who, after coming down from Oxford, had become an English teacher. She told me that my mother no longer liked having Guy around and that, in a way, Rees did not want him there, either. It was difficult to know what to do with him. She thought the same thing had happened with Guy as it had with Rosamond: 'Rees wanted both of them out, but did not think it was the right thing to do to simply cut people off because you do not like them any longer.' Mary watched Guy – 'He was disgusting, his clothes were dirty, he smelt, he was extraordinarily unattractive' but he had a hold over Rees, she thought. Rees had known him for a long time and could not bear to bring to an end what had been a close friendship, even though Guy's presence upset my mother. 'One of their overriding things was loyalty,' Mary said, 'and it was the same in Margie and in Rees. In that sense, Margie was very proper and I admire it. So, she put up with Guy . . .'

Anthony Blunt, who had been a close friend of Louis MacNeice's at school and had remained so, was also a visitor to our house, though I have no personal memory of him; he had become Surveyor of the King's Pictures in 1945 and left MI5 the following year. He invited my parents to Buckingham Palace and had plenty of amusing stories to tell about his job. Mary recalled that she did not like him: 'I don't think Rees did, either. There was a curious thing about Blunt. When you looked at where he was sitting, there was just a black hole, a kind of nothing. He was creepy.'

My parents were relatively well off during these years, and we were able to take a holiday in Switzerland, in a house on the shores of Lake Lugano which had been lent to Rees by a friend. My sister developed glandular fever and sat on the terrace swathed in blankets but when she was better we went out with the boatman and watched small black snakes swimming in the lake and in the evenings went with my parents and my aunt Susie to a small restaurant, where customers danced under a vine-covered pergola. All around us were the mountains of the Ticino, and there was not a sign anywhere that a war had taken place in the rest of Europe. There was wine and milk chocolate and clean fresh air and my parents used to go cycling together in shorts and disappear in the evenings to a local hotel, where one of the specialities of the house was to permit guests to spin gramophone records across the surface of the lake. Meanwhile, my father was writing his third novel, *Where No Wounds Were*, which was published by Chatto & Windus in 1950. It was the story of the interrogation of a captured Luftwaffe pilot and he dedicated it to my mother. A review in the *Times Literary Supplement* described it as an 'investigation of the German mind'; it was a 'mixture of philosophic argument and Kafka-like fantasy'. In concentrating on his 'subtle points about the nature of Nazism', Rees, according to the reviewer, had produced a 'rather static and unexciting' novel, though in the intellectual quality of its approach and the skill with which it developed the emotional involvement of the interrogator, it was 'a distinguished piece of work'.

In August 1950, just after the start of the Korean War, Guy was posted to the British Embassy in Washington as a second secretary with special responsibility for Far Eastern affairs. Rees and David Footman went to his farewell party at his flat in Bond Street. At the end of October, at a special meeting at All Souls, Rees's name was put forward with that of another Fellow to succeed Geoffrey Faber as the college's Estates Bursar and he won the vote. Many people have assumed that this appointment was somehow 'swung' for him by his friend John Sparrow, but Sparrow did not become Warden of All Souls until the following year, following the sudden death of Warden Henderson. Geoffrey Faber, who had always been very taken with Rees and whose family firm had published his first two novels, wanted my father to have the job, but not everyone felt it was such a good idea. In *All Souls in My Time*, A.L. Rowse remembered his own reservations: 'But was Goronwy the right man for the job? Neither Sparrow, who was his friend, nor I thought so. I had taken his measure long ago. When he came into College, handsome and seductive, a playboy, everybody fell for him. I was sympathetic as a fellow–Leftist, though mistaken in thinking him a fellow-proletarian; we were both Celts, for he was Welsh, but middle-class. Faber noted how very different we were, but all his affection was for Goronwy ...' Rowse 'couldn't fancy Goronwy, impecunious yet extravagant, looking after the College finances'. He brought up the story of Rees adjourning for oysters at Prunier's after addressing a socialist gathering; he could not see him dealing with the college's tenant farmers. But when the deed was done and Rees was duly voted Estates Bursar of the college, Rowse decided that he was not so unsuitable after all. 'To be fair, it appears that Goronwy was quite good at office work, and he was clever enough at presenting the estates business at College meetings. Also he had a good war record in the Welch Fusiliers,' he wrote.

It was a demanding job and it got off to a troubled start. As Estates Bursar, which he became in April 1951, Rees was the senior college officer after the Warden and the Sub Warden. By then, we had moved from Cavendish Avenue to a house in Sonning-on-Thames, near Reading, where, only a month after taking on his new responsibilities for All Souls, a very alarming sequence of events was to unfold. During Guy's absence in Washington, something had happened to unnerve my father. One evening, he and my mother were in the Gargoyle Club when Donald Maclean, whom Rees had not seen for fifteen years, lurched up to their table and, addressing my father by name, said, 'I know all about you. You used to be one of us, but you ratted.' This was not an incident that Rees tried to hide in any way; it has been told many times in the books about the Cambridge spy ring and there were witnesses, but it was Rees's own story.

He was puzzled by Maclean's outburst. 'It could only mean, it seemed to me, that he thought that I had once been a communist, as he had been, and was no longer,' he wrote. 'But I hardly knew Maclean ... and there was no reason why he should be any more interested in my political ideas than those of hundreds of young men who had gone through the same process. And why the slightly sinister: *I know all about you*, as if he shared some secret about me which was unknown to the rest of the world. This could not have any reference to my political opinions which, after all, had never been concealed from anyone. A dreadful suspicion began to dawn upon me that Maclean had been a collaborator of Guy's in his espionage activities and that Guy had told him he had enlisted me also. So far as I could see there could be no other explanation which was at all possible, yet I shrank from accepting it because of the appalling consequences it entailed. It meant that Guy had been telling me the truth about himself; for surely he would not have troubled to tell the same lie to two people, and in particular to Maclean, who by now held a very senior appointment in the Foreign Office? It also meant that Guy had been telling me the truth when he said there were others associated with him in his work, though he had not mentioned Maclean's name. But two spies in the Foreign Office? It seemed preposterous . . .' There were even more ominous conclusions to be drawn. 'If Guy was a spy, what was I to make of the fact that several of his most intimate friends held important posts in the intelligence service?' Rees wondered. 'Was I to assume that he had told them what he told me? It seemed hardly credible. Or was I to assume that he had not? In which case I had also to assume that, as a spy, Guy had successfully deceived them, even though some of them knew him a great deal better than I did; or at least, so I had always believed . . .'

He searched for an explanation: perhaps, for a while, both Guy and Maclean had acted as Comintern agents and regarded Rees, who said he had 'broken' with the Soviet-German Pact in 1939, as a 'political renegade who had deserted to the forces of capitalism and reaction'. It was not a satisfactory answer, but it was the only one which would allow him to avoid the conclusion that Guy and Maclean were members of a spy network that had penetrated the Foreign Office and, possibly, the intelligence services. 'As such, with some relief, I accepted it. Guy was, after all, my friend; and besides, I had no ambition to be the British Whittaker Chambers, and even if I had, I had nothing like the mass of evidence which Chambers had at his disposal. I had, at the most, a suspicion, which might prove to be entirely without foundation.'

In the spring of 1951 Rees received a letter from Guy, telling him that he had got into trouble in Washington after letting a young man to whom he had given a lift drive his car. A further letter informed my father that he was being sent home in disgrace. Guy had been away less than a year. He wanted to come and see Rees as soon as he arrived back at the beginning of May. I remember him coming to Falcon House; he brought me a pair of blue jeans and there were presents for everyone else as well. My aunt Mary was staying with us at the time; she was then head of the English department at Bedales School but taking a sabbatical, and had been instructed by my grand-mother to come and help her sister with the children. There had been a 'furious' row with Rees, Mary remembered, because she refused to take any money.

She overheard my mother and father talking about Guy coming back from Washington and saying how 'ghastly' it was and how impossible it was to get rid of him. 'I heard Margie say to Rees that she knew how much Guy made him drink and she was worried about his new job and some very important articles he was writing and it was very bad for him to drink so much,' Mary said.

Rees noted when he saw Guy that he was 'labouring under a tremendous sense of excitement, as if he were under intense internal pressures'. He launched into a 'fierce indictment of America and American policy and the menace of McCarthyism, the imminence of war and the total inability of our Washington Embassy and the Foreign Office to comprehend the catastrophe with which we were all faced.' He also showed Rees a long draft despatch, as from the Embassy to the Foreign Office, that he had written about the political situation in America, which, Guy contended, constituted an 'immense danger to peace', Guy was furious because the Ambassador, Sir Oliver Franks, had refused to send it on, but as Rees observed, 'in all this there was not the slightest awareness that a Third Secretary [sic] is not expected to have independent political views and certainly cannot hope that, even if they are brilliant, they are likely to have the official endorsement of his Ambassador'. He suddenly had the 'slightly queasy feeling' that he was speaking to a lunatic. But Guy was very happy to be back in England and he and Rees walked down to the White Hart pub in the village and talked about Guy's possible future. He told Rees he had been offered a job by Michael Berry on the *Daily Telegraph* but was not sure whether his 'conscience' would permit him to follow the newspaper's Conservative views. According to my father, he spent the night at our house, and he and Rees went up to London by train together the following morning and then proceeded from Paddington to a pub, where it was arranged that Guy should come and stay again the following weekend. It was the last time Rees ever saw him.

According to my aunt Mary, she had been taken aside by my mother on the day Guy arrived. 'Margie said: "I want you to do something for me, Mary, Guy is coming this afternoon and we cannot put him off. He's been a friend of Rees's for years and he has rung to say he has got presents for the children which he wants to deliver. You are to go into the sitting-room and you are not to leave Guy and Rees alone. You are to keep an eye on the drink and you are not to leave the room",' she told me. So Mary went into the sitting-room and managed to give the impression that she was very involved in doing something or other behind the sofa. She remembered: 'Guy told Rees that he had got into trouble with the car on purpose, to rile them, because it was such fun annoying Americans when you have diplomatic immunity. He said, about two or three times, that he wanted to annoy them, and how he was able to cock a snook at them when they thought they had got him. Rees was talking to Guy like an elder statesman, in a cautionary way, asking him whether this had been the right way to go about things. Guy talked masses about America and Rees did not drink very much ...' But when Guy left, Mary again overheard my father talking to to my mother about him. 'I heard Rees say that it was an extraordinary thing, but he had a very nasty feeling that Guy was a spy,' she said. 'He told Margie absolutely everything, he always did. I think that was the understanding they had – he should tell her everything and she would tell no one else. It was those two against the world.'

This particular ground has been gone over again and again by everyone who has written about the Cambridge spies, but, taking artistic licence into account, the following version reveals a little more about how Rees viewed the event. In a screenplay, *Influence*, which Rees wrote with scriptwriter Paul Mayersberg in the seventies, the Guy-character arrives at the front door of our house 'in a picture postcard English village', carrying a Foreign Office attaché case and a large brown paper parcel wrapped in string. My mother welcomes Guy and says he has lost weight; Guy replies: 'For what doth it profit a man if he gain the whole world and yet doth not lose weight?' In the 'cosy' sitting-room cum den, the Guy-character, over a glass of whisky, explains that he has been 'expelled, sent down, suspended' and it is not until much later, in the village pub, that he begins to relate how this happened and rants and raves about America: 'It's like a concentration camp over there. The whole country. America is completely in the grip of McCarthy. You can't be seen having dinner with another man without being labelled queer. You can't open your mouth to criticize anything or anybody American without being a Commie. Actually, they've become utterly identified. If you're a queer you're a Commie and if you're a Commie you're queer. America is a Fascist nation ...'

The exchange between the two men continues:

RICHARD (*Rees*): Come now, Dexter, I may not have been to America, but I do know who McCarthy is. I don't believe the majority of people in America accepts what he says.

DEXTER (*Guy*): Oh, but they do. They have to, you see, for fear of not being on the right side. So they go so far to the right that they're on the brink.

RICHARD: On the brink of what? Really, Dexter, you talk as if the world's flat.
DEXTER: The Senator from Wisconsin says it is flat.
(*Cut to interior, courtroom, Washington, a hearing of the House Committee on Un-American Activities*)

In the pub, Dexter tells Richard that Senator McCarthy is 'merely a symptom of the disease which is American aggression, anti-communist aggression throughout the world' and Korea is just the first victim.

In his own version of events, Rees wrote that he was not looking forward to having Guy to stay the following weekend, as had been arranged. He did not want to hear any more of Guy's anti-American ravings: 'They annoyed and depressed me, and yet they seemed the only thing that really engaged his interest or feeling.' So he rang Guy to postpone the visit: 'There was nothing in his voice or manner during the conversation to indicate that he was in any way disturbed or distressed; rather, he seemed more than usually cheerful and happy.'

On the evening of Thursday, 24 May, Rees was at All Souls, where he was preparing a report of the college's finances to present to a general meeting. On Saturday morning, 26 May, he received a telephone call from my mother to ask whether Guy had come to see him in Oxford; she had heard that he was missing from the young man who shared his flat and 'seemed rather hysterical about the whole matter'. My mother went on to explain that the previous day she had received a telephone call from Guy which 'had been so incoherent and so little of it had made any sense to her that she had assumed he was either drunk or under the influence of drugs and she had not really paid much attention to what he was saying'.

Rees returned to Sonning on Sunday evening, when my mother told him more about the telephone call from Guy. 'My wife said it was difficult to give a coherent account of it because Guy had sounded so strange that she really hardly understood what he was saying,' Rees wrote. 'Among other things, he had said that he was about to do something which would surprise and shock many people but he was sure it was the right thing to do ... Guy had gone on to say that he would not see me for some time and that this was really for the best, because we no longer saw eye to eye politically ... But I would understand what he was going to do, and indeed was the only one of his friends who would ...' According to Rees's own account, he had told only 'one other person', Rosamond Lehmann, of Guy's confession to him that he was an agent before the war. This may have been an instance of his being 'economical with the *actualité*', to borrow a phrase from Alan Clark, but what is certain is that, that evening, my mother learned all there was to learn about my father's relationship with Guy, and so The Secret was born.

When he heard about Guy's twenty-minute telephone call in greater detail, my father, according to his version of the story, suddenly had an 'absolutely sure and certain, if irrational, intuition that Guy had gone to the Soviet Union'. He wrote: '. . . the explanation seemed to be crystal clear. So much so that to my wife's utter bewilderment, and almost without thinking, I said: "He's gone to Moscow." Yet even as I spoke the words I felt how wildly improbable and fantastic they would sound to anyone else, and I had only to look at my wife's face to see that this was so . . . Yet, after so many years of doubt and speculation, I felt that this time it really was not for me to decide what was the truth of the matter, even though anything I did was likely to involve me in ridicule or perhaps worse. If I was right about what Guy had done, then it seemed to me that even the claims of friendship did not allow me to be silent any more, because the consequences of his action might be in innumerable ways disastrous. I had no choice, I felt, except to inform the proper authorities of Guy's absence, and of what I thought to be the reason for it, even though I didn't much look forward to the polite incredulity with which my story was likely to be received. I explained to my wife what I thought I should do and my reasons for doing it, and even then felt how very odd my explanation sounded, even to a sympathetic listener. It seemed to come out of a past that had vanished, and conjured up a present and a future that bore no relation to our own lives . . .'

On that Sunday evening Rees rang David Footman, with whom he worked at MI6, and told him that Guy had 'apparently vanished into the blue' and he thought MI5 should be told. David said that he would tell someone at MI5. (The following day, Monday, David left a message to say that someone from MI5 would be in touch with Rees.) After speaking to Footman, Rees then rang Anthony Blunt, who had been in MI5 during the war and was still closely associated with the service: 'He was greatly distressed and said he would like to see me.' So, on Monday, Blunt came to our house. He and Rees went for a walk by the river and my father told him where, and why, he thought Guy had gone, about his violent anti-Americanism, his certainty that the United States was about to start a Third World War and 'most of all the fact that he may have been and perhaps still was a Soviet agent'.

Blunt pointed out that these were not very good reasons for going to MI5: lots of liberal-minded people were anti-American; Rees's belief that Guy might be an agent rested on one single remark made years ago and never repeated to anyone else; and a professional agent was hardly likely to make public professions of anti-Americanism. But then came Blunt's strongest argument to dissuade Rees: Guy was a very, very old friend and friends do not denounce friends. 'He was the Cambridge liberal conscience at its very best, reasonable, sensible, and firm in the faith that personal relations are the highest of all human values,' Rees wrote. 'He reminded me of E.M. Forster's famous statement that if he had to choose between betraying his country or betraying his friend, he hoped he would have the courage to betray his country. I said that in the appalling political circumstances under which we lived, to betray one's country might mean betraying innumerable other friends and it might also mean betraying one's wife and one's family. I said Forster's antithesis was a false one. One's country was not some abstract conception which it might be relatively easy to sacrifice for the sake of an individual; it was itself made up of a dense network of individual and social relationships in which loyalty to one particular person formed only a single strand. In that case, he said, I was being rather irrational because after all Guy had told me he was a spy a very long time ago and I had not thought it necessary to tell anyone. I said that perhaps I was a very irrational person; but until then I had not really been convinced that Guy had been telling the truth. Now I was, and I was tired of the deceit he had practised over so many years and was only anxious to get rid of all my doubts and suspicions and speculations and pass them on to those whose business it was to say what they were worth . . .'

Blunt told him that MI5 might wonder 'what on earth I was up to in coming to them with so curious a story'. But Rees repeated his intention to go to them: 'At least it would not be my problem any more.'

What followed is difficult to establish, because of Rees's muddled recollection of dates. My aunt Mary remembered that as a result of David Footman's intervention, Rees received a telephone call from Guy Liddell, the deputy director of MI5, and that there was a 'strange atmosphere' when Blunt left the house. 'Rees and Margie went into another of their huddles,' she said. 'They were really worried and Rees was desperate; he felt it was the right thing to do to go to MI5 and tell them what he knew about Guy and Margie was behind him, of course. Rees felt that he knew something terrible and he agonized about how he could possibly "shop" his friend, but if Guy was really a spy and selling the country's secrets then someone had to be told.' But Rees had to wait ten days to see Guy Liddell; they did not meet until 7 June, the day the news broke that two diplomats were missing. It later emerged that MI5 had intended to question Donald Maclean on Monday, 28 May, about leaks from the British Embassy in Washington, and that Guy and Maclean had, indeed, left England for France on the evening of Friday, 25 May – Blunt had made all the arrangements for their defection.

Shortly after Guy and Maclean had disappeared, Stuart Hampshire met Rees at a party near Oxford. Rees, he told me, came up to him in a 'great state' and said something like 'It's terrible, I am terrified ... I am going to see MI5 ... What am I going to say?' Rees told Stuart that Guy had told him that Anthony Blunt was an agent, too, and he felt he should tell MI5 about that as well. They had been in touch with him; he was going to see Jim Skardon, MI5's senior interrogator. He wanted advice. Stuart told me that he bitterly regretted what he had then said to my father. 'I'm afraid I gave him a very bad piece of advice; I said, "Look, Goronwy, just do nothing. Let them find out what they want." I had been in MI5 myself and I told Goronwy that I knew how it worked. I did not think he ought to run round and volunteer anything. I thought that ... if they interrogated him and said, well, what about Anthony Blunt? ... then he might as well tell the truth, but otherwise do nothing.' Rees, he said, was frightened, and he considered that 'natural'. Stuart's own feeling was that the professionals knew how to conduct these interviews and it was more prudent to leave things to them. 'These intelligence people have big maps in their heads,' he told me. 'They write everything down ... they do things their own way ... But what I did was not right and it played a very significant part in the whole story ...' Indeed it did, because Rees equated his advice to do nothing with the advice he had received from Blunt, and when he was finally interviewed by MI5, as well as naming Burgess and Blunt as spies, he claimed that not only Stuart, but another Fellow of All Souls and ex-MI6 undercover agent, Professor Robin Zaehner, and Guy Liddell, whom he had seen at the flat in Bentinck Street, were all associated with the Cambridge ring, though he had no proof. According to Peter Wright, writing in *Spycatcher*, no one had followed up any of the claims Rees made in 1951 and he, Wright, opened up the file again in 1964, when Blunt confessed and was given immunity against prosecution.

When Rees met Guy Liddell, on 7 June, he was surprised to learn that the meeting was not to take place in an office, but at an informal lunch. When he arrived, he was even more surprised to find Blunt there, too. According to Rees, who was not at all happy to confront these two, whom he did not trust, Blunt and Liddell took up where Blunt had left off. 'They did their level best to convince me that I'd be wasting everyone's time if I went along and submitted the nebulous kind of evidence against Guy Burgess that I seemed determined to offer,' he wrote. 'Maclean was the person MI5 had been after, not Burgess. Against the latter there was no case. Besides, how could I or anyone else be sure whether Guy had accompanied Maclean? I'm afraid I dug my heels in hard: I was wise enough, perhaps, to refrain from even hinting at the long-held grounds for my suspicions, so in the end Liddell said somewhat reluctantly that he'd see to it that I had my wish. He added sternly that it might go hard with me when I did volunteer my statement. I thanked him and said I took note of the warning...'

A few days later my father kept his formal appointment with MI5 and saw Guy Liddell again, this time with Dick White, the head of B Division and in charge of the investigation. Later that month he was called back for a second and longer interrogation, at which, Rees was to tell Andrew Boyle whose book, *The Climate of Treason*, precipitated Mrs Thatcher's public statement in 1979 that Anthony Blunt had been a spy: 'They treated me as if I were a spy and a traitor with lots to hide. I held nothing back this time. I revealed the name of Blunt as the only other conspirator given to me by Burgess when I'd asked for one...'

My aunt Mary recalled how distressed Rees was throughout that summer. She told me that he felt he was caught up in a situation that was like something out of Kafka. The impression she gathered was that no one would believe him. 'Nobody would listen and every time he put his foot on a solid plank to cross this raging river, the plank was a dud,' she said. 'He wasn't saying, "What shall I do?", he knew perfectly well what he wanted to do, he wanted somebody to tell him whom he should go to. But nobody wanted to know. It may have been that they thought he was a lightweight, not an intellectual lightweight, but his girls and all that, but he was a serious person in that he had a serious view of life. I think he had a very raw deal . . .'

Rees's screenplay, *Influence*, contained a long interview at MI5 between the Rees-character, Richard, and a man called Jones – a Cambridge man – in which Richard is talking about Oxford and Cambridge in the twenties and early thirties. He says: 'Oxford and Cambridge were like two neighbouring countries. But as different as chalk from cheese. Oxford was very smart and worldly. Cambridge was rather provincial, but high-minded . . . Cambridge was like a great church. The Cambridge tradition of the Natural Sciences was a religion. The undergraduates were the congregation . . . and the Society was the ministry.' Jones says he has not heard of the 'Society' and Richard explains: 'It was the club of intellectuals. It included some of the most distinguished men in Cambridge. Each year a few, very few, undergraduates were elected to its membership if they came up to the required intellectual standards. It had no premises and none of the usual rituals associated with University clubs. It met simply once a week to discuss things . . . the things that occupy intellectual people. Politics, painting, education, scientific research, literature . . .'

Jones asks if Richard has any concrete evidence that the 'Society' existed and when told that people just 'knew' about it: 'Is it possible that this mysterious Society is a figment or creation of your imagination?' On his next visit to MI5, Richard is seen by a man called Mr Smith – another Cambridge man. He tells Richard that Mr Jones has already filled him in on some background and says that he is particularly interested in the 'personalities involved' and Richard's 'involvement' with them. But as Richard begins to speak – 'All right. I first met . . .' – he is interrupted by Mr Smith who says: 'One moment, Dr Owens. I'm sorry to interrupt you so rudely. I'd like to adopt a rather different method of inquiry from your conversation with Mr Jones. You see, in this office everything that is said falls under the Official Secrets Act. But please don't be alarmed by that. It's merely a matter of procedure . . .' Smith tells Richard that he does not want him to volunteer information, he wants him simply to answer his questions. He then asks Richard questions about a Maclean-character called Rooks – of whom Richard knows virtually nothing – and the incident in the Gargoyle Club:

RICHARD: The only thing I can think he meant was that he thought I was a communist but had left the party.
SMITH: Were you ever a communist?
RICHARD: No.
SMITH: But you were a sympathizer.
RICHARD: Yes, but then so were thousands of others.
SMITH: Quite so. But I don't understand why Rooks, whom you didn't really know and who presumably didn't know you, would make such an accusation even if very drunk.
RICHARD: I don't understand it either.
(*Mr Smith stares at Richard.*)
RICHARD: But this is incidental to what I want to talk to you about.
SMITH: I'm not at all sure that it is.

The interview ends with Smith telling Richard that he finds him a 'very rum fellow indeed', coming to the authorities to inform on a friend. Richard replies: 'I am no longer a friend because of what he has done, because he has betrayed me, and a great many other people. I still have great sympathy for him. I can guess at the pressures that have been brought to bear on him. But he is no longer my friend. You are right when you say friendship implies loyalty. But where is his loyalty? He defected. I didn't. Quite apart from that, I don't believe that one's loyalties are confined to people one knows personally. Nor do I respond to the idea that one's friends are granted special privileges or special immunities from one's judgment . . . May I remind you that I went to Oxford. We did not enjoy the finer feelings of Cambridge. We had our ideals, but they weren't terribly high. They were ones you could conceivably reach. We were a rougher lot, I suppose. In my case, not being a public schoolboy or being a disciple of G.E. Moore or having a proper tie to wear, I kept, I suppose, a respectful distance from those whom society taught me were my betters . . .'

In the plot, MI5 are not interested in Richard and the Burgess-character, only in the Maclean-figure. At the end of the screenplay, one man from the Foreign Office says to another of the Burgess-character: 'I think he was something of a freak. It's not clear to me why he went. He didn't have access to anything top secret . . .'

I have been told that Dick White, who died while I was writing this book, disliked my father intensely, but these feelings of hostility were not, I think, reciprocated by Rees. In 1985 White apparently told Barrie Penrose and Simon Freeman, when they were writing their life of Anthony Blunt, *Conspiracy of Silence*, that Rees was as 'slippery as an eel and had a violent antipathy to Blunt'. He added: 'I thought he was a four-letter man. [*I suppose he meant a liar.*] If he had really known all these things why hadn't he come forward? Then he went into all this explanation of how he thought we had known it all. So I said to Rees: "You assumed we knew? Burgess was working for the Russians and we did nothing about it? What can you mean?" ... He said: "Why don't you ask Blunt about these things?" But he did not say that Blunt was our man. No, he said nothing resembling that.'

Somewhere there is a file that would tell me exactly what Rees did disclose at those interrogations, but my letter to Mrs Stella Rimington. Director of the Security Services, was never answered and so, not unnaturally, I concluded that I would probably never find out. I do know, however, that in the following years my father became almost obsessed with the idea of exposing Anthony Blunt as a spy.

Guy's telephone call to my mother, on the morning of his disappearance, had been made from the Reform Club and, characteristically, he had forgotten to pay for it. The amount owing, in Guy's name, and the telephone number he called – ours – was put up on the members' noticeboard where it remained for some time and where it was spotted by some vigilant journalists. Very soon, our house was surrounded by newspapermen and photographers and Rees's name was known to all. Burgess and Maclean, the 'Missing Diplomats', were a very, very big story, and once my father's identity had been revealed it was impossible for him to escape from the press.

The *Daily Mail* of 18 June 1951 carried the following story, under different headlines for different editions – 'Burgess "One of the Nicest Men I know"' and 'Burgess Blamed US "War Drift"' – and a photograph of my mother, looking very demure. The contents are indicative of the panic that seemed to have overcome my parents and of a certain lack of grip on reality that was always to accompany The Secret. I should explain that Guy's bang on the head happened when he was pushed down the stairs at Le Boeuf sur le Toit during a drunken evening.

MR GORONWY REES, the author, of Falcon House, Sonning, Berkshire, told last night of his 20-year friendship with Mr Guy Burgess, one of the missing British diplomats.

Just before he left England with Mr Donald Maclean, Burgess telephoned to Mr Rees's wife, Margaret.

'Guy Burgess is one of the nicest men I ever knew,' said Mr Rees. 'To my knowledge he is not a Communist.

'I have known him since I was at Oxford and he was at Cambridge, between 1930 and 1933. He is godfather to my youngest child.

'When he phoned my wife he said "I do not want to speak to Goronwy because I know we should quarrel and we would only upset each other."

'I think he referred to an argument we had had a week before about American policy. He was convinced that the Americans were provoking a third world war and I did not agree with him.

'He said he would not see me for some time but that she and I would both understand why this was so eventually.

'He has always been a Leftist but he has had an enormous admiration for British foreign policy.

'He was in some ways one of the most patriotic Englishmen I have ever known and was entirely free from the kind of denigration of British social life and political policy which is typical of most communists. He was absurdly sentimental about England.

'Two years ago he had a very serious fracture of the skull after falling down some steps and has been in almost continuous pain ever since. To this everyone who knew him well would attribute the eccentricities of his conduct in the past two years.

'He is a sick man. I do not believe all the unpleasant things printed about him.

'He is a patriotic Englishman, but he is also a Marxist and it was because he has such a rare grasp of Marx's theory that his views were sometimes of extraordinary originality.'

Mrs Rees said: 'I have known Guy Burgess for ten years. His disappearance is due to social reasons and certainly not to political reasons.

'Before the last war all the university youngsters were communists. If a man of forty was a communist when he was twenty surely you're going to give him credit for growing up?'

# 9

What's become of Waring
Since he gave us all the slip,
Chose land-travel or seafaring,
Boots and chest or staff and scrip,
Rather than pace up and down
Any longer London town?

    Robert Browning


I wish I could recount how, once Guy had bolted, our life returned
to the way it once was. But I cannot. This was only the beginning of
the hunt that was to go on over the following months and years for
the Third Man, the Fourth Man, the Fifth Man . . . At the age of nine
I became used to hearing my father described as Goronwy Rees,
'who is heterosexual'; my mother was once approached by a newspaper
reporter, who, hoping to gain her confidence introduced himself by
saying, reassuringly: 'It's all right to talk to me, Mrs Rees, I'm
bisexual,' In high places, the disappearance of Burgess and Maclean
created alarm and panic which was to take a very long time to calm
down; it also caused consternation among those, in all the disparate
parts of the Establishment, who had been touched by what my father
described as Guy in his self-appointed role of Figaro – the go-between,
the fixer, the man who was all things to all men and the tireless
meddler in other people's affairs.

  Harold Nicolson, who had become very attached to Guy after
meeting him through the BBC during the war, wrote in his diary on
7 June: '. . . I am horrified to read headlines in the evening papers that
Donald Maclean and Guy Burgess have absconded. If I thought Guy
was a brave man, I should imagine that he had gone to join the
communists. As I know him to be a coward, I suppose that he was
suspected of passing things on to the Bolshies, and realizing his
guilt, did a bunk. Apparently he and Maclean went off by car to
Southampton and took the night boat, I fear that all this will mean a
witch-hunt.'

  The following day he returned to the subject: 'Everyone is discussing the Maclean–Burgess affair; I mind dreadfully because (1) it
shames my dear old profession; (2) because it will enrage the Amer-

icans; (3) because it will make everyone suspicious of quite innocent people; (4) because I fear poor Guy will be rendered very unhappy in the end. If he has done a bunk to Russia, they will only use him for a month or so, and then shove him quietly into some salt-mine. During my dreams, his absurd face stares at me with drunken, unseeing eyes.' Nicolson was to tell his wife, Vita, in a letter a few days later that their son, Ben, who was Blunt's deputy as Surveyor of the King's Pictures, was 'speechless with horror and disgust'; Ben, he told her, felt that Guy had 'betrayed Anthony'.

In his memoirs, Rees acknowledged that he went into a state of shock, from which, in a sense, he never really recovered; for Guy's ghost was to go on stalking him for the rest of his days. He wrote of hallucinating; imagining that he saw Guy's tall, slightly hunched figure disappearing around street corners. But while Guy had gone, Anthony Blunt remained, and he knew that Rees knew the truth about him, and he knew that Rees had told – or, at least, had tried to tell – what he knew to MI5.

However, of course, life of some sort did go on, though there were telephone calls in the middle of the night from newspapers and more and more absurd theories were circulated about what had happened to the 'Missing Diplomats'. In the autumn of 1951, Labour lost the general election to the Conservatives and Churchill became Prime Minister, with Eden as his Foreign Secretary, and the following February the King died in his sleep at Sandringham. When his daughter was crowned in Westminster Abbey in June 1953, we flew the Welsh flag from the top window of Falcon House. Rees was still working for Pontifex and busy looking after 30,000 acres of agricultural land that made up the estates of All Souls; he used to come home filled with stories of how he had visited the college farms on Romney Marsh and as far north as Yorkshire, which made him think of his own family connections with small farms in Cardiganshire.

Of that period, Rees wrote, revealingly, as if he had been visited again by Mr Nobody: 'My wife and children; a pleasant house with a large garden on the Thames; a business that was itself interesting and allowed me leisure to write what I wished; the academic life of All Souls, combined with the mundane realities of managing the college properties; all this was enough to provide me with an active and satisfactory life and should, I suppose, have been sufficient to keep me happy. And yet it was not. Somehow my life had taken a path I had not intended and chance had cast me in a part which I could not play with conviction. I seemed to have become a different person and regretted the one I had been. I was not unhappy but I was vaguely dissatisfied and disorientated, as if forces beyond my control had set me on a course which I had not chosen for myself and from which henceforth there would be no deviation. Such feelings, I am sure, were quite unjustified. In my case, at least, the difficulties of living had never arisen out of pursuing too settled and regular a course, but rather out of failure to remain on any course at all except for the briefest periods. It was always the unexpected and not the expected that had happened; even my marriage had taken me by surprise; and winds, storms or soft and scented breezes had never come from the quarter in which one had looked for them. There was no reason for me to regret that, for the time being, life had treated me almost too kindly or to have felt that I was overburdened with security. All I had to do was to wait for the hand of chance to reveal itself once again, and in the meantime enjoy the good things which life had given me.'

Then, indeed, two years after Guy's disappearance, something did turn up: Rees was asked if he would be willing to be considered for the appointment of Principal of the University College of Wales, Aberystwyth. Years later, with hindsight, he wrote: 'If I had been wise, I would have recognized in the letter a most dangerous form of seduction; and if I had had any sense I would have realized that such letters, particularly if they come from Wales, are never quite what they seem and are usually the product of long hours of not entirely disinterested thought and deliberation . . .' But, as so often, he did not make a wise decision and, in the summer of 1953, my sister and I said goodbye to the old henhouse in the garden where we used to conduct planning meetings for our games and the toads in the pond which, cruelly, we used to bury in deep holes so that we could wait, expectantly, for them to dig themselves out. We left Falcon House and exchanged the Thames Valley for the small seaside town in Wales where our father had been born.

For us, it was the start of a great adventure, but for my parents it was the dawn of a disaster.

My father wrote that he saw his return to Wales as a challenge. There was something stimulating, he said, even exciting in the idea that there, in Aberystwyth, stood an institute of learning which had already played a large part in the life of the Welsh people and which now, with patience and persistence, he might help to play an even greater part. He had his own ideas on the role of universities and felt that 'perhaps of all things' what his people most needed was a university that 'genuinely' fulfilled its function of educating young Welshmen. There were other considerations, too.

He thought that we, his children, would enjoy the hills and streams where he and his brother had roamed as boys: 'I had never quite lost the belief that, whatever might be the case for grown men, Wales was the only country for children . . .' But my mother was wary about the project right from the start: 'She was astounded and looked at me with that incredulous look, so familiar to me, which meant that she thought I had once again taken leave of my senses . . .'

My mother knew she was not going to like it. As my father related: '. . . partly because of me, she thought of the Welsh as of some primitive tribe which spoke an unintelligible language, practised savage rites and customs, and was in general shiftless, untrustworthy and hostile to strangers. To her, Aberystwyth represented a kind of Welsh ghetto, in which she would feel as much at home as in some Patagonian settlement full of naked savages . . .' But she agreed to support him and told him that if he knew what he wanted he must do as he wished, though, Rees felt, she did not understand why the prospect of returning to Wales was attractive to him. 'She acted out of the kind of generosity which in the end hurts oneself as well as others.' he wrote, 'and by self-sacrifice made it possible for me to persist in my folly . . .'

There were six of us and an assortment of German maids when we settled into our new house, Plas Penglais, the Principal's residence up on Penglais Hill that overlooks the little town and the sea. My youngest brother, Matthew, was born in October of the following year. My sister and I were delighted with our new surroundings; there was a large garden and acres of dense woodland up on the hillside behind the house, which we set about exploring with our cat, Burgess, and my mother's Pekinese, Puff, and beyond that there was open countryside and the cliffs. For a wonderful moment, it looked as if the 'other' life that we led with our grandparents would happily coalesce with our real life; there were fields nearby and grazing for ponies. I had just passed the eleven plus examination, and so I was to go to my father's old school, Ardwyn, and my sister, with my twin brothers, would attend the primary school at the bottom of Penglais Hill.

The first difficulty, I remember, was that my mother absolutely detested the house. The Plas, where the previous owners of the estate had lived, had only recently been acquired by the college and had been renovated, at some expense, to make it suitable as the Principal's residence. With total lack of any aesthetic sense, it had been rendered on the outside with what looked like cement and the interior had been stripped of all its architectural features so that each room was a kind of cell, with as much elegance as a bunker or a gun emplacement. My mother felt powerless in the face of such bleakness: there was nothing she could do to make the place pretty. But worse, I suppose, was the matter of the garden; almost as soon as we arrived, this became a battleground and is the most appropriate symbol of everything that went wrong for us in Aberystwyth. For, beyond the lawn in front of the Plas, a section of the large grounds was being marked out into botanical plant-specimen beds and as time went by these marched closer and closer towards the house, to threaten what my mother considered to be *her* garden.

I think any gardener would understand my mother's position; her own style was romantic and somewhat on the wild side, while the botanical beds, with families of plants arranged mathematically in rows, each with its name logged on a small white wooden label stuck into the ground by its side, created the very reverse of the effect she wanted to achieve. In no time at all, war had broken out between my mother and Professor Lily Newton, head of the Department of Botany. This was very unfortunate, for Professor Newton had been Acting Principal before my father arrived and would have dearly loved the job. She was to become a prime mover in the forces that gathered against him later on.

We were very isolated from the town up there in the Plas on the hill; to get to and from my school I found myself going in the opposite direction to the other children, who lived in the town. From our house, I would follow a cinder path alongside a stream that ran through the grounds, go out through a five-barred gate on to the main road, cross over towards the National Library of Wales, go down a flight of steps, round a corner and then through the main gates of Ardwyn. I was put in the bottom class, because I did not speak Welsh, but as just about everything was new to me I was not at all aware of any discrimination. What I loved was the morning assembly, and the glorious sound of the whole school singing Welsh hymns. As I began to make friends and learn Latin and returned home for tea to exchange stories about school with my sister, I was quite unaware that there might be any hostility to my father's appointment or to my mother.

It had been pointed out to me, only recently, that my father arrived in Aberystwyth only thirty years after his father had more or less been driven out and many of the families who had disapproved of his father were still there. The whispering campaign had already begun: Rees's Welsh, because he had been in England, was not going to be up to scratch; he had mixed with *louche* and decadent people in London before the war; he had been away too long. Aberystwyth was not like Oxford; in Aber town *was* gown. There were people there who remembered what had happened to R.J. in the great by-election saga of 1921. In time, Rees was charged with even worse sins: wearing suede shoes, not paying bills, consorting with homosexuals and drinking in public houses. He wore *white* socks. Possibly worst of all, he mixed socially with students and had the walls of one of the college buildings painted pink. My mother, too, was an object of criticism; she, with her passion for large American cars with wings and fins, drove around in a Chevrolet, and did not have much interest in 'coffee mornings', where little cakes were served on paper doilies. But I was not to learn about how unhappy she had been until much later.

We should never have gone to Aberystwyth at all. My aunt Mary, told me that probably the worst aspect of it was that, for the first time in his life, Rees became 'pompous' but, looking back, that was one of the lesser of the problems.

My father delivered his inaugural lecture on 3 October 1953, in which he spoke of how, during his childhood, principals of the college appeared as 'figures of almost superhuman greatness' and of the function of a university, which he did not consider to be the 'practical and utilitarian one of satisfying the needs of the state for good lawyers, good technicians, good teachers, good managers' but 'the pursuit and advancement of knowledge for its own sake'. However, before appearing for the first time in his gown in front of the assembled body of the college, he had, in September, considerably blotted his copybook by giving a talk on BBC radio entitled 'Returning to Wales', in which he quoted one of his favourite poems by Gerard Manley Hopkins that contains the lines:

Lovely the woods, waters, meadows, vales,
All the air things wear that build this world of Wales ...

It would have been politic not to quote the line, 'Only the inmate does not correspond' but Rees was not in a cautious mood. One way and another, his talk was a fairly fierce attack on his compatriots. An absence of thirty years, he said, had not made his heart grow fonder; he was returning more with curiosity and apprehension that with affection. He told his audience: 'Wales as I remembered it, and especially that part of Wales from which I come, was a highly integrated community, in the sense that certain standards and beliefs commanded, in public at least, almost universal assent; it has always been a matter of surprise to me that Welshmen, who individually tend to be highly self-assertive, in the mass are extremely orthodox. And I believe that in some people, and in young people especially, this tends to create a feeling of oppression, of wanting wider horizons, of wishing to use their limbs more easily and freely, to try other modes of experience and expression than those which are approved by the community.' He recalled the 'sense of liberation' he had experienced when he first left Wales to go to Oxford, because at last he felt that he might think as he liked, believe what he liked, without the certainty that disapproval was bound to follow. So when the moment came to take the train to Wales, he had a 'certain sinking of the heart' that in returning to his own country he was voluntarily going back to 'the land of bondage . . .'

If this was not already damaging enough, Rees then went on to comment, disparagingly, on the unchanging nature of Wales: 'What is surprising is the permanence and persistence of the Welsh way of life and belief, an intense cultural intellectual conservatism which shows itself sometimes in an almost Chinese reverence for what is established and sanctified by custom, a strange form of ancestor worship which is all the stranger because, as an articulate body of thought and belief, it is not more than a hundred and fifty years old. I would say, quite sincerely, that the most striking single impression I have received on returning to Wales is that of the strangely rigid and unchanging habit of thought and belief of the Welsh people today . . .'

Then he turned to the Welsh language: 'It seems to be so obvious as hardly to be worth saying that the strongest reason for the persistence and endurance of Welsh culture, and of the Welsh people as a people, has been the survival of the Welsh language; if it dies, the people perish. Yet if it is to live, it is not sufficient merely that the language should be protected and taught and propagated; it is necessary that the language should become, what it is not now, a medium through which it is possible to understand and master the most advanced scientific philosophical thought of our time. At the present time, this is not possible . . .' The Welshman who not merely speaks, but instinctively thinks, in Welsh – certainly the Welshman who thinks exclusively in Welsh, as the Welsh National Eisteddfod presumably wishes us to do – is debarred from understanding and mastering the fundamental problems with which we are faced; he has neither the materials nor the tools for such a task, Rees said. And if he is to be given the tools, then it calls for an immense creative intellectual effort devoted to the development of the language itself. It seemed to him that the difficulties involved in the Welsh language, at its present stage of development, might partly explain why in many fields Wales seemed to be living on an intellectual heritage which was fast dwindling away under the impact of modern conditions; that this reflected itself sometimes in an obsession with problems that had long ceased to be real problems; sometimes in a passive acceptance of such changes without any effort to adapt them to local and national conditions. 'To a native returning,' he said, 'Wales seems to lie like a ship becalmed, waiting for some fresh breeze which will bring it once more under full sail . . .'

The selection committee that appointed Rees in June 1953 was chaired by Dr Tom Jones, the man who was known as the 'King of Wales'; a former civil servant who had been adviser to Baldwin and Lloyd George, he was a figure of considerable influence in the principality, someone who pulled strings. According to Dr Ted Ellis, the college's official historian and the biographer of 'T.J.', Dr Jones felt he could not consider Professor Newton for the appointment because of the 'prejudice of the so-called educated male professors', or Richard Aaron, the professor of philosophy – who was to gang up with Professor Newton against Rees – because he was 'infected with Welsh nationalism' and would not be strong enough to withstand its 'currents' which were then in full flow. The committee met on eight occasions and considered the claims of fourteen candidates.

According to Dr Ellis's history of the college, Rees, 'outstandingly able, distinguished in appearance, impressively sophisticated, blessed with winning charm and brilliantly articulate', seemed 'to be marvellously equipped for his new responsibilities'. He made an instant appeal to the students and 'many people were impressed, even captivated, by his Inaugural Address . . . which, beautifully expressed in his usual limpid style, made it plain that his academic credo was one which could be endorsed heartily by those who cared deeply about universities. He viewed the State, "which does not belong to those who believe that it is more blessed to give than to receive", with a healthy suspicion. And he was prepared to fight to the death the dangerous implication that the duty of universities is to produce the kind of men, in sufficient quantities and in the right proportion, which a modern state needs if it is to survive; a heresy which seemed to him to be implicit in the government's later open-handedness to universities. Everything looked set for a brilliant principalship . . .'

A year later T.J. then eighty-four – he died in 1955 – retired as President of the college and Sir David Hughes-Parry, a man my father was later to describe as a 'distinguished lawyer of impeccable virtue, a dull mind, and ardent Welsh patriotism', took over. There were other changes, too. A year after we arrived in Aberystwyth, my sister and I were taken out of our respective schools and sent away to Huyton College, where my mother and her sisters had been; I always understood that my father felt, by then, that the growing hostility towards him by certain members of the university staff was creating such a difficult atmosphere that it was better for us and our education if we went away. I remember things being very tense when we came home for the holidays, but, of course, nothing was ever said in front of me to indicate just how unhappy both my father and my mother were.

In his own account, Rees wrote at length of the difficulties presented to him by the Welsh nationalist faction at the college: 'It would perhaps be absurd to say that during the few years in which I remained at Aberystwyth the college became a battlefield between two dia-metrically opposed conceptions of what a university should be. To say so may seem to give too great an importance to what was happening in this obscure little corner of Cardiganshire. And yet the conflict made itself felt in almost every matter, important or trivial, which came up for discussion during my period as Principal . . .' First of all it came up, he said, in the question of appointments: which should come first in one's assessment of a candidate, his qualities as a scholar or as a Welshman? It made itself felt in the degree of liberty which should be permitted to students; for was the college really an institute of learning or a preceptor of Welsh morals? It affected the admin-istration of the college's inadequate resources; should whatever there was to spare be devoted to departments with potential for making original contributions to learning, or to the provision of additional lecturers who would teach through the medium of Welsh? It even arose in the question of providing a community house for the academic staff: if they had a house, would not its amenities include a bar, and would not a bar be in itself a betrayal of the Welsh Nonconformist ethic, and, even worse, would it not set a dangerous example to students? 'Most of all,' Rees said, 'the conflict entered into the question, none the less important because it could never be explicitly formulated, what kind of a person the Principal of the College should be? Should he be one who put the pursuit of knowledge about the preservation of the Welsh language, reason above Nonconformity, lowered his dignity by making friends with students and junior lecturers, was not greatly concerned with their morals so long as they did their work, and even helped to corrupt them by offering them a drink when he had invited them to his house?'

It is impossible to know how long my father could have kept this up. Something had to give. Many of Rees's friends felt the outcome was inevitable. Stephen Spender told me: 'There was a sort of anarchism about him. It was ridiculous really for him to have been the head of a university, because, for him, it was a kind of role-playing in which he could not accept the role.'

The seeds were sown, I think, in 1955, a year of great excitement for the college, because, in August, the Queen came to Aberystwyth to open the newly completed National Library of Wales, the foundation stone of which had been laid by her grandfather in 1911. My father accompanied her around the Welsh Plant Breeding Station at Gogerddan, where I, in a frock my grandmother had made for me and white cotton socks, presented her with a bouquet, after being given special lessons at Huyton in how to curtsey.

Freddie Ayer came to stay with my parents and during his visit, Rees happened to show him an account he had written of his friendship with Guy Burgess, about his habits and his character, and about the famous flat in Bentinck Street. Freddie advised Rees to lodge a copy in the British Museum and my father said he would think about it.

It was at the end of that year that Richard Cobb arrived in Aberystwyth from Paris to be a junior lecturer in Modern European History. He was to become a close friend and ally of my parents, who felt, by then, under siege from the hostile group of professors to whom my mother gave the collective name of the 'Llanbardarn Road Mob' because many of them lived in a part of the town where, like north Oxford, there was a concentration of academics.

Cobb told me how he first met Rees. 'I was very unwilling to leave Paris, where I had been for eleven years,' he said, 'and Aber was a stinking place. My interview was held in a rather beautiful room in that old college building, overlooking the seafront, and I sat down facing a horseshoe-table, with Goronwy in the centre ... As the horseshoe fanned out there were more and more pseudo Lloyd Georges, with absolutely marvellous heads of white hair, some in dog collars. I could easily spot him, because he was absolutely stunningly good-looking, wearing his gown,' Rees, he recalled, put him totally at ease by mentioning the name of a mutual friend. Cobb got the job and arrived in September. The first six weeks in Aberystwyth, he said, were 'absolute hell'. He lived in the Talbot Hotel and used to go the station every day 'just to remind myself that there was a link to Shrewsbury and London and that I was not completely stranded ...' He also took out a year's subscription to *Le Monde*. After a while, he met Dick Spilsbury, a philosophy lecturer and son of the pathologist Sir Bernard Spilsbury, and the two became firm friends. 'We used to share a flat and from the kitchen window we could see the Plas up on Penglais Hill,' Cobb said. 'Dick would say that so long as he could see the white house where Goronwy and Margie lived he felt sure there was some element of sanity and culture in the place ...' Fairly soon, he and Spilsbury and Rees had established an arrangement to meet before lunch every Saturday in the back bar of the Belle Vue Hotel, on the seafront.

Cobb recalled: 'As we left, you could see one or two professorial figures with notebooks, writing something down about how the Principal had been seen drinking and accompanied by Cobb and Spilsbury ... Goronwy would always make a point of going up to them and making a friendly remark of some kind.' At the bar, he said, the three of them would talk about anything under the sun; mutual friends in Oxford or German literature, about which he knew nothing and Rees had a very good knowledge. Cobb also used to go on outings with my parents to pubs in the country outside Aberystwyth, where, he told me, they went in the 'mistaken notion that they could escape from the "Mob"'. My father, he said, was having problems: 'From the very start some of them had it in for him because he gave sherry parties on Sundays at the Plas, but there was a pretty clear division between those who approved of him and those who did not. On the whole the scientists thought he was doing a good job and brightening up the place and on the other side was the "Mob". Goronwy was marvellously flippant,' Cobb said, and this did not go down at all well in Aberystwyth. There was the story of the row at one of the women's halls of residence about a bed that had been identified as being surplus to requirements. 'The subject of this extra bed was brought up at some committee and it went on and on and in the end Goronwy said that enough time had been spent on this matter and why didn't someone just bring the bed downstairs and put it in the lounge or something. It was immediately reported back that the Principal was encouraging immorality. I don't think he realized how literally they took things.'

When I went back to Aberystwyth in the summer of 1993, some forty years later, I found, in a book on the history of the town, *Born on a Perilous Rock: Aberystwyth Past and Present*, published by the local newspaper, the following reference to my father:

After a period during which Professor Lily Newton proved a worthy Acting Principal, Morgan Goronwy Rees, the son of yet another minister of Tabernacl Chapel, Fellow and Bursar of All Souls, author, journalist and having a distinguished war record, was appointed Principal in 1953. But Goronwy Rees and Aberystwyth College did not see eye to eye with one another and in 1957 he resigned.

If only it had been as simple as that . . .


On 12 February 1956, the news was broken by the Sunday newspapers that Burgess and Maclean had surfaced in Moscow and, on the previous day, had held a press conference at the National Hotel, where they had read out a spurious statement in which they claimed they had never been 'communist agents' but had gone to the Soviet Union to 'work for the aim of better understanding between the Soviet Union and the West'.

Although an official government report on their disappearance had been published in 1955, it was the first time Burgess and Maclean had been seen in public since they had vanished nearly five years earlier and the effect was electrifying. On 11 March *The People* newspaper began a five-part series under the garish headline: 'GUY BURGESS stripped bare!' and trailed in the following fashion:

HIS CLOSEST FRIEND
SPEAKS AT LAST

• This is the first of a profoundly disturbing series of articles. They reveal appalling facts about Guy Burgess, the missing diplomat, that the authorities

HAVE NOT DARED TO LET THE PUBLIC KNOW.

• These disclosures come from the one man in a position to know the complete story. He was Burgess's closest friend for more than 20 years and now occupies a high academic post.

• Only he can reveal the full depth of corruption that lay behind Guy Burgess's treachery. Now he speaks about the friend who was the greatest traitor of all.

The tone was, of course, highly sensational, befitting the mass-circulation broadsheet newspaper, the pages of which, in the mid-fifties, were filled with advertisements for constipation remedies, columns by Gilbert Harding, features about teddy boys, Laurence Harvey writing about how tedious he found Hollywood parties, and exposés such as how calves were crowded into lorries and sent 'hundreds of miles to be turned into pies'. The anonymous author had plenty to get off his chest about Guy Burgess, who 'wrought more damage to Britain than any traitor in our history'. But first he put himself in context: 'I have known Guy Burgess for twenty-four years. We were constantly in each other's homes. We shared anxieties and joys. We went to parties together. We had the same friends. He is godfather to one of my children. He wrote to me frequently when we were separated. He had even sent me messages of friendship from Moscow. He deceived me about only one thing – his treachery to Britain. And it is the way he duped me, his other friends, the Foreign Office and our Security chiefs that is the most astounding and terrifying part of my story . . .' The author went on: '. . . I must take you right back to the beginning when Guy Burgess was a communist at Cambridge University. It was there that I first met him in 1932 [*Rees's memory was not any better then* . . .]. I was a Fellow of one of the most famous Oxford colleges. Guy was on a visit from Cambridge, where he was the most brilliant undergraduate of his time. He was not only brilliant; he had compelling charm. He was the most fascinating conversationalist I had ever come across. And, since I am going to be perfectly frank, I want to avow here and now that I was exceedingly fond of this strange and in many ways terrible man . . .'

The first article even stated that the mysterious anonymous author had been a journalist on the 'Conservative weekly *The Spectator*'. Over the weeks, the articles revealed how Guy had advised the Rothschilds and worked for a Conservative MP, and had confided to the stunned author 'very slowly and with the utmost gravity': 'I WANT TO TELL

YOU THAT I AM A COMINTERN AGENT AND HAVE BEEN EVER SINCE I LEFT CAMBRIDGE.' Burgess's 'friend' laid bare Guy's depravities and 'the whole sordid tale of his private life'; how he kept every letter written to him so that he could blackmail influential people, how he 'indulged in practices that repel all normal people', had numerous friends who shared his 'abnormal vices', how he was 'up to his neck' in spying. He introduced into the story Guy's fellow Comintern agent, named X, who was 'ONE OF BURGESS'S BOON SEX COMPANIONS AND HE HOLDS A HIGH POSITION IN PUBLIC LIFE TODAY' and one of the 'country's most celebrated academic figures'. This sounded remarkably like Anthony Blunt. However, Guy Liddell, formerly of MI 5 and, in 1956, head of security for the Atomic Energy Commission, was named as was Victor Rothschild, owner of the Bentinck Street flat.

One of the *People* articles told of a curious incident at the Gargoyle Club when a drunken Donald Maclean tottered up to the author's table and said, 'in an extremely menacing and belligerent voice': '*I know all about you. You used to be one of us, but you ratted.*' The series ended with a severe warning from 'Burgess's closest friend': the Foreign Office had concealed the whole story of the Missing Diplomats and the public must be warned about the dangers still to be faced from men like Burgess and Maclean. They were not the only Britons in positions of trust to be recruited into the Soviet spy ring. The author continued: 'I believe that Burgess and Maclean staged their recent public appearance in Moscow as a warning to those remaining traitors – a warning that they can be exposed if they do not continue in the service of Russia. The traitors must be rooted out before the long-range blackmail begins to work. Only then will Britain be saved from another Burgess and Maclean scandal...'

The mystery writer told readers that he had received two messages from Guy Burgess since his flight in 1951. The first, a postcard at Christmas 1953, stated that he was well and sent his love. A second communication had been received since Burgess's reappearance: 'He asked me to write to him at Poste Restante, Central Telegraph Office, Moscow, USSR. I do not know what kind of reply he expected. This story and my verdict on Guy Burgess will serve as an answer...'

Reading through these articles, written so long ago, to select excerpts for this book, a shiver ran up my spine as I tried to imagine what could have driven my father to commit such a self-destructive and extraordinary act of folly. I was thirty years old when I was able to read his own explanation in *A Chapter of Accidents*, in which he wrote of the effect upon him of Guy's reappearance in Moscow and the public statement which Burgess and Maclean had made: 'They were like some chilly official announcement that every suspicion I ever had of Guy had been correct and that all the theories, excuses, explanations, which I had found or invented in order to exorcize them, had been merely self-deceptions practised in order to conceal the truth from myself. It seemed extraordinary to realize at last that Guy had in fact told me the truth and that for nearly twenty years I had *known* that Guy was a Soviet agent but had been unable to acknowledge the fact; or had I, and merely evaded the issue?' It was difficult, Rees said, to accept: 'Especially because, as a result, many people had suffered, some perhaps in ways I did not like to think of. It was equally difficult to accept that for all those years Guy, apart from his one single moment of self-revelation, had consciously and consistently betrayed all the affection which his friends had for him, in spite of all the strains to which he had so often exposed it.'

But there was something else, Rees wrote: 'It is perhaps not necessary to explain here the process of disillusion by which one comes to see a cause in which one has placed one's highest hopes as an embodiment of evil. Others have done it better than I can: the story of *The God That Failed* is one of the fundamental stories of my generation and it has been told in so many different versions during the last thirty years that my own version of it would add nothing to the others. It is perhaps enough to say that, far from seeing Guy as one who had sacrificed himself for higher ends, I saw him as one who had advanced an unworthy cause by equally unworthy means. Even more, he had become in my eyes one who had voluntarily engaged in the cruel and murderous operations of an organization which was directly responsible for the destruction of millions of people by death, torture, starvation and any other means which its ingenuity could devise to achieve that purpose. He was, no doubt, my friend; he was also a man with blood on his hands...'

Rees expressed the hope that he could finally rid himself of a nightmare by having the articles published: 'I did not think that my own account would do me very much credit. At best I would look foolish, perhaps absurd, and at worst tainted by my association with Guy. And to some, I knew, the mere act of committing to paper what I knew about him would be regarded as treacherous and dishonourable. I did not much look forward to such consequences but in the end, I thought, to tell the truth was the only alternative left to me . . .'

It was in the *Daily Telegraph* of 29 March 1956 that the author of the 'strange series in *The People*' was identified as Rees, but many people knew who he was immediately the first instalment was published. The 'Peterborough' column of the *Telegraph* commented: 'The series is not at all the scholarly analysis one would expect from a Principal. For the most part it consists of gossipy jottings bringing in the names of well-known people or describing them sufficiently for easy identification by their acquaintances. Mr Rees is careful to acquit them of knowledge of Burgess's activities. But a little mud always sticks. There is a revelation, typical of this kind of journalism, about a character named "X", who is, or was, a Comintern agent. "He was one of Burgess's boon sex companions. And he holds a high position in public life today." In that case is it not Mr Rees's duty to report him?'

Many years later, Michael Berry, now Lord Hartwell, wrote a letter to his own *Sunday Telegraph* in which he described Rees as someone who could not be counted on to be loyal. Rees, he said, wrote a series of anonymous articles for *The People* in which he 'smeared the names of well-known people or described them sufficiently for easy identification by their acquaintances' and was then sacked by the University College of Wales, Aberystwyth.

In the summer of 1993, I wrote to Lord Hartwell, who had been a friend of Guy's at Eton, and asked him if he could explain why he had felt so bitter about Rees. I was a little apprehensive before our meeting, but he seemed to enjoy talking about what had happened all those years ago. He said he thought Rees had behaved 'shabbily'. 'He identified friends of mine, such as Victor Rothschild,' he told me. 'That was automatically a crime, because it was very, very disloyal. Victor was terribly upset. It did not matter being disloyal to Guy – no one took his defection very seriously, anyway.' Lord Hartwell said he was 'upset' but also actually rather 'relieved' when Guy disappeared. He had seen him in Washington and Guy had asked him for a job because 'they weren't very pleased with him at the Embassy there.' Shortly before Guy vanished he had received a lunch invitation from him.

Lord Hartwell continued: 'At school Guy was clever, he had been the youngest boy to win the history prize and our history tutor, Robert Birley, later to be the Headmaster, said he was the most brilliant student he had ever examined. I knew he was extremely well-read and I thought he might be able to do something at the *Daily Telegraph*.' When they met, Guy had told him he had been fired and asked if his friend could do anything for him. Lord Hartwell had asked Guy to show him something he had written. He remembered Guy turning up with Rees and that they both had a glass of vintage port. 'Guy gave me a document to read, marked Top Secret,' he said. 'That was typical Guy. It was a report he had drafted for the Ambassador at the embassy in Washington on the state of American opinion on something or other, but it never got passed on. I was appalled when I read it. His writing had certainly gone to seed. He wasn't seedy, but his writing was. So I felt relief when he went, because I no longer had to find him something to do.'

On the day following the publication of the first article in *The People*, two MI5 officers arrived at the Plas to see Rees, which pleased him because, as he said, he hoped they might pay more attention, this time, to what he had to say. In Aberystwyth, his unmasking by the *Daily Telegraph* had, in his words, 'something of the effect of the bombardment of Fort Sumter in provoking the American Civil War' and, of course, Oxford had also been hit by the blast. Stuart Hampshire remembered it well: 'I was at All Souls, when I got a telephone call from a friend, who said someone had rung him about this article and could I go and get a copy of *The People*, which I did. When I saw it, I sat down and wrote a very angry letter to Rees, which I have regretted ever since. I would never do such a thing again, but I was upset. The stuff about Bentinck Street was very damaging to them all. Victor Rothschild was a great friend of mine and so I wrote an abusive letter and told Rees that I really could have no more relations with him and we all sat around speculating about why he had done it.' Everyone, he said, knew that the author was Rees; it could not have been anyone else. 'Then stories began to emerge about the Aberystwyth life,' he said, 'and how Rees had no money and had unpaid bills and there was a very dramatic situation developing there as his enemies had been ganging up on him before these articles appeared.' It was generally acknowledged that Goronwy was 'frightened' about something, Stuart told me; he was frightened that stories might appear in newspapers that could be used against him in Aberystwyth by his enemies. Rees, Stuart said, was 'very angry' when he received his letter and they never spoke again.

Isaiah Berlin told me that he had known for some time that Rees had written something about Guy. About a year before the articles appeared, Rees had, he said, gone to their mutual friend, Sylvester Gates, then deputy chairman of the Westminster Bank, and asked if he had a confidential secretary to whom he could dictate a story he wanted to tell. In the end, he never used the secretary, but appeared to have written whatever it was himself. Of the *People* articles, Isaiah commented: 'Of course, Rees did not write them as they were published, they were written by somebody on the newspaper. If Goronwy had had them published in a reputable magazine like *Encounter*, absolutely nothing would have happened ...' Isaiah knew of the first article because a friend of his, unable to find any other newspaper at Paddington Station, had bought a copy of *The People* and had shown it to him as soon as he arrived in Oxford. 'I was horrified,' he said. 'It was very terrible about Guy. I asked Goronwy why he had done this and he replied, "You have no idea about Burgess, he is a very wicked man, much worse than you think. He really is very sinister." ' Isaiah did not reply to a letter Rees wrote to him and after that there was a 'certain *froideur*, a certain coolness between us because I thought it was an awful thing to write an article saying that people in the Foreign Office were communists and homosexuals. Oddly enough, having the government that we do have, nothing happened. But what did happen was that Goronwy lost his job. It was a curious result and one that was acclaimed by the MacCarthyites.'

I asked Isaiah if he had any ideas as to my father's motive. 'Some people think he did it for money,' he said, 'but I think that, although he might have had debts, that was not the reason. It was a kind of insurance policy. I think it was because he was afraid, he was afraid of Burgess spreading disinformation and telling terrible stories about him and everyone one else and he had to get in first. That is my hypothesis. I think Goronwy was frightened. I think he thought that anything could happen and he panicked. Goronwy was easily panickable ...' Maurice Bowra, then Warden of Wadham, wrote to Rees to suggest that he should plant Judas trees around the college athletics field. As the social invitations were withdrawn and more disapproving letters arrived from those he had once considered his friends, my father was made to feel, with no uncertainty, that he was in disgrace and, in their eyes, beyond the pale. This time he had gone too far. One of the other unfortunate effects of the articles was that much sympathy was expressed for Anthony Blunt, who found himself, once again, the target of gossip and speculation. In the papers of my uncle, Geraint, I found some notes about my father scribbled on a piece of fading blue paper: 'After 1956, Blunt and friends always "cut him dead" when they met...'

My father's apparently reckless determination to walk into trouble was as much a puzzle to Nat Rothman, the deputy editor of *The People* at that time, as it was to everyone else. A lawyer, he was called in by the managing editor of the paper, Sam Campbell, to advise on how to handle the manuscript they had bought from Rees's literary agent, Jean LeRoy. Nat told me that he thought it was a 'very strange thing' for Rees to be doing: 'I thought, why on earth has he come out with this now? From our point of view, it did not add a great deal to the story, as far as I can recall, but the reason we were interested was because the spies were in the news again as they had turned up in Moscow. I do remember thinking – God knows, it was over forty years ago now and I may have formed the wrong impression – that he might have been concealing more than he was disclosing ...' However, Nat was 'astonished' that Rees had lost his job as a result of the publication of the articles. Thinking back, he remembered that he could not understand why Rees had wanted the articles to be anonymous, particularly as he was easily identifiable to anyone who knew him. 'I thought he paid the price for his anonymity rather than for what was in the articles,' he said. 'If he had put his name to them, then people would have said, well then, OK, there it is, there is dear old Goronwy who let his pals down or whatever. But to do it anonymously seemed to be cowardly and I think that put people's backs up.'

Rees went into the office every week to look at the proofs of the articles and Nat Rothman recalled his visits. 'I only saw him a few times, I think,' he said, 'but he struck me as a most lugubrious, not to say tragic, man. His face was long and furrowed as he sat there and everything about him seemed to be sad. He did not enjoy anything about what he was doing. It was as though he had been dragged reluctantly to do all this. I don't know why, but somehow or other I thought afterwards that he had some terrible guilt feeling.'

The journalist Tom Driberg, who had hurried over to Moscow to see if he could 'scoop' the first interview with Guy, recalled the visit in his autobiography, *Ruling Passions*, and had raised the question of Rees's behaviour when he subsequently returned to Russia to show Guy the proofs of the book he had written about him, published later that year. Driberg related how, at an open-air cocktail party at the Indonesian Embassy in Moscow, he had come across the 'celebrated

Oxford don' Isaiah Berlin, an old friend of Guy's. He had heard that Driberg would be seeing Guy and asked him to give Guy his 'warmest love' and to tell him that 'none of us are speaking to Goronwy ...' Driberg said that when he reported Isaiah's comment to Guy, Guy was pleased, but did not take a censorious view of Rees's behaviour, simply saying: 'He probably needed the money. He always did.'

Four years later, Guy asked Stephen Spender why Rees had written the articles. Was it just for £5000? Stephen recounted in his *Journals*: 'I said I thought this figure was exaggerated: there was a view that after Guy's reappearance in Moscow and the publication of his own articles, Goronwy panicked for some reason or other; perhaps he thought that Guy would start disseminating articles from Moscow about his past and his friends.' Stephen explained that Guy had replied: 'Well, in that case, the most likely thing to make me do so would be for him to write an article "provoking" me.' Continuing the conversation, Stephen suggested: 'I dare say that is so, but all the same he might have wished to tell his side of the story first.' Guy wanted to know why and Stephen replied: 'Well, supposing he thought you had given away secrets. Then he might have wanted to dissociate himself from that.'

Harold Nicolson was particularly incensed with the article in which Rees described how Burgess kept letters that he could use for black-mailing purposes. According to his biographer James Lees-Milne, Nicolson was devoted to Guy: 'Harold's "respect" for Guy Burgess amounted to his brain and courage of his convictions. He had no respect for those convictions. But his loyalty to his friend was unwaver-ing. Nothing a person, who had once been a friend, could do, however offensive, erased in Harold's sentimental mind the memory of that friend when he had first known and been attracted to him. To Harold, the drink-sodden, crapulous traitor which Guy Burgess had become, remained in his vision the bright-eyed, fresh-looking, brilliant and promising youth of the very early thirties.' Apparently Nicolson was 'sickened' when he read the articles: 'He thought it so filthy that he felt the author (Goronwy Rees) must have gone mad ...'

Reactions among Rees's friends and acquaintances encompassed shock, disbelief and disapproval. However, not everyone took a high moral tone. Henry Yorke, in a letter to a friend in Canada in October 1956, reported that Rees was in 'bad trouble'. He had left Pontifex, he said, to go to Aberystwyth 'still convinced that his dearest friend Guy Burgess had not gone to Russia but was vacationing in Algeria'.

He went on: 'When Guy gave a newspaper interview in Moscow to say in effect that he had deflected [*sic*] to the East, it broke Goronwy's heart and for £2700 he sold material to *The People* Sunday newspaper which provided five scurrilous articles with every kind of sexual imperfection in them. As a result the University asked him to resign. He refused. A lot of other people then resigned because he had refused to resign. There is now a Commission of Enquiry sitting to decide who is in the right. And poor old Goronwy's hair has gone dead white and he has lost a lot of weight . . .'

In Aberystwyth, the row over the articles dragged on, almost unbearably, for nearly a year until it was finally resolved by Rees's resignation in March 1957. At first it looked as if the affair was not, mercifully, going to be drawn out; in June 1956, the college council, meeting in private, decided that no action was to be taken and the matter was closed. The students voted, by a massive majority, in favour of a resolution that their body would 'view with extreme concern and alarm any action that would result in the dismissal or resignation of the Principal'. But from the point at which two members of the college council resigned at the prospect of the Principal being forgiven his sins, Rees's position became more and more precarious, though he carried on with his duties, receiving members of the University Grants Committee in June 1956 and conferring honorary degrees on Frank Lloyd Wright, the architect, and his friend, the writer Richard Hughes, at a Congregation of the University of Wales at Bangor in July. In June, however, he resigned from the Wolfenden Committee on Homosexuality and Prostitution, on which he had been sitting.

I have taken a resumé of the mood of the moment from Dr Ellis's history of the college: 'Many members, past and present, lay and academic, were profoundly disturbed, some deeply outraged by the course of events. Some of the members and many of the senior academic members of the College believed strongly that the affair should not simply be ignored . . .'

A major move on the part of the anti-Rees lobby came on the day of the degree ceremony on 19 July, when Professors Richard Aaron (logic and philosophy) and Reginald Treharne (history) left a letter on the table in the robing room which began: 'Dear President, We, the undersigned, desire to inform you that in our opinion it is essential in the interest of the college that an independent committee of enquiry be immediately set up to examine the present situation in the College ...' This had gathered twelve signatures by the time the degree assembly had dispersed and, when finally presented to the President, had been signed by fifteen professors out of a total of twenty-eight; two professors, in Iceland and New Zealand, could not be rounded up in time. Very briefly, Rees said he 'welcomed' the setting up of an independent committee of inquiry, to be nominated by Sir Keith Murray, chairman of the University Grants Committee, and Sir Emrys Evans, Vice-Chancellor of the University of Wales.

Three Englishmen were chosen to adjudicate on the battle that was being fought in the small Welsh seaside town: Henry Willink QC, Master of Magdalene College, Cambridge, chaired the committee; with him sat Dr J.W.F. Hill, president of the council of Nottingham University, and Dr W.J. Warboys, chairman of the Council of Industrial Design. At the next stage in the proceedings, the inquiry committee invited members of council and Senate to submit written statements or 'offer themselves for oral examination', and sat eight times. Richard Cobb volunteered to be orally examined by what he described as the 'Star Chamber'. It did not go very well: 'Willink asked me, "Mr Cobb, what are your relations with the Principal?" and I replied – I was being quite serious – "Sir, I was employed by him." Willink said that he took that to be a frivolous answer. I told him that I saw the Principal most Saturdays. "Where?" he asked. I said, well, in the bar at the Belle Vue Hotel, and I was told that that would be all and I could leave. I did not think I had let Goronwy down, but it was obviously a terrible thing to have said.'

Cobb was living in a hotel on the seafront at the time and, on one occasion, was accosted by a reporter from a tabloid newspaper, who asked him if he was employed at the college. When Cobb said he was, he was asked whether he thought the morality of the students had declined since Rees had taken over as Principal. Cobb told me: 'I said that undoubtedly it had. The students had barbecues on the beach. He became very cross with me. But it was all very silly, because nobody really cared about the articles, they were just a pretext to get at Goronwy. The whole town was split. I remember the beachcombers who used to look for what had been washed up by the tide were all pro-Goronwy, as were the dustmen. One of the two Presbyterian chapels was pro-Goronwy, because it had been his father's chapel.' Cobb was as bewildered as everyone else by Rees's extraordinary decision to publish the articles: 'Goronwy was one of the most charming people I have ever met. But there seemed to be some elements that were just missing from him, in the moral sense. On the other hand, I would have thought he was the sort of person whom you would forgive for almost everything. He did not seem to think there was anything wrong with writing articles about very close friends of his and showing up what sort of bounders they were. But in Oxford, what they did not like was the high moral tone he used about those wild parties with people drinking red wine out of saucepans. A lot of people wondered why Goronwy should have taken that line.' My mother had told him, Cobb said, that Rees had to do it; he had to tell his side of the story before Guy told his. 'But what amazed me most of all,' he said, 'was that Goronwy was a Welshman and he had spent his childhood in Aberystwyth and he should have known. I suppose that if there is a *morale de cette histoire*, it is do not be flippant when dealing with provincials. They do not understand it.'

Relating the story of Rees's articles in his book about his contemporaries, *Our Age*, Noël Annan said that 'Rees was alarmed that Burgess would implicate him in public and was determined to get his blow in first . . .' He had written the articles – 'an indictment not only of Burgess but of his friends, and in particular of those friends who were in high places or had been in the security services' – in a 'moment of madness'. In these articles Rees had maintained that Burgess had blackmailed people to obtain secrets; that he was protected by his homosexual friends in MI5; and that he should have been expelled from the service on several occasions. The 'explosion', he said, 'detonated' by these articles was 'atomic': but the 'blast walls of the Establishment are so cunningly constructed that the person most hideously wounded was Goronwy Rees himself . . .'

The Willink Report was published in February 1957, and on reading it my father resigned the following month. A report in *The Times* on 15 March said that the council had 'acceded to a request of the Principal, Mr Goronwy Rees, to terminate his office as Principal, for which he has given six months' notice, and that he ceases to carry out his duties as requested in his letter'. The report went on: 'Mr Rees told your Correspondent yesterday that "after having a perfectly horrible time for a whole year mainly due to accusations concerning my personal behaviour", he wanted nothing more than to leave the university. His only sorrow in leaving would be for the students. He denied that any group of newspapers had made him offers of a job. He would be only too happy to accept them if they had. He had no plans for the future . . .'

# 10

During the whole of that day I was in great
distress and alarm and disturbance of mind,
because I felt that now it really was
necessary to do something...'

Goronwy Rees


The Willink Report was never made public and even if it had been,
at Huyton College we would have been as protected from its findings
as we were at home. My housemistress carefully examined each
morning's copy of the *Liverpool Daily Post* and cut out every story and
article that was considered unsuitable for our eyes in our small, Pym-
like enclave. I was therefore very grateful when, in the summer of
1993, I was given permission by the college Principal, Professor
Kenneth Morgan, and the Registrar, Daniel Gruffydd Jones, to read
the report.

One morning in August I found myself walking to the old college
building – an ornate Victorian mock castle – from the Belle Vue
Hotel, scene of my father's Saturday morning sessions with Cobb and
Spilsbury, along the seafront, which looked exactly as it did when I
lived in Aberystwyth forty years previously. Nothing appeared to have
changed; even the train of donkeys, carrying small children along the
promenade, looked much like the ones my sister and I had persuaded
our parents to let us borrow and keep up at Penglais one winter,
when we rode them around the garden paths and battled with their
formidable wills.

In the Registrar's office, which, like my father's in his time, looked
towards the sea, I found, laid out on the table for me, the 43-page
limited-circulation report, marked 'Strictly Confidential', which, it
specified, was the result of a letter signed by eighteen heads of
department and presented in 1956 to Sir David Hughes-Parry, the
college President, asking for a Committee of Enquiry to 'consider the
present situation in College and such matters as may be raised by the
President or the Principal'.

The 'situation', it explained, had arisen from the publication of
articles in *The People*, in March and April 1956, which were 'admittedly' based on material supplied by the Principal of the College,

Goronwy Rees, and 'described in detail in the first person, but anonymously, his close and friendly association over a period of many years with Guy Burgess, a man who since that period has achieved notoriety and who has just made a sensational reappearance in Moscow'. The introduction added that the 'situation' had brought about a 'serious cleavage of opinion within the college and in a wider field and an outbreak of gossip defamatory of the Principal'. Sir David Hughes-Parry had asked the committee to consider Rees's 'irresponsibility' and the 'harmful effect of the publication in creating divisions among staff, council and students' and the 'injury done to the reputation of the College and the harm done to its well-being', and Rees himself had raised a number of matters for investigation. The buff-covered report did not make pleasant reading but it produced some facts which helped to illuminate my father's behaviour, about which I had, until then, been able to gather only snippets of gossip and a wealth of speculation.

The 'cleavage of opinion', said the report, had been, of course, due to the publication of the articles: one view was that it was 'no more than an error of judgment' and, in the interests of the college, Rees's apology should have been accepted; others were more critical, considering the articles' 'clear evidence' that he was unworthy of his office. Figures were produced; twenty-six members of the academic staff, including twenty professors, had given evidence. The committee noted: 'Most realized there were aspects of the matter on which they were inadequately informed, and all realized it was a matter for council.' Nine people were in favour of forgetting the articles, fifteen took a 'grave view' of the Principal's conduct, and two could pass no opinion without further information. Some witnesses said there were 'shortcomings' in Rees's administration of college affairs, while others said he was an 'exceptionally competent, sympathetic and successful' head of a college. The committee found, however, that 'The net effect of what we have read and heard leaves us with the impression of an academic community that was running well and smoothly'.

The report opened by covering the background to the 'situation'. Rees told the committee that on 12 February 1956 when Sunday newspapers published the news that Burgess had reappeared in Moscow, he spent the day 'in great distress and alarm and disturbance of mind, because I felt that now it was really necessary to do something', and, according to his evidence, that evening he telephoned David Higham, his literary agent. In a letter he wrote to Higham following the telephone call, he asked for professional advice and assistance: 'I should say that Guy Burgess was perhaps my oldest and best friend and for the last five years I have resisted every temptation to make any kind of statement about him ... I have become more and more interested in the case and more and more under a compulsion to say what I know about it ...' Could it make a book or a series of articles? If David Higham agreed to act for him, Rees added, he could say that Guy was 'perhaps my greatest friend for twenty years' and that he had 'precise and accurate knowledge of his activities as a communist during that period'. He suggested the matter would need 'careful handling' and he did not want his name mentioned at that stage. On 22 February he went to London to see Jean LeRoy at David Higham's office and agreed to sell his account of what he knew about Guy to *The People* for 2000 guineas, on condition that they would submit proofs to him for approval and that his identity would not be revealed. A manuscript of between 5000 and 6000 words, written in 1955 for 'his own amusement and for the record', became the basis for the final narrative of 28000 words. According to the report, the manuscript was typed by my mother and completed by 2 March.

The Master of Magdalene and his colleagues observed: 'It is not too much to say that we found it a very shocking document. In it, the Principal recounts his association with Burgess, whom he describes as "perhaps my oldest and best friend" ... even before they met, he knew he was a homosexual, and that within twenty-four hours of their first meeting Burgess had attempted to seduce him ... Over many pages, Burgess is described as a particularly vicious homosexual, a corrupter of men and boys, a pimp and a procurer in this unsavoury field. Burgess is characterized as "quite exceptionally gross and coarse in his approaches to other men", as a retailer of scandalous homosexual incidents and as a heavy drinker and addicted to drugs ...' It was noted that Rees had said that Burgess kept a bundle of letters *which he never destroyed*. The manuscript also described Burgess as 'completely promiscuous, physically dirty, notoriously untrustworthy and unreliable, a reckless and irresponsible public servant', and in it Rees revealed doubts in his own mind about whether he was a 'loyal British subject'.

But, the committee said, 'There is no syllable in the document to suggest that Rees ever attempted to reform his friend. To the end they are represented as continuing in the original pattern.' Worse than that, possibly, was the fact that Burgess was godfather to one of Rees's children. Also held against Rees was the 'tenor' of the narrative, which was 'more reminiscent of a scandalous novel than a serious record or a balanced biographical sketch': the description of Guy's homosexual adventures was 'flippant' and the attitude of the author was 'immoral'.

The committee recorded: 'It has been assumed by some that *The People* had sensationalized the information. This is not the fact. Those who prepared the articles changed the style, but the narrative is quite equally sensational . . . contains long passages dealing with homosexual promiscuity which are shocking in the extreme and of which *The People*, wisely as we would think, decided not to make use.' The report does not contain a copy of Rees's original manuscript. The committee explained that the Principal 'prohibited its reproduction', and the panel agreed, both because it was 'defamatory' and could have been leaked to the press and also because 'it would be distasteful of us to include it for council members to consider'.

The report then dealt with the mysterious matter of Rees's insistence that, in preparing his narrative and having it published, he 'sedulously inculcated' a belief – 'which he must have known to be untrue' – that by doing so he was 'in some way carrying out the behest, or complying with the expressed wishes of the authorities responsible for the security of the country'. In May Rees had written to Sir David Hughes-Parry, stating: 'It is my duty . . . to do all I can to protect the interests of the country. The method by which this latter was achieved, so far as I could contribute, was not of my choosing, but I unequivocally support the end which, as I have reason to know, fully justified the means . . . That which I did recently was done advisedly and with the full knowledge and approval of those persons and organizations whose duty it is to protect and preserve the security of this country.'

From the Willink Report it is clear that the committee strongly disapproved of this line: 'The truth is that none of it owed anything to the instigation or approval of the security services. It was entirely his own initiative . . . We cannot escape the conclusion that Mr Rees endeavoured to create the erroneous impression that in procuring the publication of the articles he had in some way been the mouthpiece of the security authorities and was embarrassed by his inability to disclose the nature and degree of their responsibility for his action; and that he intended to deceive and did, in fact, deceive such members of the council and Senate as felt this might be a good reason for his failure to produce any other satisfactory explanation of his action . . .'

Moving on, the report said that Rees's course of conduct was so 'unusual' and had been so 'embarrassing' that the committee felt it essential to inquire into his motive.

He had admitted to being 'hard up' for the past three years and this, the committee felt, would have been the normal explanation. In a statement to the Senate in June 1956, Rees had said that out of a 'very much reduced income' he had had to pay 'heavy demands' for surtax on his earnings before he was appointed Principal. He explained: 'In the last two years alone, these have amounted to £1300 and I admit it has not been easy to meet them, but even so matters have never been so serious as to force me to make money out of betraying my friends. It was not because of money but because, rightly or wrongly, I thought it my duty, that I allowed the articles to be published...'

It was with a 'feeling of relief', apparently, that the committee found themselves satisfied that Rees's motive was not 'primarily or mainly for financial gain'. Looking more closely at the reasons which had led my father to 'feel such alarm and such a sense of urgency' when Burgess reappeared in Moscow, the panel were suspicious of his explanation that he had felt Guy capable of doing 'great harm' because he possessed 'an appalling fund of information to the discredit of numerous persons in prominent positions in the country and that his collection of such information, though made primarily for purposes of gossip and private amusement, constituted, with Burgess and Maclean in Moscow, a formidable weapon of pressure and blackmail'. According to the report, Rees explained to the committee: 'After a great deal of trouble and distress of mind, I had come to the conclusion that he must have been a spy (and once he reappeared there was no more possible doubt about that) and I thought that if he reappeared he would try in some way or other to renew his previous activities ...' He went on: 'From all the experience I have, it is clear to me that a spy never does, and can never, operate alone. He must have other associates. When Burgess reappeared, I believed he might try to renew his previous contacts and I wanted to warn anybody whom he approached precisely what kind of dangers they would be running if they renewed contact with him, or did anything as a result of contact with him ... I thought he might do an enormous amount of personal and political damage – simply by writing down or telling someone else what he knew about other people...'

The Master and his colleagues rejected the 'security' motive, even though they were prepared to accept that Rees had not sold the articles to make money. They concluded: 'Mr Rees cannot have been anxious to save from exposure those who had been, and were still willing to continue to be, in Soviet pay. Nor can he have had such pressing anxiety with regard to persons who had compromised themselves in any way; Burgess's reputation was already such that innocent persons would be very unlikely to yield to advances from him ...' On the other hand, Rees himself was one of those of whom Burgess could tell a highly damaging story; he had, as he had written to David Higham on 12 February, precise and accurate knowledge of Burgess's activities as a communist during a period of twenty years. 'No doubt,' the report said, 'there were others compromised to a greater or lesser extent than himself, with regard to whom Burgess might make, or threaten to make, highly embarrassing relevations; people who could in some degree, be protected if Burgess were himself exposed as utterly depraved and utterly untrustworthy.'

The report stated: 'We have been unable to escape the conclusion that Mr Rees was moved to take the course he did by the thought that it was essential, in his own interests as well as in the interests of others, to discredit Burgess completely, even at the cost of exposing himself as embarrassingly compromised and surprisingly gullible. The urgency of his anxiety to discredit Burgess is proved not only by his conduct, but by the fact that when examined he had to admit that in a number of the more lurid parts of the narrative his description of Burgess is exaggerated and in part untrue. While, therefore, we are able to say that Mr Rees was not primarily moved by a commercial motive, we are unable to say that his motive was patriotic or altruistic. It was, in a very large degree ... self-regarding and there is not from first to last any hint or suggestion that he gave a thought to the effect upon the College.'

Summing up, the committee found fault after fault with the conduct of a Principal whose tenure had promised to be so successful: 'His record shows him to be a man of great intellectual ability; his attitude to staff and students was helpful and sympathetic and, though it would seem that some of his more liberal changes would cause controversy, we have had no evidence to establish that such controversy would go beyond that which is to be expected in any university institution.' But they had to consider his conduct in the light of the fact that he was Principal of a university college and that 'the college is in Wales where university colleges are held in special esteem'. The acceptance of the appointment 'implies the acceptance of a duty to take into account these considerations', for the Principal 'must be trusted and respected by members of college and may have to adjudicate upon a serious moral matter arising within the college'. He may also have to address the student body on questions relating to character and behaviour or to conduct periodical religious services.

Taking all this into account, the committee decided that Rees had acted in a manner 'incompatible' with the standard of conduct required by his office, both in making his contract with *The People* and in the way he had fulfilled it. In offering material that was 'lewd and scandalous', which he had admitted was partly 'exaggerated and unfair', he had shown a 'wanton disregard' for the interests of the college...

As if that were not enough, there was also criticism of his behaviour towards the President, Sir David Hughes-Parry, in the wake of the publication of the articles. According to the report, the President had known by 20 March, that Rees had been identified as the author of *The People* articles and on Easter Sunday he was visited at his country home by a party of professors, led by Professor Newton, who wanted to express their concern. By then, Rees had confirmed that he had also written to the *Western Mail*. On 10 April, Rees and my mother went to discuss the matter with Sir David over lunch at a hotel at Talyllyn, outside Aberystwyth, when, the report recorded, my father had said he would resign and Sir David had intimated that he would recommend that the college council pay him one or two years' salary if he did so. On the same day, the President was able to write to Professor Newton, giving her the news that at the 'friendly discussion over lunch ... on what was best for the future of the college' he and Rees had come to a 'friendly understanding which was most satisfactory from all points of view in the circumstances'. They had both agreed, he said, that the proper time and place to make this understanding known was at the next meeting of the college council and, in the meantime, had undertaken to say nothing to anyone. Sir David ended the letter to Professor Newton: '... I can assure you that I am confident that all is for the best ... I apologize for being cryptic, but I must honour my word...'

The whole dreadful affair could have ended there instead of dragging on for many more months and prolonging the agony for my parents. However, on 22 April Sir David Hughes-Parry received a letter from Rees, which said: 'I have thought very carefully about the suggestion you make, but I cannot help feeling that, quite apart from myself, it would not be in the interest of the College for me to offer you my resignation now. Since I last saw you, it has been repeatedly suggested to me that I am being forced to resign and I am quite sure that if my resignation were to be announced to council in June it would inspire a very violent hate campaign against the College. I ought to say that I have already had to write to one editor, who wished to attack the College and defend me, asking him to say nothing and he has been good enough to do so . . .' Rees said that if he were to resign, it would inevitably be assumed that he had been forced to do so and he would not find another appointment. He could not possibly find a new home and a new job within six months and he was worried about my mother's health. He suggested instead that he should resign in September, by which time he hoped he would have managed to make alternative arrangements.

Rees ended his letter: 'There is one thing I would like to add. Until now, no single person connected with the College, except yourself, has discussed or even mentioned this subject to me and I had had no opportunity whatever for explaining the motives, which I believe to be good ones, which impelled me to do what I have done. I am perfectly prepared to give such an explanation and, indeed, if the matter is to be discussed in public at all I feel it is only right that I should have the opportunity to do so . . .' His letter had a sting in the tail: 'I hope you enjoy your visit to Israel and will return refreshed by the spectacle of other people's troubles which are, after all, very much more serious than our own . . .'

According to the report, the President replied stating that the matter could not wait until September. In response he received a letter from my father, written on his London solicitor's writing paper, in which, so the report claimed, he went back on the Talyllyn agreement. Rees dug in his heels and said that he could not be 'associated' with a joint statement in June because it could not contain the 'full facts'. He reiterated that it had been his duty to write the articles and that the end fully justified the means. He was not prepared to compromise: 'I am not and cannot be influenced by ill-considered and rash obser-vations of those who necessarily are uninformed and who, in the very nature of things, are only able to take a limited view from which no proper or fair deduction can possibly be drawn. To be so influenced will militate against the true well-being of the College and suffice merely to resuscitate a matter now dead save in the minds of those who permit prejudice and partisan consideration to obscure the true issues.'

Mr Willink and his colleagues took a dim view of this intransigence: 'It is sufficient to say that by this letter ... the Principal repudiated the arrangements to which he had agreed at Talyllyn. Rees's *volte face* created a situation of 'great difficulty' for the President because the Principal had 'gone back on his word'. More letters were exchanged before the President wrote to the Principal saying: 'I note you are going back on all you arranged with me at Talyllyn ... I would remind you that you opened your talk with me with the words "I have decided to resign", and we amicably agreed that, having regard to the interests of the College, that was the best course in the circumstances. I have taken you at your word ever since and have kept to mine. You must realize that you are putting me as President in an impossible situation. So I must reconsider my own as well as your position ...'

With a final letter, from Rees to the President, stating, 'I am sorry that you should say I have gone back on our agreement at Talyllyn. I really must deny this totally and completely and also say that your recollection of my "opening words" is incorrect', the report noted that all hope of a joint statement was gone. The committee was very critical about the behaviour of this loose cannon on the college deck: 'Our findings as to his conduct subsequent to publication are, to our regret ... adverse. He went back on his word, after making an agreement with the President on 10 April. The measures he took to secure his continued tenure of the principalship and to avoid a Committee of Inquiry were discreditable. His repeated representations that all he had done was with the approval of the security authorities were, to his knowledge, untrue. His attitude to the President was discourteous, offensive and, to his knowledge, unfair.'

Finally, a special meeting of the college council in March 1957 accepted Rees's resignation and granted him his request to leave immediately. It was agreed that he was to be paid his salary until September. All copies of the Willink Report were returned to the Registrar. Minutes of the council meeting in June confirmed the action of the Registrar in deducting income tax from Rees's salary and it was decided to advertise for a new Principal, offering a salary of £3000 a year.

Recording Rees's departure from Aberystwyth in the official history of the college, the author, Dr Ted Ellis, perhaps understandably questioned my mother's view that the Welsh were poisonous and malicious. Of Rees's own account of the affair in *A Chapter of Accidents*, Dr Ellis wrote: 'It is a highly subjective version; some of the criticisms he made of the College are not without their point, but the picture he presents can scarcely be described as balanced; indeed, here and there, it falls away to caricature. Certainly the charitableness that governed his attitude to Guy Burgess over so many years is conspicuously absent from his (and even more his wife's) comments on Aberystwyth and more especially on the supposed frailties and limitations of the Welsh people. He insists that he and those at Aberystwyth who opposed him were irreconcilably at odds as to the true purpose of a university. It is open to conjecture whether anything more than a very small minority of the Principal's critics would accept this apparently antithetical definition of the affair. What is certain is that, once the articles had appeared in print, a serious challenge to his position would be mounted. In the vivid account he has written of his boyhood in Aberystwyth, Rees described the town (and the College can only be partly divorced from it) as a "theocratic society, ruled by priests and elders", who formed a "sort of unofficial Sanhedrin which exercised an absolute dictatorship over the morals and behaviour of the town." This is perhaps too much a view from the manse to be completely accurate, even for the years he had under consideration. But it has its validity, and even after the lapse of thirty years it was evident that the life-style of the Principal's close friend, Burgess, was utterly unacceptable to many members of the college. Given all the circumstances, it is difficult to see any other outcome to this painful episode, which occasioned so much distress in so many quarters . . .'

Fortunately, Rees could still count on the support of a few friends. In *The People* of Wales, the poet Keidrich Rhys came out fighting for him, under the headline: 'This Secret Trial Was A Disgrace'. He wrote: 'It is with the deepest regret that I learned that the University of Wales in Aberystwyth had accepted the resignation of their Principal, Goronwy Rees. I think they should be thoroughly ashamed of themselves. They have lost a man of great academic distinction. They have hounded from office a scholar who has already as a Welshman contributed much to our international reputation. The tragedy is that he had a great deal more to contribute. And now we have lost him . . .' The resignation was brought about, he said, by the Willink Report, but Mr Rhys had other ideas: 'I know he has been the subject of attack from certain people ever since he took over the job of Principal four years ago . . . I know the reasons for those attacks – the real reasons. They were not his articles in *The People*. They were his somewhat unorthodox views on Welsh life. He resented the narrowness of Aberystwyth. And I agree with him. That town has always given me the willies! Soon, no doubt, the post will be advertised. I suggest that it should be phrased in these words: "*Aber wants new Prinny, Knowledge of Welsh necessary – and regular attendance at Methodist Chapel compulsory.*" One thing is certain. This stealth behind closed doors makes Wales and her college look supremely foolish.'

I do not know how my parents left Aberystwyth, with Thomas, Daniel and Matthew in tow, for Lucy and I were away at school and were hardly aware of the pressures my father and mother had endured. In *A Chapter of Accidents*, Rees gave some kind of rationale for what made him destroy his academic career, and, of course, it was all bound up with Guy: '. . . the guilt I felt in regard to Guy and my dealings with him was exacerbated by a more general sense of guilt, which was inspired by the support and approval which, in the 30s and even later, I had given to the Communist Party of the Soviet Union.' Indeed, he said, in his attitude to the Soviet Union he had behaved in much the same way as he had to Guy: even after he had sufficient evidence to recognize it for what it was, he had continued to make every kind of allowance for its conduct, however evil the consequences. 'It would perhaps have been easy to forgive oneself on the grounds that one had been under the spell of an illusion to which thousands of others had also fallen a victim,' he wrote. 'One always finds it easy to forgive oneself.' What he had wanted to do, he said, was in some way to try and limit the amount of harm he had done, even if, in relation to the 'monstrous evils' for which the Communist Party had been responsible, his own contribution had been so minute as to mean little except to himself: 'I felt something of that wholly irrational sense which involuntarily recurred to Rubashov in Arthur Koestler's *Darkness at Noon* and which he expressed in the almost meaningless words: *I must pay*.'

As he stood on the platform at Aberystwyth's 'grim' little railway station, ready to board the train for London, on the morning after the college council meeting at which he had resigned, he observed: 'The future seemed bleak in the extreme. At the age of forty-five, with a wife and five children to support, I found myself homeless, without visible means of subsistence, unemployed and, in any academic capacity, henceforth virtually unemployable ... Even so ... I could not repress a sense of happiness and liberation at this second escape from my birthplace.'

It was a miserable time for my parents. Mr Nobody, for whatever reason, had made an unwise decision and everything had fallen to pieces in his hands. Later my mother and father were to tell friends that Rees *had* written the articles for the money: they wanted to get away from Aberystwyth and in those days £2000 was enough to buy a house. However, John Morgan, the Welsh journalist who was to make a television documentary about Rees two years before he died, said that my father had told him that the root of the quarrel between himself and the college authorities was a land deal. John was not sure just how mischievous Rees was being when he had maintained that the trouble had arisen when he had decided to sell some college land and had brought in an English agent to handle the business. 'Being a Cardiganshire man himself,' said John, 'and generally familiar with the ways of Welsh politics ... he thought that, to put it delicately, the arrangements might be better carried through with a "neutral" in command. If in his youth he was to learn a lot about the wrath of women scorned, it was nothing to that of men who saw their commission melt away, and, more, into the pockets of the English.'

There are those who knew Rees later in his life who believed that he was motivated to write *The People* articles because he was sincerely concerned about the damage Guy might have done from Moscow. Diana Trilling, the American writer and critic, who, with her husband, Lionel, had been one of a group of New York intellectuals that became 'fellow-travellers' in the thirties and later turned against communism, knew my father and mother well in the sixties. She told me: 'Rees's anti-communism was serious and I believe what he said. The overall picture of his life may not be serious, but each moment was of the utmost seriousness to him.'

It will now be impossible to establish definitely why my father did what he did. But, having gone so thoroughly through Rees's account of his friendship with Guy, I cannot stop thinking of his reference to Guy's habit of keeping letters. Did Guy have a letter that could have incriminated Rees in some way?


When I next came home for the holidays from Huyton, I found my parents in very reduced circumstances in a furnished ground-floor flat in Westcliff-on-Sea, Essex. We had absolutely no connections with the place but my father, in partnership with an unreliable character called Derek Verschoyle, a publisher with whom he had worked at *The Spectator*, had invested what little money he and my mother had in a local company that sold prefabricated doors. It very soon turned out to be a failure. If Westcliff-on-Sea was a disaster, what followed was a catastrophe.

In May, returning to Essex from my aunt Mary's house near Reading, with the twins, my father was knocked over by a Volkswagen minibus when my mother stopped at a garage for some petrol. Rees suffered a serious head injury and his left leg was shattered.

On the day of the accident my aunt and her husband, Jack Hardy, a doctor, were holding a large party for the christening of their first child, Jane. My mother had spent the day at the house helping her sister to prepare the food for the reception. It was early evening when she, my father and the twins, Thomas and Daniel, who were then nine, left the big blue Chevrolet. They not been gone long when the telephone rang at the Hardys' house and my aunt Mary answered it. She recalled: 'There was a strange, flat voice that said, "May I speak to Dr Hardy?" and I said, "Is that you, Margie?" She did not seem to recognize me at all, she just went on asking for Dr Hardy.' My mother managed to explain that something dreadful had happened at a place called Littlewick Green, on the road between Reading and Maidenhead, and Mary and her husband went to the rescue immediately. It had not been Rees's fault, Mary told me. My mother, who had been standing all day, had taken her shoes off and could not put them back on again. There was petrol rationing, and she asked Rees to go round to the back of the car to check that the right amount of fuel was put in. Just then Rees was hit by the minibus and his body dragged up the road. When he did not get back into the car, my mother, unaware of what had happened, started wondering where he was. 'Margie told me,' said Mary, 'that one of the twins pointed out to her that there was something lying in the middle of the road that looked like an old coat. It was Rees. Margie was marvellously composed. She scooped up the boys and rushed, with them, into the hotel that was there. They had a television there and she stuck them in front of it, where they just sat.' Rees disapproved of television and would not have one in the house, so the twins were still happily sitting there an hour and a half later.

Rees was taken to a hospital in Ascot, and my mother went with him. 'His face was a terrible mess,' Mary told me, 'and he kept saying that he did not want anyone to see him like that, with his teeth knocked out . . .' My mother and the boys were reunited later at the Hardys' house, where, quite unexpectedly, she found Bingo, her mother and Susie, who had forgotten their petrol coupons and had not been able to drive back to Devon where they lived. 'I remember Margie saying to them, "Look, I know that none of you ever thought anything of him, but he is the most wonderful man and I love him and I could not bear anything to happen to him . . . If he is dead, then I am going to die, too."'

Rees spent about six months in Heatherwood Hospital, Ascot, and was very happy there. In *A Bundle of Sensations*, he called it 'The Great Good Place' after a story by Henry James; he was very interested in his fellow patients and the nurses spoiled him and said they thought he looked like James Dean. When he improved, they used to let him sit in the sun on the balcony; he got browner and browner over that summer and, when he finally came home, he looked as if he had just returned from a cruise in the Caribbean. His face was relatively unmarked by the accident although there were little pit holes left by the gravel off the road; his leg never regained its proper shape, however, and he limped ever after. For months my mother went backwards and forwards between Westcliff and Ascot and my grandfather, Bingo, generously provided the funds to keep us all going, somehow. At the end of that summer term I was taken away from Huyton College and the following September joined the Sixth Form at Westcliff High School. By then, with her usual ingenuity, my mother had found a house for us all at Marine Parade, Leigh-on-Sea, which looked over the Thames estuary and from where, in the mornings, a small army of commuters, with briefcases and umbrellas, set off for their offices in the City, to return *en masse*, with another day under their belt, to their neat semis in the evenings. Everywhere there was a faint aroma of mud.

By the time my father came out of hospital, my mother had painted the whole of the inside of the house white and had sat for hours at her sewing machine making curtains for the windows. I had developed a passion for mice, and, as their numbers expanded, at night one could hear them exercising on their wheels in their cages. I was allowed to keep them in the dining-room, for my parents' once so busy social life had, for the time being, been brought to halt. Only the most loyal and faithful of their friends visited us in our new surroundings. It was wonderful to have my father home again, but he was very fragile and changed by the accident. It was difficult for him to walk the long distances that he had enjoyed in the past and, instead of being able to take a large amount of alcohol, he found that he was 'drunk' after one or two small glasses. I remember that he frequently suffered from headaches and my mother often used to say, 'He's had all the stuffing knocked out of him, poor Rees.' Looking back now, I am struck by how much my father had to carry at that time. He and my mother naturally spent much time behind closed doors, having those long, long discussions that formed such an important part of their alliance. They were broke, he had no employment. Somehow he had to get back on his feet again and find some work and earn some money. Now and then he would take the train to London from the little station at the bottom of the steep bank of gardens that lay between our house and the railway line, to see who was speaking to him and who was definitely not.

One evening, I remember, he returned from London with a young BBC television producer called Catherine Dove, who was temporarily standing in for the producer of weekly *The Brains Trust*: as its name implies, this was a gathering of heavyweight 'talking heads' sitting on some rather uncomfortable-looking chairs and sofas in a studio and, if the programme went well, having an argument about ideas. Among those who appeared on it were members of the intellectual Establishment such as John Betjeman, Noël Annan, Freddie Ayer, Rebecca West, Dr Jacob Bronowski, Alan Bullock, Marghanita Laski, Harold Nicolson, Lord David Cecil and Pamela Hansford Johnson, many of whom strongly disapproved of my father. Catherine Dove, who later became a family friend, was a very welcome visitor to Marine Parade. As we did not have a television, we did not know very much about the programme, but Rees was delighted to be invited to appear on it. His appearances, however, did not last long.

Catherine told me that she had met Rees through Louis MacNeice, who had been sent to 'do a little stint' at Lime Grove, where she was working at the time. Of Louis, she said: 'I thought he was wonderful; for my generation, he and Auden and Day-Lewis were the poets we cut our teeth on at school. So, when he turned up at Lime Grove, I was delighted and I immediately began to leave the straight and narrow and spend far more time in the pub than I should have done.' Inviting Rees to appear on *The Brains Trust* was entirely Louis' idea, she recalled: 'Louis, not missing a trick for his friend, said, "I tell you somebody you ought to have and that's Goronwy Rees. He is an absolutely wonderful talker, you won't regret it. He's down on his luck, he's had a rotten time, he's got a large family to support and you will be doing him the most enormous favour, but it will be good for the programme.'' Louis had told her about the car accident and made it quite plain that he was asking her to help rehabilitate Rees; she thought Rees had invited her home so that she could see for herself how many people were dependent on him, but I think it was because he was grateful and knew how much it would please my mother.

Catherine had heard a great deal more about Rees from another mutual friend, Freddie Ayer: 'Freddie told me how much he loved Goronwy, what an incredible charmer he'd been at Oxford, how nobody in the world had been as charming or beautiful, but that he had been unlucky and foolish, though he thought he was still a wonderful chap.' It was through Freddie that Catherine heard about the repercussions from the articles, about the people who had turned their backs on Rees, though he and Louis had not. Catherine said she had found Rees 'engaging, charming and intelligent' and so she was very surprised when her boss at the BBC, Leonard Miall, who was head of Talks, sent for her and gave her what she described as 'the worst ticking off of my career' because she had put Rees on the programme. She remembered: 'Leonard Miall was liberal, intelligent, very sophisticated and cool. He had been a foreign correspondent, so was very worldly, and he had been at Cambridge. What he said was, "Catherine, I am surprised that you should have such ill-judgment as to to put this man on *The Brains Trust*", and I said, "Oh, why?" He said that Goronwy was a man that nobody should have anything to do with — I'm trying to recall the tone — that he was a traitor to his friends and no decent person would want any dealings with him.' Catherine told Miall that she was very sorry but she thought Rees's situation was a bit more complicated than that; he had been very harshly treated, he had no money and he had a large family to support. 'I told him that I had been assured by people who knew Goronwy that he was absolutely okay,' she said, 'and that I knew people who thought very highly of him and that I considered him to be a good talker. The line, however, was that no decent person would put on this man who had betrayed his friends — nothing to do with spies or being a communist, which is really interesting if you think of the implications.' She could not remember how many more times Rees appeared on the programme or whether he was dropped 'like a hot cake'. It was, she said, as if the 'tiny world that ran things, the Establishment, just did not want any more of Goronwy'.

After speaking to Catherine I wrote to Leonard Miall, who had worked at the BBC with Guy during the war, and asked him if he could give me an explanation. I received the following reply:

Dear Miss Rees,

Thank you for your letter of the 17th August. I am sorry that I am not in a position to help you with your biography of your father. I did not know Goronwy Rees personally and I now have only the vaguest memory of my conversation with Catherine Dove some thirty-five years ago. So I have nothing useful to contribute. I regret having to write in such negative terms.

With best wishes,
Yours sincerely,
Leonard Miall

In the late spring of 1958, leaving me to stay with neighbours while I finished my school year and sat for some more O-levels, my mother put the contents of the house on Marine Parade into packing cases and, with my father, moved to a Victorian house she had found in Highgate, North London, which was to be our new home. For some months beforehand, my father had taken an evening walk through the public gardens in front of the house, where he had befriended a small and bedraggled stray cat that lived under some bushes. He called her Suky Tawdry and often fed her with scraps of chicken or other titbits, but he had never brought her home. Coming back from his walks, he always had a tale to tell about her. Leaving her behind proved impossible for him and, as the removal van was about to leave for London, she was caught and put into a box and left Leigh-on-Sea for a new and far more comfortable life.

In Highgate, my mother planted her garden and put up the bookshelves and, I feel sure, trusted that the worst was over and that, with care, caution and a great deal of good luck, Rees would be able to make a fresh start, writing. Stephen Spender, who was then with the American writer, Irving Kristol, a co-editor of *Encounter*, had helped Rees by publishing some pieces of his in the magazine, largely as a result of which, in November of that year, my father signed a contract with Chatto & Windus for an 'autobiographical work'. *Encounter* was published by the Congress for Cultural Freedom, an anti-communist organization funded by various American trusts and charitable foundations. The magazine had made a name for itself in 1955 by publishing an article by Nancy Mitford entitled 'The English Aristocracy', in which she gave a handy guide to U and non-U usage of the language, but its serious business was fighting the Cold War, which it did with great effect until the Berlin Wall came down and there was no longer an enemy left to fight.

In 1958 Kristol left *Encounter* and his place was taken by Melvin Lasky, a New Yorker who, after serving as a combat historian in France and Germany during the war, had been the founding editor of the intellectual journal, *Der Monat*, which was sponsored by the US High Commission in Germany. Mel was to edit *Encounter* for more than thirty years and he became a close friend of Rees. He told me about how they had met: 'Stephen brought Goronwy around to the office in 1958, when the entire Oxford Establishment were against him. I admired him and I liked him; he was enormously talented and he represented the spirit of the magazine. I think I knew that Rees was a man with a burden to bear, he had a price to pay for all the intimate details he gave about Guy Burgess and I recognized him as a classic case of someone who had once sympathized with the communist cause and had changed his mind and turned, without there being any stages on the way. But it was not something that he talked about, he was secretive.'

Stephen Spender explained to me that he had brought Rees to *Encounter* because he thought he would be good for the magazine. They had never been very close friends, but he liked Rees. 'I felt sorry for him,' he said, 'and did not hold it against him that he had been sacked from Aberystwyth. I remember getting a letter from him saying that I had saved him and he would never forget what I had done for him and he would be grateful to me for ever and ever.'

My own age of awareness, I suppose, coincided with this stage of my father's life, for the Rees that I knew in my adolescent years was ferociously pro-American and anti-communist. I remember a fierce argument raging about the Aldermaston marches, which I passionately wanted to go on; not because I had any deep political belief at that time, but because lots of people I knew were going and it all sounded very exciting. But my father would not allow it; absolutely not. I tried, as usual, to stand my ground, but he would not budge and I could not understand his state of high agitation. His objection was that if I went on the march, I would meet communists and all communists are proselytizers.

No such dangers were to be found at the secretarial college in Hampstead where I was sent at the insistence of my practical mother who said I would always be employable if I knew how to type. I was then sent off to learn French in Paris, where I stayed with some friends of Rees's Aberystwyth ally, Richard Cobb. I could not have been more fortunate; Jean Meuvret was a professor at the Ecole Normale and his wife was a librarian at the Ecole des Langues Orientales and they lived at the top of a tall, narrow house on the Quai de l'Horloge, which runs off the Pont Neuf. Cobb had a little bolt-hole in the Rue de Tournon and when he was in Paris I saw a great deal of him. As is his way, he talked incessantly about France and the French and I could not have had a more learned, or amusing tutor. I had momentarily escaped from the troubles of home, but not for long.

I was summoned back to England in the early summer of 1960, when my father's 'autobiographical work', *A Bundle of Sensations*, was published. He had dedicated it to my grandmother, Peggy Morris, who had died of cancer at the early age of sixty while we were living at Leigh-on-Sea and whose death had come at a particularly distressing time in my mother's life. In his acknowledgments at the beginning of the book, my father said how grateful he was to the editors of *Encounter* for permission to reprint two of his sketches which first appeared in the magazine; he wrote: 'I owe them more than a formal acknowledgment for their generous help and encouragement at a time when these were not easy to find.'

The book was well received, which was very pleasing to my parents. The *Times Literary Supplement*'s reviewer had already read my father's second novel, *A Bridge to Divide Them*; he found Rees's description of his visit to Germany on the eve of Hitler's assumption of power 'quite the most successful thing in the book' and perhaps even better than Christopher Isherwood. Mr Nobody did not go unmentioned: 'Mr Rees has found it easy to pass from himself to objects surrounding himself. He claims to have found no trace within himself of "that *something* simple and continued which most autobiographies take for granted"; and he concludes a provocative foreword with the challenge – not quite fair, though not unanswerable – that his reader find a *something* if he may. He quotes Hume in his support; he might also have quoted Keats on the "poetical Character": "It has no character – it enjoys light and shade; it lives in gusto, be it foul or fair, high or low, rich or poor, mean or elevated." Here is a writer – intelligent, witty, humane – who can peck with Keats's sparrow. Have we not found a chameleon autobiographer?'

The *Sunday Times* gave *A Bundle of Sensations* to Cyril Connolly to review; he felt that 'so cool, so collected, so analytical an arrangement of consciousness as Mr Rees's will certainly, after this autobiography, tempt the Establishment to woo him again ...' Mr Connolly was not taken in by Mr Nobody assuming the colour of his circumstances: 'If one accepts this view of the mind as a theatre of illusory perceptions, it must lead to a becoming humility, but one of the Mr Reeses whom I used to know was not without a capacity for intellectual arrogance and moral indignation quite inappropriate to the ephemeral floating bird's-nest which he purports to be his true self.' But he found the book to be 'delightfully refreshing and intelligent' and offered his own interpretation of Rees's autobiographical sketches. *A Bundle of Sensations* was, he said, a book about a man's relation to authority, in which Rees finds a series of fathers, such as the reactionary Baron von Reichendorf, the 'father of all fathers' Field Marshal Montgomery, and Sir William Strang. Montgomery was the most successful: 'It speaks well for the vein of nonconformism and for the psychological insight of the Field Marshal, that he knew how to appreciate the first-rate mind and qualities of Mr Rees and so win his undivided allegiance, where his other father-figures had to be content with a qualified submission.'

But Connolly wanted to know about areas of Rees's life which were not covered in the book. He wrote: 'I am so drawn to Mr Rees and his predicament. He seems to gravitate to all the sources of power – All Souls, *The Times*, the advisership to the Political Adviser, Big Business (after the war) and finally the direction of a new university – only to end in conflict with them.' He suggested that Rees resembled Dylan Thomas as a private in the army, slovenly and anarchic, but was nothing like him when he joined the Territorials in 1939 or rising to be some 'hush-hush colonel'. Connolly went on: 'There were two types of Englishman who were right about Hitler; the Left who opposed him – and Mussolini and Franco – throughout the thirties, and the men of the Right (Duff Cooper, Hailsham, etc.), who, after Munich, started learning how to fight. Mr Rees was one of the very few left-wing intellectuals to join the Territorials and so find themselves in the army when war was declared. He writes best (and that is saying much) about his idyllic visit to Germany before the war, and about the extraordinary fellowship among the military untouchables of his Territorial years . . .'

The reviewer for *The Times* described *A Bundle of Sensations* as a 'chronicle of one to whom things happen, rather than of one who chooses to do things': 'It is no use . . . expecting Mr Rees to reveal many central facts about a personality of whose very existence he is so uncertain. His book . . . disowns the impedimenta of personal feeling, whether romantic, domestic or merely ideological, that are the main weight of most men's lives . . .' The critic appeared flustered by Mr Nobody and did not like the fact that several of the sketches had appeared elsewhere: 'The fact that they have done so emphasizes the episodic nature of Mr Rees's book. This is, in fact, one's main disappointment; for while each episode is written with the utmost distinction, as well as charm, so that the mind and eye are constantly pleased, the absence of a humanly recognizable narrator means that the *rapport* with the author is constantly being interrupted. The blanks between the episodes, about which we get few clues, begin to concern us; what is happening is certainly very interesting, but to *whom* it is happening?' He spotted something else. Describing Rees's visit to Silesia to tutor the son of the baron, the critic noted: 'Nevertheless, the experience . . . seems to have been the beginning of an increasingly familiar pattern, one which, depositing him in "the wrong set", both in and out of the army, has raised him and dumped him down, with equal force and fickleness throughout his life.' The final sketch, 'The Great Good Place', about the hospital that put my father together again after his road accident, went down particularly well as 'an example of what Mr Rees can achieve when he extends himself'. There was a glowing final sentence: '*A Bundle of Sensations* may have been felt by anyone; in fact these particular ones were felt by Mr Goronwy Rees, and it is our great good fortune.' The headlines of two of these reviews were most perceptive: 'Fragments of the Self' (*TLS*), and 'A Man of Feeling Caught in the Current of Experience' (*The Times*). It was Rees's first book for ten years and it looked as if a fair wind was with him as he began his new life as a professional writer.

# 11

Things said or done long years ago,
Or things I did not do or say
But thought that I might say or do,
Weigh me down, and not a day
But something is recalled,
My conscience or my vanity appalled.

*Vacillation*, W.B. Yeats.

However, that was not to be. Some time very shortly after I came back from Paris my father broke down. Whether it was the first indication that he was not well or there had been others, I do not know, but one morning, sitting at the breakfast table, he put his head in his hands and wept. My mother was clattering about with dishes in the kitchen and the younger children had left for school. I was sitting at the table with him, in the dining-room, but I did not know what to do. I was very frightened and when I remember the sound of him sobbing the fear returns. I cannot recall exactly what happened next, but my mother came, as always, to his side, and, with her arms around his shoulders, walked with him out of the room. Many telephone calls followed and, later that morning, he was admitted to a psychiatric hospital. I used to go and see him with my mother, for whom this was a very grim period.

Much later, I asked Rees how he had felt during his breakdown and he told me it was as if he had lost his soul. Very soon, however, he had become most interested in his fellow patients and I recall that there was one who particularly fascinated him. He was a man who found it difficult to make any decisions. By his bedside he had a small locker in which he kept an orange. Rees told me how he would spend the morning opening and closing the locker door to look at the orange while trying to decide whether he should eat it. If he ate it, it would no longer be there; if he left it there, he could not enjoy eating it. The man could often be seen standing by the swing doors, trying to decide whether he should walk through them. This small psychiatric hospital, called Halliwick, was a new but self-contained part of Colney Hatch, a vast Victorian institution in Southgate, north London, which has now closed. My father felt a special sympathy for the many middle-aged women who were being treated for depression. I remember him saying that, once they had been 'patched up', they would simply be returned to the lives that had depressed them so much that they had become ill and nothing would change.

I am grateful to Michael Wharton, for many years 'Peter Simple' of the *Daily Telegraph*, for reminding me of the curious character of Halliwick in his second volume of autobiography, *A Dubious Codicil*. It was no ordinary mental hospital, he said. Although it operated under the National Health Service, it had a high proportion of middle-class patients, including writers, musicians and people from the BBC and so could have been described as the 'sick bay of Hampstead'. There was a wing for 'serious cases' but the part that my father was assigned to was for cases of 'mild clinical depression'. Wharton suggested having a Halliwick tie designed, but nothing came of it. In the afternoons he used to sit in the large patients' lounge, where my father sat, too, and talk to a 'sad woman of my own age from Hampstead' who lived alone and had fallen into a mild depression after the death of her dog, whom she had loved in a way I could not understand until, late in life, I kept dogs myself . . .' Michael Wharton was, he recalled, at Halliwick for about ten days. I think my father was there for longer and he was to revisit Halliwick later in the sixties when his depression returned, as it did with varying degrees of intensity.

It was on one of his visits to Halliwick that Rees met a young poet called Nick Willey. A thoughtful intermediary had felt they might like to talk about writing. My father, however, did not much like 'talking about writing', though he loved talking – or arguing – about books and their authors. Over the years that I spent at home I remember answering the door to earnest American Ph.D. students who had come all the way from Columbia or Berkeley to consult Rees about writing, only to find that by the time I had made tea the interview was already breaking up and I was showing the visitor out. I asked Rees, once, why he could not spend more time with them, as they were young and inexperienced, wanted advice and had come such a long way to see him. He said that all he had to tell them was that 'talking about writing' does not help anyone to write; he believed that you only learn about writing by doing it, by sitting down with a blank piece of paper and writing on it, and by reading. The Halliwick meetings between Rees and Nick did, however, lead to some of Nick's poems being published in *Encounter*. Some years later, my father

pinned the final verse of one of Nick's poems, which I think he found
comforting, on the wall beside his desk:

> Cherish yourself. Sometimes quite late at night
> Pretend that you could take off your own head
> And hold it, weatherbeaten, in your arms.

In May of 1993 I drove down to Wiltshire, where Nick, his wife,
Sarah, and their two children live in a little square stone cottage, and
found him digging in his garden surrounded by fields full of cow
parsley. I wanted to find out what Nick could remember about my
father at the time of his breakdown. He decided that they must have
been in Halliwick together twice and told me: 'I remember going up
to him in the canteen and introducing myself to him. I went up to
him and said: "You are that chap with the funny name, aren't you?"
He was very nice and we got on very well together. I always called
him Gunners.' While in Halliwick, Nick went to the public library
across the road for a copy of *A Bundle of Sensations*, which he found
'enchanting' because it was so vivid. Something odd had happened
recently, he said, when he lent the book to an 'extremely intelligent
and delightful colleague' at work. She read a great deal and her father
was a vicar and Nick thought she would enjoy Rees's book because
of the essay on his childhood in the chapel. But when his colleague
returned the book to him, she had not shared his enthusiasm. 'She
told me she found Rees's presence in it very disconcerting,' Nick
said. 'She found it almost chilling because it was so detached, there
was a coldness in the way he described things that had happened in
the war. I was very taken aback to hear her say that because it never
occurred to me to think of him in that way. In my memory of him in
hospital, the nicest side of him, is, I think, the depth and genuineness
of interest in everybody around him.' He and Rees went on meeting
in pubs around Broadcasting House, where Nick later worked, and
my mother often invited him home for supper. 'I don't think we ever
talked about anything of any significance,' he recalled, 'but I was very
fond of him and I certainly think of him as somebody important in
my life. My great memory is of being made to feel valuable and
worthwhile by him. After coming back from an evening with him, I
would think, oh, well, I had better do some writing...'
    In the context of my search for enlightenment about my father's
life, it was tempting for me, at first, to think that his breakdown was

a particularly dramatic breaking-out of The Secret. Naturally, it was not a subject that was ever discussed with me in any depth. I just knew my father was unwell. Even without The Secret, my mother had a very highly developed sense of what should, or should not, be discussed in front of us. She was what is often described as a 'private' person. At that stage, both she and my father were very conscious that there were five of us to be prepared for life in the outside world, where, somehow, we had to be able to hold our own and survive. For many reasons, the diving-board from which we were going to have to launch ourselves into the big pool was pretty rickety and my father's idiosyncratic *Weltanschauung* meant that the messages that I subliminally picked up were not always very helpful. It was due to my mother's careful protectiveness that I did not think of him, at that time, as a rebel or a misfit. Now I understand that if we had, indeed, known of his past it would have been impossible for him to have even tried to play the part of a father. That role was hard enough for him as it was. I think I had a very muddled set of values as a result, for, in a way, reality was more or less closed off to me. My mother, like a hen gathering her chicks under her wing, quite clearly felt that if she was not very careful the sins of the father might, by others, be visited upon the children, which was why we were to know as little as possible about his 'other' life.

Thus I was never able to learn about the relationship between actions and consequences until I made my own mistakes. With my father, nothing was ever very clear. At a time when I badly needed some direction, it was difficult to make any sense of the messages that came through from him. For example, I did not quite know what to make of his advice that one should be wary of the Establishment, or another of his favourite sayings, that just because someone is intelligent does not mean that he is nice, although the basis of these opinions is clear to me now. In fact I realize that there in Highgate we had a walking, talking Cautionary Tale; but, because of the undercurrents of fear, it was a tale we were never to be told.

My father's heavy drinking was another thing that was never discussed, though I had been carefully trained by my mother to prevent him from becoming drunk in company too early in the evening. The operation began in the kitchen, where I would watch my father pour out a large glass of neat whisky for himself, as he prepared the drinks for his guests. My mother also drank whisky, but she added quite a lot of water to hers. Usually, just before dinner, while I was helping my mother put the finishing touches to the meal or to the table, she would instruct me to go into the sitting-room and, while Rees was not looking, exchange her glass for his, so that he would find himself with considerably watered-down whisky. I was always surprised by how smoothly the operation worked and I became quite an expert at this sleight of hand. My father was usually so excited and pleased at having friends around him and so busy talking and smoking that he really did not notice me lurking about at his side, furtively swapping the glasses. I might have to do this two or three times during the evening, on my mother's instructions. But such was her love for him and her loyalty to him that she would never, ever admit to me that he could be very upsetting when he was drunk. I never heard her utter a word of criticism about him, nor, as things went from bad to worse in the years to come, did I ever see either of them show any signs of self-pity. They battled bravely on, and though my father's drinking and his not very subtle romantic adventures deeply distressed my mother, she would not hear a word against him.

Unable to extract any sensible explanation from my mother, for years, I imagined that the reason why my father had broken down that morning at the breakfast table was something to do with guilt. However, as there seemed to be so many aspects of his life that he could have felt guilty about, I found it impossible to narrow down the options. In my quest to find out more about him, I am most indebted to the psychiatrist at Halliwick who treated my father and in whom both my parents confided and who, after all these years, felt able to tell me what he knew. In the framework of my father's immensely complicated life, the clinical explanation seemed relatively simple: at just turned fifty, he was troubled by what he considered the repressive condition of his childhood and how, having escaped it once he had equated his return to Aberystwyth, felt he had gone back to his family and the same restrictions. Dr X described it as the 'naughty boy syndrome': as a young man Rees had deliberately rejected the values of his family and set out to shock them and he had done it again when he went back to Aberystwyth. As a patient, Rees was 'very secretive and very compartmentalized' and revealed little about himself, so much so that sometimes Dr X did not know which Rees he was talking to. 'He was very guilty about what he had done to his family,' he said. 'He was a rebel without a backbone, a weak person. He needed something to believe in, he went from one cause to another . . .' His feelings of guilt were the cause of his depression.

These deep, dark depressions were to continue to dog him. The death of his father in 1963, at the age of ninety-five, was another difficult moment for him. Nick Willey told me that Rees had talked to him about being at his father's deathbed, when his father had been telling him about how glad he was to be leaving 'this vale of tears' because he was going to be reunited with his wife, Apphia. As he was lying there talking about how much he was looking forward to what lay ahead, he really seemed to have died already. 'But then, Rees said, he came back again, like someone who had left a room and thought, well, this is rather insensitive, and so put his head, as sit were, around the door and said, "But, of course, I shall miss you . . .", so that Rees should not feel he had been forgotten.' It is a strange little story, and one I had not heard myself; in it, Rees appears to have been forgiven by his father.

The ten years that lay ahead of my parents at that time were hard and painful for both of them. They were plagued with financial problems – with the Inland Revenue hard on my father's heels – and although Rees wrote four books in that decade – *The Multi-Million-aires*, *The Rhine*, *St Michael: a History of Marks and Spencer*, and *The Great Slump* – his intellectual commitment was to *Encounter* magazine. There is an irony in the fact that while Rees was writing about the rich and about money, which he did very well, his own financial affairs could not have been worse. He was always behind with his income tax and hopeless at paying bills. The brown envelopes would arrive and he would first stuff them in the pocket of his dressing-gown and then put them somewhere else where they would inevitably be lost. My mother attempted to bring some order into this particular area of chaos in his life and there was a long-suffering accountant who would regularly come to see my parents and go through all the drawers in the house himself, gathering up anything with the words Inland Revenue stamped on it. But, even if the paperwork had been done, the bottom line always, was that there was not enough money to meet all the demands. My mother's house-buying activities, of course, helped to generate capital; they moved three times during the sixties, always in great haste.

From Highgate we all moved to a tall house in South Terrace, just off Thurloe Square in South Kensington, where the rates finally became too expensive and then, as we children moved out in stages, my parents were able to buy a lease on a top-floor flat near Kensington High Street. By then I was married and, while expecting my first child, trying to establish a slightly more settled and less fraught house-hold than the one in which I had been brought up. It was something of a struggle, for the news from my parents was, at that stage, par-ticularly dire. I remember my mother telephoning me one morning – she always rang very early and usually in a state of some agitation – to tell me that her car had vanished from its parking place outside the flat and she thought it had been repossessed by the hire purchase company. It had. The flat had to be sold next, but my mother remained remarkably cheerful throughout all this and kept telling me never to worry about bailiffs because the ones she had met were always very pleasant.

For a while they had no home at all but lived on a rented houseboat on the Thames, by Battersea Bridge, with their two black cats, until they were able to buy the flat next to ours in Holland Park. My mother had turned herself into a very proficient medical secretary and valiantly gone out to work, for the first time in her life, to help them through the hard times, but I think what really saved them from penury was the kindness and generosity of their many friends.

One of the regular features, I recall, of my parents' wandering existence were the evening sessions of bridge that they played with Freddie Ayer and his second wife, Dee, who became a very close friend of my mother's. First there would be supper, then they would clear the table and get out the cards and play for hours on end. I would often call in and find them in a fug of cigarette smoke working out their bets. I wondered how much my mother told Dee of their trials and tribulations, but I learned that she was discreet and gave little away. Of the time they spent together, Dee told me: 'The playing of bridge was an indication that things were nice and tranquil because it was a sort of normal, family activity.' They played bridge together for many years. At first it was whenever they could and then the New Year's Eve session became the special evening. Nobody, said Dee, ever got any better. Freddie was the best player, but he could not always be counted on. If he did not pay attention he was, she said, 'as bad as the rest of us. On these evenings, Freddie and Goronwy would discuss the current Oxford gossip, which did not affect either of them very much. They would talk about the good old days, their peak moment in the thirties. They did not talk about philosophy.' It never crossed her mind to wonder why they liked each other so much; they had known one another for so long that their friendship just seemed perfectly natural. Since those happy days of the bridge parties Dee had often thought how cut off both of them were from any world apart from the one they both knew, Freddie perhaps more than Goronwy, who had greater elasticity. Freddie, she said, was 'terribly fond' of Goronwy: 'You could not not be, really. He was so charming, intelligent and such fun.' Dee used to enjoy arguing with Rees; she liked making him 'rise to the bait'. But Freddie did not like her doing it; he disliked anything confrontational. Dee remembered: 'Goronwy would, in that stubborn Welsh kind of way, take an absolutely unsupportable stand and then stick to it and I would be pushing and pushing to see if I could move him. Sometimes, Margie would join in, too, but most times she was too kind and well-mannered to do so . . .'

Dee knew my mother exceptionally well, and I had always assumed that she had told Dee about their trials and tribulations. But I was mistaken. 'With Margie, the only way that you knew there was something wrong,' she said, 'was by seeing that she was a little more worried than usual. After a while, she would suddenly blurt something out. But it was never along the lines of let me tell you about our latest misfortune or anything like that that you get from your other friends. She was very brave and very gallant. She loved him and she was the most patient, good person I have ever known . . .' My mother, she said, had her own way of making things seem happy even if there were terrible underlying strains and tensions 'that would leave the rest of us screaming'. Dee remembered the car being repossessed. 'Margie made nothing of it.' she said. 'She was very fastidious about things like that. Goronwy was never to be criticized for having failed as a provider.'

In May 1966, on the day I gave birth to my first child, whom we named Sam, at the old Charing Cross Hospital in the Strand, my mother, who had been diagnosed as suffering from cancer, underwent a mastectomy at the Middlesex Hospital. Nurses at both hospitals considerately exchanged messages for us, so that my mother knew the baby had arrived safely and I knew that her operation had gone satisfactorily. She always maintained that her cancer had developed from a fall she had had in the bath at South Terrace. But many years later, when I was living in France, I read a book called *Mars* by a young Swiss-German writer, Fritz Zorn, who diagnosed the tumour that had developed on his neck as an accumulation of 'swallowed tears'; I wondered if one could have made a similar diagnosis for my mother. She once told me, in an unguarded moment as I was helping her in the garden, that marriage had not quite worked out for her as she had expected; when she was young, she said, she had a picture of herself, as a married woman, sitting on the lawn of a large house wearing a white dress. I could see this picture in my imagination, as she spoke, and accompanying it was a sense of leisured calm; reading between the lines, at which I became quite accomplished, I knew what she was trying to tell me.


Rees's obsession with Anthony Blunt had begun to manifest itself overtly when he was recovering from his breakdown, though I suspect he had been brooding over it for years. This was when, at private gatherings, I started hearing stories from third parties about Rees accusing Blunt of being a spy. Since being ostracized by many of his Oxford and academic friends after the Aberystwyth disaster, he and my mother had found a new circle of friends, who were either not at all interested in spies or whom Rees had got to know through *Encounter*. Several events took place in 1963 which made it a significant year. In March Kim Philby disappeared from Beirut and was named in the House of Commons in July as the Third Man. Some months later Guy Burgess died of a heart attack in Moscow: whatever it was that Rees was frightened of him saying would never, now, be uttered. In fact, Guy never spoke about him.

That summer, their financial situation had permitted my parents to take a small flat in Cap d'Ail, in the south of France, for the second year running. I had spent several holidays there in a student camp on the hillside overlooking the sea, from where a steep flight of hundreds of steps led down to a little beach that was perfect for swimming. Below the camp, on the *cap* itself, where Beaverbrook had a villa and I once saw Greta Garbo walking across the rocks by the sea, there was a hotel which always reminded me of the one described in *Tender is the Night*: 'On the shore of the French Riviera, about half-way between Marseilles and the Italian border, stood a large, proud, rose-coloured hotel. Deferential palms cooled its flushed façade, and before it stretched a short dazzling beach . . .' It is not the same place as Fitzgerald was thinking about but I recommended Cap d'Ail to my parents because I could somehow see them there, rather like the Divers. In 1963 they had invited David Rees, then literary editor of *The Spectator*, to go at the same time. David is not a relative, though of the same tribe, I suppose; he and Rees got on very well together because David was also a Cold Warrior. He was just beginning his research for a book about Harry Dexter White, the Assistant Secretary to the US Treasury and a 'fellow-traveller', who worked for the Russians and died shortly after testifying to the House Un-American Activities Committee.

For many years David was a very close friend of both Rees and my mother, who did confide in him about The Secret. In the summer of 1993, thirty years later, David told me about what had happened when he had met up with Rees and Margie at Cap d'Ail. He said: 'They came to meet me at the airport at Nice and sat me down while Rees said to Margie: "I think we'd better tell him, don't you?" She agreed and then Rees told me that he knew that Anthony Blunt was the Fourth Man, but it was all a terrible secret. He seemed very cross that Blunt was still being protected.' Blunt was obviously in their minds that summer, he said, because of Philby. He remembers that on one of his visits to South Terrace he met a man there who was writing a book about Burgess and Maclean. 'We all went out to the pub to have a drink,' he said, 'and Rees told him all about Blunt. I remember thinking when we went back to the house for supper that Rees wanted to get it out. The name kept coming up over and over again.'

The man in the pub with Rees was the journalist Douglas Sutherland, who was gathering information for the book that he was writing with Anthony Purdy. Published by Secker and Warburg in May, 1963, the book created a sensation because the authors said that a mysterious and unnamed former 'senior' MI5 officer made a telephone call to Burgess to warn him that Donald Maclean was about to be arrested. The man, the authors claimed, was a homosexual who, since leaving MI5, had 'won honours in another field'; there was 'some reason to believe' that Burgess would one day publicly name the man, in a book or when he returned to England. According to Sutherland and Purdy, Guy had already named the man privately. The book said: 'He has told many people that if he ever stands trial in Britain he will subpoena a number of well-known names for his defence, as well as two not so well-known ones – two of the friends who were then officers of MI5. One of these two men is the Third Man.'

The following year there were a number of significant developments, at home and abroad. In the summer of 1963, Michael Straight, who had been recruited by Anthony Blunt at Cambridge, had been selected to take over the chairmanship of the newly-created American Advisory Council on the Arts and was told that he would have to be vetted by the FBI before his candidacy could be put before Congress for approval. Straight subsequently told the FBI all about his Cambridge past, naming Blunt as the Fourth Man, who at the beginning of 1964 was interrogated by MI5. But although Blunt had been implicated, it was considered that there was not enough information to provide the basis of a charge which could be brought against him. However, as we now know, Blunt confessed, and was given formal immunity from prosecution.

According to Peter Wright, writing in *Spycatcher*, he met Blunt 'every month or so' for the next six years at the Courtauld Institute. Wright also reopened the file containing information about Rees's visit to MI5 in 1951, when he had told them about Guy, which, according to Wright's book, had since 'lain uninvestigated'. Wright noted that Dick White, MI5's head of counterespionage, 'disliked Rees intensely and thought he was making malicious accusations in order to court attention, if not publicity.' He went on: 'Dick's view of Rees seemed confirmed when, in 1956, Rees wrote an anonymous series of articles for a popular newspaper . . . the Rees articles, detailing some of the salacious activities of Burgess and those close to him, caused a sensation.' But when Blunt confessed in 1964, Wright said, 'the colour of Rees's 1951 testimony changed'. He thought it prudent to look at Rees's file again, 'if only to satisfy myself that Rees had not been lying when he claimed to have given up all thoughts of the Soviet cause before the war'. According to Peter Wright, Rees was 'reluctant' to talk to him, and my mother, apparently, accused Wright of 'Gestapo-style tactics' in trying to resurrect the past after so many years. He observed: 'They had both suffered grievously for the newspaper articles. Rees's authorship had become known and he was sacked from academic life. Since 1956, they had eked out a miserable existence, shunned by the Establishment. Eventually Rees agreed to see me, and went through his story again.'

Peter Wright also followed up the accusations made by Rees against Stuart Hampshire and Robin Zaehner back in 1951, but found nothing that could be held against them. Stuart had, of course, already let Rees know what a low opinion he had of him when the articles in *The People* were published, but Robin Zaehner, who was very fond of Rees, had spent much time at our house at Highgate. It is painful to imagine how Rees must have felt, knowing that Wright was going to investigate the reliability of the 'Prof', as we knew Zaehner.

In the summer of 1964 Rees went to Prague on behalf of *Encounter* to write about the Kafka exhibition which was taking place there in September, forty years after the writer's death. Kafka was one of those for whom Rees always kept a special place in his heart and his mind, along with Solzhenitsyn, Cardinal Newman and Monty. It was the first trip that my father had made behind the Iron Curtain and this caused my mother a considerable amount of anxiety which a curious incident that occurred at about this time did nothing to diminish. Rees had, for some reason or other, been invited to meet someone at a hotel in Bloomsbury and he set off looking forward to the appointment. I remember him returning home looking very alarmed and I overheard him explaining to my mother that he had left the hotel almost as soon as he arrived: 'It was all wrong, there were Russians everywhere. I got out as quickly as I could.' I never found out precisely what had happened, but it had frightened him very much.

As Rees's trip to Czechoslovakia approached, my mother became more and more apprehensive, as if some dreadful fate awaited him there. She used to talk about how the Russians had all kinds of ingenious ways of 'bumping off' people, and how accidents were often not accidents at all. She would warn Rees to be careful when he crossed the street and to watch out for buses; she warned me, too. My father went off to Prague, as arranged, leaving my mother with the promise that he would telephone as soon as he could and send postcards at regular intervals. One evening I returned home to find my mother talking to someone on the telephone and, by the tone of her voice, I knew something was wrong. I gathered from what she said – she was, as always, being very guarded – that Rees was 'lost', and that was all she would tell me. One of the friends to whom my mother turned in her distress was David Rees, who when I visited him, told me all he knew of what had happened. 'Margie used to talk to me quite a lot because she was worried about Rees and the Blunt thing,' he said. 'I told her that I was a completely different generation to Rees and that people like myself had difficulty understanding why it was necessary to become a communist in the thirties. There were plenty of people who didn't, like Hugh Gaitskell.' He and my mother had the same views and they used to share jokes about liberals: 'We used to laugh at a certain type of high-minded person who regularly made ingenious excuses to justify Soviet expansionism, and that sort of thing.'

My mother told David that Rees was two days overdue at the Kafka exhibition and she thought it possible that 'They' had got him, or even that he had gone. 'She seemed to think that he might have defected,' David told me. 'She made me promise to say nothing. I think there always was this query in her mind about '39 and whether he really worked for the Marxists. She never seemed to be quite sure if he had "broken" as he said he had . . .' I learned from David that my mother had got on to the intelligence services at the time of Rees's 'disappearance' and he understood that the Americans had been informed about it as well.

The storm blew over, however, and Rees returned home, with presents – I still have a crystal necklace as a souvenir of this episode – as if nothing untoward had happened. Many, many weeks later, some postcards arrived from Prague. Talking to David Rees in the kitchen of his cottage in West Wales, I was struck by how many times he spoke about Rees being a man with a 'burden'. Rees, he said, was often 'mysterious'. David did not know whether the fact that he had been a communist or that he knew the truth about Blunt weighed upon him the more heavily.

Rees's article about his visit to Prague appeared in the September issue of *Encounter* and he was as nasty as he always was, then, about communism. The exhibition was a very surprising event, for, as Rees commented, no writer was less suited than Kafka to being tamed and domesticated to Marxist requirements. About the strange phenomenon of the rehabilitation of Kafka, he wrote: 'For who would have thought that the Soviet Union or her satellites would ever have exposed their citizens to the risk of the kind of infection which can be caught from Kafka, of a view of life in which every moment is a source of innumerable and endless ethical and intellectual complexities, in which every event has so many facets that we can never rightly profess to have grasped them all, or perhaps not even one of them, because each is so bewilderingly coloured by the reflection of all the others? In a communist society, where men must, if they are to survive, submit themselves to the most brutal of simplifications, what time or justification can there be for all the doubts, hesitations, perplexities, deceptions offered to anyone who follows one of Kafka's heroes along his tortured path through life or through the dense labyrinth of problems he must penetrate before he can find even the feeblest ray of light to guide him on his way – and then only to mislead? What relation have the stumblings of Joseph K. to the confident onward march of history or to the obstacles which are so easily surmounted by any proletarian hero? . . .'

He quoted from a book called *Conversations with Kafka* – which he was later to translate from the German – by Gustav Janouch, whose father had worked in the same insurance office in Prague as Kafka and who, as a boy, had accompanied Kafka on his walks around the city and left a record of what they discussed. The Russian Revolution and the 1914–18 war, Kafka told Janouch, 'seems to be like a flood of evil. The war has opened the flood-gates of chaos. The buttresses of human existence are collapsing. Historical development is no longer determined by the individual but by the masses. We are shoved, rushed, swept away. We are the victims of history . . .' Such ideas, wrote Rees, are dangerous in a communist world, 'an invisible worm which eats at the heart of the rose'. He was very moved by the exhibition, held in the baroque Strahov Museum, and by the photographs of the Kafka family, many of whom were exterminated in the Nazi concentration camps, but was uncomfortable with the idea of Kafka being welcomed back to Prague.

Rees concluded: 'Kafka's world has indeed been destroyed. If one looks through a list of his friends and acquaintances in Prague one will find few indeed who escaped death, exile, extermination in the concentration camps. The society out of which he came quite truly died like Joseph K., like a dog. So that if he is now offered a "permanent visa to the socialist countries", it will be as an alien that he will return. And if he is to become acclimatized in the new kind of society which has grown up in Czechoslovakia, it will only be after he has been tamed and domesticated to Marxist requirements, for otherwise he might prove a very unwelcome visitor indeed to those who now rule there. Yet no writer was ever less adapted to such treatment than Kafka. Perhaps it is more likely that now, as before, his works will continue to fructify in silence until Central Europe will once again be ready for what he has to say, like one of those stories which the ear takes a very long time to be ready for. Perhaps then at last his spirit may find in Prague a home which he never found there during his lifetime.'

Rees regarded *Encounter* as a kind of lifeline; it provided him with intellectual company and an office in the middle of London and he shared its convictions. It was somewhere where he 'belonged'. He was delighted when he was invited to join the advisory board and, in 1966, wrote the first of his regular columns, signed 'R', which he was to continue to contribute until almost the end of his life.

But, first, there was the unpleasant *Encounter* row about whether the magazine was funded by the CIA, which ended with the resignation of

Stephen Spender, a founder editor. In fact, the row had been rumbling on for years, as *Encounter*'s other founder editor, Irving Kristol, related in his political autobiography, *Reflections of a Neoconservative*. Kristol, who left *Encounter* and returned to America in 1958, said that if he had known *Encounter* and the Congress for Cultural Freedom – which my father described as an 'intellectual Marshall Plan' – were subsidized by the CIA he would never have taken the job. 'Not, I hasten to add, because I disapproved of the CIA or even of secret subsidies (at certain times, in certain places, under certain conditions, for specific and limited purposes). Aside from the fact that the CIA, as a secret agency, seems to be staffed to an extraordinary extent by incorrigible blabbermouths, I have no more reason to despise it than, say, the Post Office. (Both are indispensable, both are exasperatingly inept.)' He was jealous of his reputation as an independent writer and thinker, Kristol said, and also, while in the army during the war, he had sworn to himself that he would never again work as a functionary in a large organization and especially not for the US Government. He had managed to keep his oath inviolate, except for those five years when he was, unwittingly, on the CIA payroll.

There had always been rumours of a CIA association, Kristol recalled, mostly from left-wing, anti-American sources, but he discounted them in advance. The fact was that the magazine's sponsor was the Farfield Foundation, which subsidized *Encounter* through a grant to the Congress for Cultural Freedom. Its president was a millionaire industrialist called Julius Fleischmann, on whose yacht some *Encounter* parties were held. Kristol said that both he and Stephen questioned Mr Fleischmann several times over the rumours and he said that if anybody ever printed 'the barest hint of such a libel' he would sue. In any event, wrote Kristol, the magazine had been promised editorial freedom and the promise was honoured. He and Spender made their editorial decisions in London, where the Congress had no office or representatives and 'there was no one to look over our shoulders while we did so' and, according to Kristol, no trace of anything resembling political censorship of the magazine by its sponsors. When a left-wing American magazine, *Ramparts*, printed allegations of the CIA sponsorship in 1966, plenty of denials were published in response.

In May 1967, however, Mel Lasky admitted in the *New York Times* that he had been 'insufficiently frank' with colleagues and friends about the magazine's funding. Stephen Spender, who felt he had been misled and put in a position of misinforming others, resigned, while my father backed Lasky. The row went on for months, causing many angry words and much bitterness, Stuart Hampshire, a friend of Stephen's, told me that he thought Rees had behaved 'appallingly'. He said: 'Stephen got Goronwy that job at *Encounter* at a time when the chips were down and then Goronwy did not give Stephen any help when he needed it. He joined up with Lasky in the most awful way and caused trouble.'

All this happened a long time ago and Stephen Spender was less harsh when I spoke to him. 'The thing is that Goronwy panicked,' he said. 'I really don't hold it against him so terribly. He was not under any obligation to resign, it would have been honourable on his part if he had, but he didn't.' At the beginning of the affair, Rees did 'make a great fuss about it' and there was a 'lot of yelling' in the office, Stephen recollected. 'What is rather bad is not that Rees did not resign but that he should have turned against me . . .'

Mel, of course, took the opposite view. He told me he was very grateful for Rees's support: 'Goronwy was 100 per cent on the personal loyalty thing; perhaps 99 per cent would have been more human, but that Calvinist absolute rectitude came out in him and he stood by me.' When, in 1978, *Encounter* celebrated its 25th anniversary with a special issue, the cover of which was designed by Henry Moore, Rees was asked by Mel to provide the leading article. This was called 'On Intellectual Reviews' and in it he wrote: 'A review which, like *Encounter*, is committed to a belief that a free exchange and discussion of ideas is an essential feature of any civilized society has to recognize that, as things are today, it operates under conditions which are not favourable to its success. Some of those conditions are, from the point of view of Western society, external ones. They arise in general out of the existence, in the Soviet Union and its satellites, of an alternative society and ideology which, by its own standards, the West cannot hesitate to characterize as barbarian, both in the sense that they are hostile and alien, and in the sense that they lack those minimum guarantees of individual freedom and security in the absence of which no society can claim to be civilized.'

*Encounter*, Rees explained, had been founded as a result of a growing realization, on the part of many people, that this alternative society constituted a threat to the liberal intellectual tradition of the West which was in danger of going unchallenged, simply because the means did not exist to do so. A voice had to be found, and the venture that brought *Encounter* into being would not have been possible without the generous assistance and support of the United States. There were some who, for that very reason, regarded *Encounter*'s claims of unrestricted freedom in its choice of subject matter and contributors as being 'vitiated' by its very origins. 'To believe this,' Rees said, 'would be as absurd as to deplore the post-war reconstruction and recovery of Europe because the original initiative towards it came from the great Secretary of State and of the Army, General George Marshall.'

Many of those who wrote for *Encounter* in the early days had once been communists or 'fellow-travellers' and, on the principle of 'knowing the enemy', they made the most discerning critics of the system. They were of the generation described by Richard Crossman in what might be called their Bible: a book entitled *The God That Failed*, published in 1950. Crossman wrote in his introduction: 'It so happens that, in the years between the October revolution and the Stalin–Hitler Pact, numberless men of letters, both in Europe and America, were attracted to communism. They were not "typical" converts. Indeed, being people of quite unusual sensitivity, they made most abnormal communists, just as the literary Catholic is the most abnormal Catholic. They had a heightened perception of the spirit of the age, and felt more acutely than others both its frustrations and its hopes. Their conversion therefore expressed, in an acute and some-times in a hysterical form, feelings which were dimly shared by the inarticulate millions who felt that Russia was "on the side of the workers" ...' The intellectual in politics, Crossman said, is always 'unbalanced' in his estimation of his colleagues. He peers round the next corner while they keep their eyes on the road; and he risks his faith on unrealized ideas, instead of confining it prudently to humdrum loyalties. He is 'in advance', and, in this sense, an extremist. If history justifies his premonitions, well and good. But if, on the contrary, history takes the other turning, he must either march forward into the dead end or, ignominiously, turn back, repudiating ideas which have become part of his personality ...

Mel Lasky had changed his mind about communism, he told me, with the Moscow show trials in 1936 and 1937. What he could not understand was how Rees, who had professed to have 'broken' with the pact, could have gone on seeing Burgess and Blunt during the war and afterwards. 'You would not mix and mingle with these characters, and they would not want to mix with you ... For me the only explanation was, that Goronwy says to himself, "I'll keep my big mouth shut, I won't say Stalin is a monster and as bad as Hitler, because I'm working for MI6 and I want to keep in touch with my old comrades so that I know what they are up to . . ." Doesn't this sound like Rees to you?' Rees, when he first met him, struck Lasky as a 'classic' case of someone who had been a communist and had then changed his mind – without going through stages on the way. 'Rees was a playful writer,' Mel said, 'and I don't know whether the mischief was better or worse in prose than in life.' He still asked himself questions about Rees: Was he a 'snitch' at All Souls? Did Burgess and Blunt 'have something on him'? Rees never said anything to Mel about these matters; he was very secretive. 'I think it was an ethical thing. I knew he had been in MI6, not because he told me, but because other people told me. I was also told he had been planted on me but I doubt that was true. I found him shadowy, but I admired and liked him. He was a good man and a good friend to me.'

Rees hated the permissiveness of the sixties and *Encounter* was the perfect place for him to state his views. He once told my aunt Mary, that he had imagined it would all be so wonderful when the conventions of respectability, which he himself had rebelled against, were thrown aside, but when this happened he loathed it. I remember the shocked faces of my father and mother one evening when a leading light of Swinging London, whom they had invited to dinner, took out a joint and smoked it in front of them. In column after column Rees attacked the 'counter-culture' of the times, and in an introduction to a collection of his articles, *Brief Encounters*, published in 1974, he said that he had felt like a spectator at the Greatest Show on Earth during those eventful years. 'The essence of the new counter-culture was that, as opposed to the repressive forces which were believed to dominate "post-industrial" capitalist society, it represented Love, Compassion, Liberation, the Flowering of the Self, "doing your own thing" without regard to the legal, ethical, sexual or economic inhibitions by which the established order tried to present the basis of its own power.' A 'debased and diluted' version of the counter-culture had established itself as a dominating influence on the mass media, he wrote. 'Here, it merged with, and became almost indistinguishable from, a feature of the contemporary scene which went by the name of the "permissive society", which represented those elements of the counter-culture which were acceptable to the enlightened middle classes. These elements might be said to include greater sexual

freedom, an increased tolerance towards divorce, abortion, homosexuality and pornography, and an almost obsessive belief in the
healing power of four-letter words . . .'

Rees saw out the decade by condemning, in his 'R' column, a
series in a Sunday newspaper about the 'new poor'. The paper, a left-
wing one, 'having temporarily exhausted, or having bored itself to
death with, the potentialities of both the Affluent and the Sick Society,
has now made the startling discovery that we are also a Sad Society,
"an expanding world where there is a blight of previously neglected
poverty: emotional poverty", and is now busily occupied with "a
major series of interlinked reports" documenting "the broken heart
of the problem of the new poor" '. Nothing, he said, could be 'sadder
or sicker' than the words chosen by the newspaper to announce its
new series. 'People who write like this should really be debarred by
law from investigating other people's broken hearts until they have
mended the cracks in their own.' He wondered if the more expensive
Sunday newspapers had, in their basements, a permanent cast of
characters with carefully selected features that could be used at any
moment to illustrate a series on the Affluent, Sick, Sad Society. The
justification for all this, he said, was the implied claim that the 'new
poor', the sad, the unhappy, the emotionally disturbed, are in a
significant way representative of contemporary society as they have
never been of any other. He continued: 'I know of no method, either
analytical or statistical, by which such a claim could be verified
and indeed rather suspect that the reverse may be true; that, in fact,
society is characterized not by the number or the condition of those
who live in emotional or material poverty, but rather of those
to whom life offers a large degree both of emotional and material
satisfaction . . .'

*Encounter* published a collection of tributes to Rees when he died
and in one of them, Jonathan Power, who had much admiration for
my father and attended the magazine's lunches of brown bread, cheese
and pickles, remarked on his singularity as a writer: 'Where did
Goronwy's keen and uncommon political sensitivities derive from?
He knew few politicians or diplomats. The George Balls, David
Owens and Louis de Guirancauds were not exactly the kind of people
with whom he had friendships or even had personal knowledge of.
But Goronwy studied, listened, took books seriously, played with
ideas, held fast to the earnest contemplation of life and society. He
was a man of priceless perception . . .' I think Rees would have felt

this was, perhaps, going too far, but his writing and his ideas were unusual in that both radicals and moderates seemed to find great interest in them.

One of his particularly successful articles was on Winston Churchill. I suppose he took Churchill under his wing because he was for many years an 'odd man out'. Anyone who was regarded with mistrust by his hated Conservative Party would have earned Rees's approval, but Churchill was special to him, indeed almost a hero. He had been watching the magnificent funeral in February 1965 and wrote: 'It is sad to think that for some time to come we are not likely to have a study of Churchill which will prefer the reality to the legend. But if it were to be written, perhaps its author would notice, as affording some explanation both of Churchill's failure and his triumph, that one of Churchill's most absorbing interests, perhaps, indeed, the most absorbing interest of his life, was one which to most of his contemporaries was profoundly distasteful and repugnant; that is to say, war ... It would be unfair to Churchill to say that, both on national and personal grounds, he welcomed the war; he could have said with some truth that it was both the country's and his own last chance. This is not to say that Churchill was ever blind or insensitive to the misery, suffering, and cruelty of war; or that policies he advocated were intended to provoke war rather than to preserve peace; or that, war having come, he ever wished to wage it for its own sake. But he would have found it perfectly natural to say, with Robert E. Lee, that it is a good thing we know how terrible war is, or we should grow too fond of it ...'

In this, said Rees, Churchill was abnormal: 'Though he saw and felt as deeply as anyone the terrible issues, the waste, suffering, and destruction, involved in war, he also saw it, as Peter Pan saw life, as "an awfully big adventure". Churchill himself was aware of his abnormality and of how much it isolated him from others; Lady Violet Bonham Carter quotes him as confessing, with a certain feeling of guilt, during the First World War, that though for others the war meant universal suffering, he could not help admitting that he was enjoying himself intensely at the Admiralty,' It was unjust to call Churchill a warmonger, Rees wrote, for he cared for peace and believed that peace could be preserved and, if necessary, restored by force or arms. He concluded: 'In fact, Churchill's acceptance of war as the ultimate reality of our time came from a profound and tragic insight into the present; in this he was far more modern than his contemporaries, and it is this above all which distinguishes him from all other democratic statesmen of his age.'

Rees returned to familiar ground in one of his 'R' columns in 1973, when he wrote about Evelyn Waugh whose previously unpublished diaries were being serialized by *The Observer*. In it he remarked: 'There is no other newspaper, unless perhaps *The Guardian*, which more perfectly represents, in its combination of mildly left-wing liberalism, its total commitment to everything that happens to be fashionable in the arts, and its belief that to be progressive and compassionate is in itself an answer to every conceivable problem, everything which Waugh detested most . . .'

Rees considered that no serious writer had ever been treated quite so shabbily as Waugh in the unedited form in which his unpublished work was presented to the public seven years after his death, and he hoped that a forthcoming biography of Waugh would be able to do something to correct the 'deplorable impression' which the early instalments of the diaries had made on many people. 'Their dreary record of adolescent and undergraduate drunkenness and debauch,' Rees wrote, 'is difficult to reconcile with the conscientious and fastidious artist which Waugh undoubtedly was; it is as if, in these diaries, he had wished, consciously or unconsciously, to be as cruel to himself as he frequently was to friends or to many of the characters in his novels . . .' Wishing that the diaries had been presented in their proper context, he went on: 'To the Bright Young Things who provided Waugh with the materials for his novels, and who continued to do so long after most of them had ceased to be Bright and all had ceased to be Young, the twenties were a period of sowing wild oats and many of them never really did anything else. But for some of them the following decade of the thirties was a period of genuine achievement in which they founded lasting reputations . . .'

It was a curious fact, he continued, that it was in the thirties, 'so dominated, as our own age is, by social and political preoccupations, so heavily influenced by Marxism, so obsessed with hopes of revolution and fear of Fascism', when the Bright Young Things were dismissed as the 'last, decadent, incurably frivolous offspring of a dying ruling class', that many of the most solid literary achievements were the work of the Bright Young Things themselves. They had remained essentially conservative, even reactionary, in their outlook, and immune to demands for political commitment or to promises of revolution. 'Indeed,' Rees wrote, 'one might say that their work has worn rather better than that of their politically minded, literary comrades, so anxious to "do Something for the Poor", and as their contribution writing novels and stories and poems which today have become almost totally unreadable . . .' In reading Waugh's diaries this should be remembered, he said: '. . . in Waugh's case, the years of drunkenness and debauch were also years which sowed the seeds both of an enormous literary talent and of friendships which lasted a lifetime, however often he offended his friends; and that they provided him with materials on which he never ceased to draw. Certainly, I cannot think of any young man who spent his youth more profitably . . .'

## 12

I am about to take my last voyage,
a great leap in the dark.

Thomas Hobbes


In an interview with Rees published in *The Scotsman* at the beginning
of 1972, to coincide with the publication of *A Chapter of Accidents*,
the writer William Foster tried to get to grips with his subject and
managed remarkably well. Under the headline 'A rebel about Celtic
backwaters', he wrote of my father: 'He has a smile that flashes on
and off suddenly, rather like the warning blinks of a strip light when
someone pushes down a switch. He says his life has been a restless one
with far too many jobs taken on, too many worlds either conquered
or left in a mild state of chaos because of his arrival on the scene.'
Foster's article was accompanied by a large photograph of Rees,
smoking a cigarette and looking sleek, confident and handsome. The
reviews of the book, which Rees dedicated to my mother, were on
the whole excellent: some of the reviewers took the opportunity to
launch into yet another commentary on the lives and times of the
Missing Diplomats while others used their space to deliver some more
personal shots. Guy's photograph was taken out of the picture libraries
and given another airing. I remember that the original manuscript
was thought to contain a number of possibly libellous passages which
had to be doctored at the last minute. There is no doubt that this was
another attempt by Rees to settle the score with Anthony Blunt, but
he could not, of course, name names.

Philip Toynbee, who had been a close friend of Donald Maclean,
was clearly not convinced by Rees's account. Reviewing *A Chapter
of Accidents* in *The Observer*, he wrote: 'One question remains – how
much is this book telling the truth? How much is it *intended* to be
taken for the truth? Misgivings began to disturb me when I came to
the description of the assault launched on Rees by the press during
the weeks that following the disappearance of B and M. I was, I
suppose, as close a friend of M as Rees was of B. Why, then, did I
receive so little attention from British journalists while Rees and his
wife were apparently the star figures in the whole investigation? It
seems unfair ...' He found *A Chapter of Accidents* 'a book of a very

odd kind indeed', 'lopsided but always fascinating', and did not like the switch from the conventional autobiography that forms the first part to Rees's description of his friendship with Burgess which follows. He pronounced the first half 'interesting and beautifully told' and likened Rees's view of Oxford to that of the young A.L. Rowse – 'both "Celts", according to our common misuse of the term' and 'both equally amazed and entranced by meeting, for the first time, those languidly self-confident products of the English upper-class machine who dominated Oxford and Cambridge so absolutely until World War II'. Then Guy appears on the scene '... he quickly becomes Rees's close friend, and, within a few months, a very strange mixture of famulus and evil genius. From this point on it is as if some great star had swum too close to a smaller one and wrenched one of the small star's planets out of orbit. Oxford had been Rees's star – indeed he has remained within that gravitational field ever since: but if one were to judge from this book alone it would seem that Burgess's effect on Rees was both shattering and permanent ...'

Toynbee said that he was not satisfied with Rees's account of why he wrote the notorious *People* articles: this he regarded as a 'sad affair' in which no more credit attached to the 'angry friends who did the cutting than to the man they cut'. But he thought that the portrait of Guy was masterly: 'Whether he deserves it or not Guy Burgess will now take his place in the gallery of immortal English eccentrics. Yet a price had to be paid for the domination exercised by Burgess during the second half of the book. To those who knew them both, Goronwy Rees was himself a character of grand proportions; the gayest of gay dogs; a bright cork which always bobbed to the surface again after each submersion. Any reader who has never known either Rees or Burgess would suppose from *A Chapter of Accidents* that Rees was no more than that earnest, responsible, wryly subordinate best friend who is always to be found in the immediate wake of a major clown. This is partly the inevitable penalty of writing an autobiography, for it is only a fatuously self-conscious egotist who sees *himself* as a colourful figure. To himself Rees is both a wiser and less interesting man than he seemed to the rest of us ...'

Writing in the *Financial Times*, C.P. Snow said that the book showed the same 'limpid talent' as *A Bundle of Sensations* and found the autobiographical chapters rarer and more rewarding to anyone seriously interested in human personality than those about Guy. Tracing Rees's development, he noted: 'Along with his talents, he has been dogged by a strong depressive streak. It sounds like the kind of depressiveness which gives a special edge and delicacy to a temperament, making it more acute, endowing it with empathy and a characteristic charm. (His history makes no sense unless one infers this.) At a very high price. For internally, the depressiveness brings a degree of self-distrust and self-discontent and, in the end, of extreme solitariness ...' Snow, too, is puzzled by Rees's articles: 'Not so sensible was to let his agent sell the story to *The People* and have it rewritten by a popular journalist. It is the latter aspect that is the most puzzling of all and one can't disentangle what possessed him. Maybe possessed is the operative word ...' He hoped that once Rees had 'discharged his feelings and conscience about Burgess' he would produce a third volume of autobiography 'nakedly about himself'.

Hugh Trevor-Roper, in the *Sunday Times*, examined the Aberystwyth disaster very closely. He also spotted Rees's reference to Blunt, though it was deliberately veiled. 'Why did he write those fatal articles?' the reviewer asked. 'His own explanation is ingenious. He was convinced, he says, that the Security Services, being a "microcosm of the Establishment", were tainted with treason, but "for reasons which were deeply rooted in the English social system" could not purge themselves of that taint. Therefore it was no good speaking privately to them. They would hearken only to a voice from Sinai, or at least from Aberystwyth, amplified a million-fold in the resonant pages of *The People*. Only thus, he hints, would the elusive Third Man in the Burgess–Maclean mystery be flushed out of his protected lair. "As later events showed," he adds smugly, "my suspicion was not unjustified." He refers, presumably, to Philby ...' Trevor-Roper continued: 'So he says; but here, as Dr Johnson would say, incredulity is ready to make a stand. There is not the slightest reason to suppose that MI5 would deliberately protect a traitor, or that Mr Rees (who had protected one for fifteen years) had suddenly become the best adviser in such matters. Philby, by that time, had already been recognized and removed. If anyone were still the victim of past illusions, it was not MI5; it was – and is – Mr Rees. How else can he still describe Burgess and Philby [*he was actually describing Blunt*] as "the brightest and best of their generation"? A charitable man will overlook these retrospective rationalizations and believe Mr Rees when he ingenuously confessed that he was "mistaken": that "common sense and practical judgment are qualities with which perhaps I am not conspicuously well endowed." ' His view was that Rees was well endowed with other qualities. He had found the book 'delightful' to read, and he admired Rees's 'delicate sensitivity, his acuteness in general analysis, his beautiful style'. There was an 'attractive freedom' from egotism, dramatization or (outside Aberystwyth) resentment ... 'Whatever his misjudgments or misfortunes, as literature and as autobiography this book is unique: the record of a poor boy from the Celtic fringe who, coming to Oxford in the effervescent 1920s, and even to All Souls College, was uncorrupted by that heady draught, and can write.'

Richard Crossman, in the *New Statesman*, said that he should have recruited Rees, not Stephen Spender, as the Englishman to add to his collection of ex-communists in *The God That Failed*, published in 1950. He took a very personal line over Rees, finding the book 'an elaborate apologia' for his failure to denounce Guy while there was still time, and objected to Rees's contention that it was almost respectable to be a communist in the thirties. Drawing on their shared experience at New College, he does not hide his feelings about Rees: 'I happened to be his contemporary and can therefore judge his picture of himself as an unspoilt, gifted Welsh boy who despite his success always felt that Oxford was unacceptable. My memory of him is of an extremely brilliant and handsome scholar who took Oxford society by storm and won as many admirers (male as well as female) as Elizabeth Longford. I thought of him as a playboy on the make. He thought of me as a bore ...' Crossman quoted a passage about Wykehamists: 'There was at New College a group of admirably serious and dedicated young men who many years later, after many vicissitudes, would provide the Labour Party with an entirely new leadership and stamp it with their own peculiar form of Wykehamist socialism ... they exuded an air of professionalism and puritanism which was somehow out of tune with the *fin de siècle* atmosphere of the twenties ... I found their ideas altogether too humdrum and dreary to fit into my utopian dreams of revolution.'

In response to those words of Rees's, Crossman commented: 'I accept the picture of Gaitskell, Douglas Jay and myself, but what I cannot accept is the impression Mr Rees seeks to give that he was always a socialist "though politics was irrelevant to the Oxford of 1928". This is surely a travesty of history. No one who has lived as a student through the American crisis, the collapse of the Labour government and the rise of the Nazis can claim that politics was irrelevant unless he deliberately made it so. This was the period when Lindsay, Tawney and Cole were at the height of their powers and when the Labour Club was a power in the land. But Mr Rees dismissed it all as boring Wykehamist seriousness and concentrated himself on the pleasures of the social swim. The communism he picked up was merely part of the social ambience in which he lived the life of an adored and somewhat spoilt young exquisite who was able to make at least two outstanding creative writers, Elizabeth Bowen and Rosamond Lehmann, feel the impact of his gay, charming cruelty. When he met Burgess he was not, as this book suggests, a famulus serving Faust but a social equal who delighted in the Burgess philosophy of cynical revolution . . .' It was a travesty of history, Crossman wrote, to suggest that everyone, apart from a very small circle of intellectuals, felt the way Rees did: 'A few of them died in Spain, but the vast majority were parlour Bolsheviks who took no part in practical politics, except perhaps an occasional lecture to a Left Book Club meeting. To describe this as the tragedy of a whole generation is ridiculous. But I think it explains the convulsion by which Mr Rees suddenly jumped out of parlour Bolshevism into the role of the fully-fledged cold warrior which he still plays today. He still cannot get over the extent to which he morally condoned communism . . .'

However, Crossman ended on a more positive note: 'As a picture of Guy Burgess *A Chapter of Accidents* is a brilliant success; as an explanation of the author's behaviour before and after the crisis it is a broken-backed failure . . .' Why did Rees not report Guy's admission that he was an agent until he had absconded? Whatever induced him to write the articles? Why does he spoil the 'marvellous story' by so much special pleading? However, Crossman dismissed all these reservations as 'old men's worries': 'For a generation which is not concerned with what really happened more than twenty years ago, *A Chapter of Accidents* provides a brilliantly readable account of what is still an unsolved mystery. Treated as a *novelle* – fiction based on fact – it is without doubt a minor masterpiece. I was reminded when I had finished it of the impression that *Death in Venice* first made on me, and what did I care whether Thomas Mann ever sat in a hotel on the Lido looking out at a boy digging on the sands?'

In his lengthy, unsigned review in the *Times Literary Supplement*, Noël Annan added his own observations about Burgess before moving on to Rees: 'In being a communist sympathizer Mr Rees was characteristic of much that was most ardent and high-minded in his generation, and it is easy to see why he was attracted to Guy Burgess . . .' He agreed with Rees that it was impossible to take Guy seriously and judged the portrait of Guy a 'triumph'. On the subject of *The People* articles, Noël wrote: 'At this point Mr Rees lost his head and his obsession destroyed him. He sat down and wrote an indictment not only of Burgess but of his friends and in particular all those friends who were in high places or had been in the security service during the war ... His friends took the line that to start a witch-hunt five years after the birds had flown was inexcusable and they put it about that Mr Rees, fearful that Burgess would make some malicious and false statement about him, had made the error of trying to get in first and denounce his former friend...'

Noël Annan did not really like the form of the book. In his view, Rees should have written about the situation and not about himself – and when Rees did write about himself he was short on plausible explanation and just plain wrong in many areas. It was unfair of Rees, Noël maintained, to be so hard on the Foreign Office and the security services: 'It is odd that Mr Rees, who is a columnist and member of the advisory board of *Encounter*, fails to recognize that what distinguishes British democracy from a communist society is precisely this unwillingness to pillory individuals and sacrifice them to the dubious value of making the state that bit more "secure". He still seems unable to grasp why, at a time when Senator McCarthy's exploits had scarcely passed into history, his friends disapproved of his articles in *The People* for making reckless innuendoes and calling for a witch-hunt ...' Nevertheless, although the book covered a lot of 'old ground', Noël considered it 'compulsive reading for the over-fifties' and noted, 'There is a frontispiece of Mr Rees looking immeasurably Welsh.'

The book had quite a different effect on Robert Conquest, who reviewed it for the *London Magazine* a few months later. He found Rees, on the subject of his own confusion about his duty in connection with his 'rather vague suspicions' of Burgess, 'natural and convincing'. Conquest wrote: 'Burgess had apparently told him, much earlier, that he was a Comintern agent. (No one seems to have pointed out that this was not illegal – in some cases, not even secret. But one would certainly not wish to find such people in the Foreign Office, let alone the security services.) Rees, as anyone might, felt first that a report of this would not be taken seriously, and second, that the security people surely knew what they were doing ... There *was* a bit of an outcry about Rees's own remarks, when he wrote his piece in *The People* about his knowledge of Burgess. It seemed to be felt by various people, including the head of an Oxford college, that it was very disloyal of

Rees not to stand by his former acquaintance. The moral lunacy of Rees's critics hardly needs rubbing in. It seems to be based in part on E.M. Forster's smug and shallow slogan of it being better to betray one's country that one's friend – just the self-applauding, sensitive "liberal" attitude Rees is so penetratingly harsh on in its earlier Oxford guise ...' Conquest's view was that Rees was, in a sense, a drop-out, 'not from tedious conformist bourgeois life into equally tedious conformist "alternative society" life, but into a genuine autonomy.' He explained: 'While Burgess, with all his ostentatious wildness, remained for years – and particularly in the period just before his death – a cog in a highly bureaucratic establishment, Rees was always beset by a Welsh recklessness and impulsiveness (understandably seen by his wife as self-destructive). When overtaken by his impulses, he has more than once infuriated establishments of all types ...'

The book's fiercest critic was the poet Harri Webb, who wrote in the Welsh magazine, *Planet*: 'In his public posturings Mr Goronwy Rees resembles nothing so much as an ageing daughter of the night, blissfully unaware of her fading charms, oblivious of the passing of the Street Offences Act, parading in the pathetic finery of a bygone day on some windy corner long deserted by the traffic of pleasure ...' He conceded that Rees could write well, but 'he loses no opportunity of decrying everything Welsh, is tireless in advocating the superior values and standards he claims to have found elsewhere'. Mr Webb concluded: 'He is a bundle of sensations, a chapter of accidents, incensed that the young of today are beginning to think well of themselves and their country, and are concerned to tackle its problems, miffed that they are not interested in the meretricious trash which has so dazzled his own eyes, offering them nothing but his obsessive chronicles of snobbery, sodomy and treachery ...'

Rees, familiar with criticism, was on the whole pleased with the reception for *A Chapter of Accidents*; but at home all was not well. My parents had, by this time, moved yet again, with my youngest brother – Matthew, to a very small house in Chiswick, near Kew Bridge. My mother had not been fortunate with her treatment for cancer and was suffering from extreme pain as her condition worsened. She hated being immobile and unable to work in her garden or carry out quite ordinary household chores and I think she knew, then, that she did not have much time left. Although she had apparently told her dentist that there was no point in him making any major plans for her teeth because she was going to die, to me, as was her way, she spoke little of her fears for the future. It was extremely hard for my father to watch her distressing deterioration: he felt helpless in the face of her suffering. He could not drive a car and although he did learn how to make a cup of tea and could boil an egg, that was about as far as his domesticity went. What he did do, though, was try to entertain my mother; whenever he came back from *Encounter* or meeting people, he would sit down by her bed and tell her stories about what he had seen or heard and describe his journey or his lunch in a restaurant in detail. My mother always became more animated when he entered the room, as if he brought life with him.

I worried about the two of them, and felt that, as I was now divorced and living on my own with my children, it would be more sensible if I could find a large house where we could all be together. I found what seemed like the perfect solution at Strand-on-the-Green; a large house on the footpath that runs alongside the Thames, with room for us all, on a short lease that was within our means at that time. My mother, I thought, would enjoy the company of her grandchildren, which, indeed, she did, and there was a large bay window in the front room where she could sit and watch the boats and the ducks on the river and the people walking past. When we moved in, I had no idea how little time she had left.

As the pain became more and more extreme, my mother spent more frequent and longer periods in Charing Cross Hospital, to which she was always happy to return; she had infinite trust in, and affection for the doctors who treated her and the nurses who made her comfortable. Freddie Ayer's wife Dee, spent a lot of time with her, both at home and at the hospital, towards the end of her life. 'I don't think Rees ever dared give any thought to how ill Margie was,' she told me. 'I don't think he ever dared tell himself that she was not going to get better because her end would be his end, too. She was so brave. I remember being at the hospital with both of them, and she looked frightful lying there, with no hair. She looked at him and said, "Am I dying?" And he replied, "No, of course not, what are you going on about? Wherever there is life, there is hope." I thought to myself, how can he say these things, when he knows they are not true? It took courage on his part and he thought it was the right thing to say to her. It probably was, but she knew perfectly well that she was not going to live for much longer. But when he told her that no one was thinking like that, it encouraged her. I remember thinking, well, maybe this is how it does work. He was so robust and persuasive.'

Dee said that she believed my mother was very frightened of dying, but that, at the end, she wanted to go. 'I think she could have lasted longer, if she had allowed them to give her more blood transfusions, but she just wanted some peace. She had had enough.'

On a beautiful summer's evening in June 1976, my mother died, leaving my father a desperately unhappy and lonely man. She was fifty-five. The last time I saw her, she asked me to look after him and told me that to love and care for others was what was most important in life.

My father was inconsolable. Without her love, her wisdom, her companionship, her comfort and strength, he was like a man abandoned, lost and desolate, and was quite unable to articulate his feelings. Trying to remember him now, the nearest I can get to an accurate description of his state was that he was like an animal that had been wounded internally and he carried about with him a deep, dull pain. I used to find him sitting in his study downstairs in the early hours of the morning, with his head in his hands and his whisky bottle by his side, and urge him to go to bed and get some sleep. 'You don't know how much I mind,' he would say to me, over and over again. One afternoon he found me listening to *The Magic Flute*, and I hoped he would sit with me as I thought it might give him some pleasure. He sat down on one of the straight-backed dining chairs and stared out of the window, with tears running down his face.

Rees had a problem with his own health, too. Before my mother's death he had undergone a colostomy at Charing Cross Hospital and, remarkably, had been able to travel to America, Canada and Australia to see the various commercial enterprises of Dalgety, the huge multinational corporation for which he wrote a company history that was printed privately for the directors. He had also spent some months working with the television journalist John Morgan, who produced an hour-long profile of him for Harlech TV.

In the programme, which was shown in 1977, Rees, looking fairly battered, was again able to bring up the subject of Anthony Blunt; he said that the security side of the affair of the Cambridge spies showed that there was something profoundly wrong with the English social structure. There was a fleeting glimpse of Mr Nobody when he told John Morgan that despite his amorous adventures in the thirties, he did not believe in love. Those people were always more in love with him than he was with them, he said. On his travels with Rees, John learned more about Mr Nobody: 'We speculated on how his bilingualism had contributed to his character and view of life. He concluded that it probably had in that his perpetual sense of non-existence, of being a bundle of sensations, sprang from uncertainties created by two languages being equal forms of expression as soon as he could speak.' John thought there was some scientific basis 'for this belief in a mild schizophrenia of linguistic origin'.

As time went by, I began to notice that Rees was finding it no easier to accept my mother's death; he looked shaken and I felt that if I could see inside him I would find bruising as if he had been wounded in a terrible accident, about which he could not speak. I remember turning over and over in my mind the real meaning of the expression 'losing the will to live'.

Every minute of the day he missed my mother and his sorrow was so great that I knew there was nothing I could do for him. I felt hopelessly inadequate and increasingly unhappy myself. He was so lonely without her, and he saw very few people. He seemed pleased when Shiela Sokolov Grant made contact with him and, with his black dog, Lady, went to visit her several times in County Cork, where he and Shiela's husband, Michael, would stay up late talking about the past.

He also went to stay with my sister, Lucy, in North Wales on a number of occasions. She lived near Micky Burn, the poet and writer, whose own wife, Mary, had recently died. Micky had known Guy Burgess and, as a commando during the war, had been captured at St Nazaire and imprisoned in Colditz, so Lucy thought that he and Rees would have plenty to talk about. It was a very successful introduction. Micky was, at that time, a Roman Catholic, and while they spoke of their wives and death, the war and Guy, they also clearly talked about faith. Rees had often said how desolate he found Freddie Ayer's atheism, but he never really made his own religious beliefs known. I always imagined this was bound up with his feelings about his father. Micky made some very perspicacious observations about Rees, as the poem he wrote after seeing his television interview indicates:

> On the Soul
> A Letter to Goronwy Rees
>
> Dear Accident, or Event, since so I must
> Address you, having seen you on the box,
> And heard you claim,

Or thought I did, we may not take on trust
Your being as an individual soul.

It seems you're composite of bombarding atoms,
For ever floating in and floating away,
A Bundle of Sensations,
'All is in flux,' Heraclitus used to say,
One can't step in the same Goronwy twice . . .


Micky was able to show me a sheaf of letters which Rees had
written to him during their short friendship and gave me an insight
into some of the more intimate feelings that my father did not wish
to reveal to me. Although the following letter is dated 21 June 1976 –
the date of my mother's death – I think this was a Freudian slip on
my father's part, for he was writing a year later.

5, Strand-on-the-Green,
London W4
21.VI.76

My dear Micky,
I am writing this late at night, so I hope you will forgive me if it is slightly
incoherent. But first I ought to thank you for your letter, and for
remembering, and to say that in all of this terrible last year you have given me
more comfort and help than anyone else I know. But that, no doubt, is because you know what it is all about, and have helped me to understand, too.
I had dreaded this Anniversary and had wondered how I could get through
it, or what devices I could think of to avoid it. But life is so strange that
somehow it has turned out happily for me, in that I have never been so
intensely aware of Margie's presence, so grateful that all her terrible suffering
was over, or so aware of her beside me, telling me that I mustn't grieve and
that somehow, somewhere, she will always be with me. I don't understand
this feeling; it must be what theologians call an Uncovenanted Grace, and
Grace it certainly is and I do not really mind very much about anything else.
[He and Micky had been discussing suicide] This brings me to Rupert and
Elizabeth, whose end disturbed me greatly, just because I understand it so
very well. I would have chosen the same path myself, if only Margie, with
much more justification, had not, and if she would not have been so angry
with me if I had.
Despair must surely be the greatest of temptations and the greatest of sins,
and I can only think with the greatest possible sympathy and charity about
anyone who succumbs to it; as I do very nearly almost daily. What saves one
from it? Freddie's and A's reaction is both shocking and characteristic,
because it is the reaction of people who simply will not admit that such a

thing as suffering really exists and is fundamental to human life. I sometimes think of Humanism and what Burns thought of Lust:

> I waive the quantum of the Sin;
> The perils of concealing;
> But Och! it hardens all within
> And petrifies the feeling!

Their reactions, and those of others, like . . ., who thought that someone like Rupert had no right to take his life when so many people were suffering so much worse in Africa, Chile, etc, etc, really horrify me more than anything else, because they really must have hearts of stone,

> Hard and cold and small
> Of all hearts the worst of all.

I had one once, and it was only Margie who cured me of it. I feel so infinitely grateful to her all the time for making me someone who, if not quite human yet, is at least not obviously and recognizably a monster . . .

Much love,<br>Goronwy

Rees had spent Christmas of 1976 with Micky at his house at Penrhyndeudraeth in North Wales, and wrote this letter of thanks on his return home:

My dear Micky,

Thank you so much for having me to stay. I enjoyed it enormously, in a way I haven't enjoyed anything for a very long time. Your house, the landscape, food and drink . . . and yourself all combined to make one happy, when one had begun to think that this would not be possible again.

But it was not only being happy. Talking to you, reading your wife's letter, were both a comfort and a source of hope, so that I felt that Margie is not altogether lost and I do not have to live entirely without her. And on Tuesday night, I dreamed about her, and she was exactly as she had been before all her pain and suffering; and I felt that the dream was meant as a kind of blessing on Beudy Gwyn [*Micky's house*], and on yourself . . .

Ever,<br>Goronwy

In May of the year before he died, Rees made another of his journeys to North Wales to see Micky, travelling, as always, with his dog, Lady. From Strand-on-the-Green, he wrote:

My dear Micky,

Lady and I came home happily and safely yesterday, especially as she was

247

petted, cosseted and fed to her heart's content by our fellow passengers.

Thank you very much indeed for all your kindness and hospitality during my visit, but most of all for the pleasure of your company, which always seems to have a good effect on me. I don't think I've talked to anyone so continuously and inexhaustibly since Margie died; you seem to understand so well everything that has happened to one . . .

I hope you know how deeply grateful I am to you for my visits; in the last two years they really have done something for me which I don't think could have been done otherwise.

I was really very exhausted and in pain when I came, but now feel very much better, and shall devote myself to getting well and try to write something worth writing.

Thank you again very much indeed,

Love,
Goronwy

PS: Lady, who is very meticulous in matters of etiquette, has asked me to say she cannot write herself, but hopes you know how enormously she enjoyed herself.

That summer he went to Ireland to see Shiela Sokolov Grant, and wrote to Micky in October:

Dear Micky,

I've only just got back from Ireland, where I sank into complete Irish indolence and lethargy and my correspondence has become completely out of hand. I'm sorry I haven't written before, especially to thank you for your poem, which I found touching, flattering, and witty all at the same time. But I think I have rather changed my mind since I was an Accident or an Event, so that now I don't quite know what I am, and I haven't found any very satisfactory answer yet. Isaiah Berlin says there is no way of disproving determinism but nevertheless we must go on believing we have Free Will. It doesn't seem a very good answer to the problem but all the same I can't at the moment think of anything better. Philosophers are sometimes very frivolous about questions that really affect people's lives very deeply . . .

I showed your poem to my hostess in Ireland. She liked it so much that she copied it out and pasted into a copy of my book . . .

Love,
Goronwy

It was at this time, like some miracle, that into Rees's bleak existence came Andrew Boyle. He could not have turned up at a better moment. One evening when I returned home from work my father asked me if I had heard of a journalist of that name. I said I had not and Rees explained that he had worked for the BBC on *The World at One*, had won a prize for his biography of Brendan Bracken, and was doing research for his new book which was to be yet another about the Cambridge spies. As my mother was no longer there to warn him to keep out of trouble, I asked Rees if he thought it was a good idea for him to speak to Boyle; indeed, what else was there to say after *A Chapter of Accidents*? However, I was not particularly surprised when he took no notice of me and began to meet Andrew Boyle in the local pub along the towpath. There were a series of meetings over many months and I gathered from Rees that Boyle was making good headway with his research. From what I understood, it was not simply that Rees had information to give to Boyle, but that Boyle, like a gundog carrying game, kept coming back to him with offerings that he had gathered from elsewhere, so that, together, they were putting together the pieces of a jigsaw puzzle. I thought no more about it, but was simply happy that Rees had found something to interest and occupy him.

Just before Christmas 1978, in a rather more cheerful mood than usual, Rees told me that Boyle had 'come up' with something and the book, to be called *The Climate of Treason*, was going to be very important. Boyle had collected everything there was to know about Anthony Blunt and had identified him as the Fourth Man. As he could not name Blunt, he was going to have to use the code name 'Maurice', but it would be obvious that 'Maurice' was Blunt. A few months before the book was published, Rees wrote to Micky about Andrew Boyle and his letter revealed the perhaps surprising fact that Rees did not know that Blunt had ever confessed: 'There's also another [*book*] on its way, by a man called Andrew Boyle, whom I've seen several times, and also, I think, quite serious. He told me, among other things, that our friend AB had actually confessed, but it would have caused too much of a scandal to do anything about it. This was on the personal authority of Dick White, but please don't mention it . . .'

At the beginning of 1979 domestic problems absorbed all our thoughts: our lease was running out on the house at Strand-on-the-Green. It was also the awful Winter of Discontent and one day, standing on Gunnersbury tube station in the sludge waiting, miserably, for a train to take me to work, I decided I had had enough of London. I conceived a plan to take my children to a somewhat primitive cottage I had bought some years before on the Cotentin peninsula in

Normandy and try to make a life for us there. It was not a wise decision.

My brothers, Daniel and Thomas, found a flat for Rees in the house of a friend in Bedford park, Chiswick. I wrote to him often, and he was good at writing back, but he seemed very confused and unsure about the future. Replying in May to a letter I had sent telling him about the local plans to celebrate the 35th anniversary of the D-Day landings the following month, my father wrote: 'Also my back seems to have got much worse and is very painful and makes sleep almost impossible. I've just had a course of twelve sessions of SUPER-SONIC RAY treatment, so I feel as if I've become a bionic man; do tell Sam and Ben; I'm sure they'll be fascinated. I've also become a transvestite, as I'm clamped in a corset; I'm thinking of buying some black fishnet stockings and a wig . . . I'm touched by the celebrations for D-Day. I landed at Arromanches on June 7 and left a few days later by motor torpedo boat with letters to London from Monty, in a most appalling storm; it was the night when one of the two artificial harbours was blown away and crossing the Channel was the coldest, wettest, roughest and fastest crossing I have ever done. It's nice that some people remember it all . . .'

In mid-October Rees wrote to tell me that his friends and colleagues at *Encounter* were to hold a party for him on his seventieth birthday on 29 November and asked me if I could manage to come. It was a sad letter, which he ended by saying: 'But whether I will be well enough is doubtful. The trouble, as you may have guessed, is one which we all know far too much about because of Margie, and in some ways I feel as if I were going through it all again with her; sometimes the pain is excruciating and makes me realize how much she must have suffered. Please do not be upset by this. There is nothing really to feel sad about, though in some ways it means a kind of revolution in one's life ... Please do not worry about me, but do write again soon . . .'

The events of the next few months are unclear in my mind, though it was my brothers and my sister, Lucy, who took the full force of the circumstances of my father's death. I learned that Rees had gone into Charing Cross Hospital when my brother, Daniel, telephoned me in France at the beginning of November. He told me that Rees had collapsed at the flat in Bedford Park and had got in touch with him to see if he could help get him into hospital. There was a strike on at the time. While lying on the floor waiting for an ambulance to come,

Rees had been reading an edition of the *Daily Mail* in which an article appeared across two pages analysing the contents of Andrew Boyle's book, *The Climate of Treason*, published that day by Hutchinson, and in which he believed he had been libelled. The libellous statement – that Rees had recruited Philby – was in fact the result of a missing line but, even so, the article was not very flattering about Rees and dismissive of Boyle's book. Rees was described as 'naive in the extreme': 'At one time Burgess told Rees that he was a Comintern agent and added that "Maurice" was one, too. Rees, though he had served as an intelligence officer in the Army, didn't go to the authorities, a fact which British intelligence is somewhat bitter about to this day. Rees's explanation some years ago was "that it didn't seem immoral then to work for the Comintern". Now he says he couldn't be sure Burgess wasn't joking. But British Intelligence itself was also behaving with peculiar sloppiness. "Maurice", despite his Marxist past, was accepted as a senior officer within MI5 during the war after only the most cursory of checks into his background, Rees got into Military Intelligence, went into MI6, where he recruited Philby, and Maclean joined the Foreign Office . . .' (As correctly printed in other editions, the sentence should have read: '. . . Rees got into Military Intelligence, Burgess went into MI6, where he recruited Philby, and Maclean joined the Foreign Office.')

The *Daily Mail* investigators considered that Boyle had written a 'useful' book: 'But whether he has unearthed two real-life spies is still open to doubt. His candidate for Fourth Man was more silly, by most accounts, than sinister . . . The fact is that the Thirties, trapped between two wars, was an unnatural and unhealthy decade. Its walking wounded, scarred by their own treachery, are still with us today. Kim Philby, the Third Man, was a spy in the truest sense of the word. The others in the continuing numbers game were so much dross . . .'

While wanting to be with my father, I was, at the same time, very relieved to be far away in my quiet corner of Normandy if, as appeared to be the case, another unpleasant round of accusations was about to begin. I wished that Rees had not become involved with the Boyle book. Meanwhile, *Encounter* had secured the services of a leading libel lawyer, Michael Rubinstein, who could not have been a more appropriate choice. My brother was far more concerned about my father's health at that time than about his misrepresentation by the press but, at his request, he went to see Mr Rubinstein at his office in Gray's Inn. When he telephoned me to tell me that the *Daily Mail* had apologized and agreed to pay £250 to charity, he mentioned a very strange coincidence. As he sat in the waiting room, he saw a distinguished-looking man come down the stairs from Mr Rubinstein's office and leave the building by the front door. The reception clerk turned to Daniel and said: 'Did you see that gentleman, sir? Do you know who he is?' After hearing that my brother's reply to the last question was negative, he said to Daniel: 'Well, sir, that was Sir Anthony Blunt, who looks after the Queen's pictures.' What Daniel could not know was that Blunt was being given protection and Rubinstein had been asked to look after his interests.

Mr Rubinstein had sent Daniel a kind and sympathetic letter when my father died, so, in September 1993, I decided to ask if I could talk to him about my brother's visit. I explained that we did not in any way wish to suggest that it was improper for him to have represented Rees at the same time as he was representing Blunt. He told me that he had been requested by the government to protect Blunt as far as was possible at that time because it was concerned about allegations in the press and the Boyle book. He said that Blunt was very 'upset' about what Rees had done, making it clear to me that Blunt had spoken of my father personally and of the part he had played in the denouement.

It was in *Private Eye*, on 9 November 1979, that the connection between Blunt and 'Maurice' was first made in print. But the press had been unable to find Blunt, who had gone into hiding, to confirm his identity as the Fourth Man. My brother Daniel, though he had not realized it at the time, had, indeed, sighted a very rare bird at the offices of Michael Rubinstein. Andrew Boyle, according to a later edition of his book, heard that two parliamentary questions relating to security had been tabled for 19 November, but that these were overtaken by a third, from Edward Leadbitter, Labour MP for Hartlepool, to which the Prime Minister had promised a written reply. And so, on 15 November, Mrs Thatcher stood up in the House of Commons and made her long withheld statement, in which she said that Sir Anthony Blunt had admitted to the security services in 1964 that he had been recruited by, and had acted as a talent-spotter for, Russian intelligence when he was a don at Cambridge before the war, and had passed information regularly to the Russians while he was a member of the security service between 1940 and 1945.

Mrs Thatcher continued: 'He made this admission after being given an undertaking that he would not be prosecuted if he confessed.

Inquiries were, of course, made before Blunt joined the security service in 1940, and he was judged a fit person. He was known to have held Marxist views at Cambridge, but the security authorities had no reason either in 1940 or at any time during his service to doubt his loyalty to his country . . .'

In the part of her statement that is particularly relevant to this story, Mrs Thatcher said: 'He first came under suspicion in the course of the inquiries which followed the defection of Burgess and Maclean in 1951 when the security service was told that Burgess had said in 1937 that he was working for a secret branch of the Comintern and that Blunt was one of his sources. There was no supporting evidence for this. When confronted with it Blunt denied it . . .'

Shortly after Mrs Thatcher had finished speaking, it was announced from Buckingham Palace that Blunt would, forthwith, be stripped of his knighthood, the first time such a thing had occurred since the trial and execution of Sir Roger Casement in 1916. My brother, Daniel, was with Rees in his room at the Charing Cross Hospital at the time of Mrs Thatcher's announcement. He told me: 'Rees watched it all on television. When pictures of Blunt appeared, he said "Got you, you swine."' Writing in *The Observer* the following Sunday, Andrew Boyle said that he had first 'stumbled' across the complicity of Blunt in the Burgess–Maclean–Philby affair on a research visit to Cambridge three years earlier, but that Rees had told him, one Saturday afternoon as they left the pub together after one of their meetings, that Blunt was the accomplice of Guy Burgess whom he was not able to name in *A Chapter of Accidents*.

That evening my father went into a coma. The corridors of the hospital were by then teeming with newspaper reporters, who were looking for him. Well, most were. I heard from my brother that one muddled representative of a tabloid newspaper had been seen wandering through the hospital looking for Anthony Blunt.

In our little house in Normandy, I was unaware of the enormous impact of Mrs Thatcher's statement and was far more preoccupied with the frightening idea that my father was dying. When I had last seen him, he had looked very ill and very old and I had held his hand. He had told me that it was very important for me to keep working and that work was something solid and sure in one's life, if nothing else was. I could not sleep at night; I used to lie stiff and rigid in bed waiting for something to happen, for some news to come through. I suppose I was waiting for the end.

On the evening that Rees lost consciousness, Daniel telephoned and told me about his condition. A doctor at the hospital, he said, was certain that the coma had been induced and that there were sinister implications. Two men had been seen near his room. It was possible that they had injected him with insulin. These two men could have been Russians. He then asked me if I knew how to contact MI5: could I give him their telephone number? It seemed a completely surreal conversation to be having, but the events of that day had been extraordinary, even given the enormous range of possibilities one had to allow for with Rees. Daniel sounded as if he had been hit over the head with a large implement; his voice sounded dazed. But it was a perfectly reasonable and practical question to ask. I told him I knew someone in Paris who could help and that I would call him later. The 'someone in Paris' was a close family friend and I woke him from his sleep, 'Something has happened to Rees,' I said. 'Daniel wants to know how to get in touch in MI5.' He did not ask why; he simply told me that Daniel should ring Scotland Yard, tell the switchboard who he was and what he wanted, and he would be put through. It all worked like clockwork. Through a series of telephone calls from my brother that night I learned that a police guard had been put on Rees's room at the hospital, though it was later found that there was nothing suspicious about his coma and that a tumour can account for a rapid fall in blood-sugar levels. The guard was removed after a week, by which time Rees had recovered.

On 20 November, Anthony Blunt came out of hiding to give a press conference; he spent seventy-five minutes in the boardroom of Times Newspapers answering questions put to him by representatives of *The Times* and *The Guardian*. He said he had been recruited by Guy in late 1935 or possibly early 1936 and, in a statement issued to the Press Association, explained that Guy had 'persuaded' him that he could best serve the cause of anti-Fascism by joining him in his work for Russia. Blunt said: 'This was a case of political conscience against loyalty to country: I chose conscience.'

Of Guy, Blunt told his interviewers: 'The Burgess I first met as an undergraduate was one of the most remarkable, most brilliant and, making a distinction, one of the most intelligent people I have ever known. He was already extremely tiresome and difficult, but he had a mind which went absolutely to the bottom of any question. One listened to him talking about politics or a general problem that was relevant, original and stimulating. He might be extremely wrongheaded. This is very difficult to realize for anyone who knew him in his last years when he was very nearly round the bend under the strain.' In reply to the question concerning his immunity, 'Were there people in the security services who wanted the affair out in the open?', he replied: 'I think it was perfectly possible. At one moment I thought it was probable. But when Andrew Boyle said my name had been given to him by Goronwy Rees I thought that was sufficient explanation and therefore one didn't have to suppose a leak by MI 5.'

A week later, on 29 November, the *Encounter* party for Rees's seventieth birthday was held in his hospital room. Among his papers in the cardboard boxes I found a Polaroid photograph of him lying in bed, celebrating, with a cigarette in one hand and a plastic cup of champagne in the other. Mel Lasky was sitting by his bedside. Towards the end of his life, there were only a few people apart from his brother, Geraint, he wanted to see: Isaiah Berlin went to the hospital, as did Freddie Ayer and David Footman. In an appreciation of Rees, written after his death, David noted that 'in spite of the pain and the discomfort he seemed to me to be more relaxed than I had known him for years. It was a profound relief to him that the Blunt affair had come into the open. He wanted news of old friends, and there were touches of the old gaiety.'

With the Blunt storm raging outside, Daniel and my sister Lucy tried to keep Rees's room as quiet and peaceful as possible and made sure there were no unwanted intruders. Lucy told me later that she 'threw all caution to the winds' and brought up the subject of The Secret. She said: 'He was in a very mellow mood and most approachable, so I was able to chatter away to him. I think he was suddenly evaluating everything a little differently because he knew he was dying. I asked him if he had been a spy and he said, no. But I said that would not do, I needed to know more ...' Rees told her about Blunt coming to the house to talk to him during the weekend that Guy disappeared but, she said, all these years later he still seemed puzzled by what had happened when he went to see MI 5 and why they had not believed him about Blunt. Lucy tried to make Rees go over it again and work it out like an 'intellectual exercise'. It was unlikely that Blunt could have covered his tracks alone; someone else must also have been involved. There seemed to be three possible names. 'I remember him saying it could not possibly have been Dick White, because he was just not that kind of man,' she said. My sister told me that she did not get the impression from Rees that he had a skeleton in the cupboard. 'He just seem puzzled. Looking back, as he was, I think he thought it was all quite puzzling and interesting.'

Rees told her that he had not been 'absolutely sure' about Blunt until Andrew Boyle came up with the other half of the evidence. 'I asked him what they were doing as spies,' she said. 'He told me that it was possible that because of them people died. I asked if he was talking about the sort of John le Carré stuff, that other spies died. He said no, quite innocent people die as a result of spies.' Then he talked about himself. 'I suddenly had a terribly strong and clear picture of a very Welsh boy, brought up in that very intellectually clean household – clean in terms of clear thinking – and with very little social sophistication, finding himself taken up by the smoothies at Oxford,' she recalled. 'He was not overwhelmed, but he decided it was not for him.' She went on to explain: 'He said what you do is . . . you say this is not for me and go your own way. It was inconceivable to him that you could embrace a whole way of life that depended upon a particular social system and then be a traitor to it . . .'

According to Lucy, Rees did not want to see Andrew Boyle before he died, though he finally agreed to do so, and the result of their talk was published in *The Observer* in January. She said: 'Boyle wanted to talk to him to see what more he could find out, but Rees said he did not know any more and there was nothing he could add.'

But despite the furore in the world outside his room at Charing Cross Hospital, my sister believed that spies were not first and foremost in Rees's mind in those last few weeks of his life. 'What was much more important to him,' she said, 'was that he had decided that he had some faith and he believed that he was going to see Margie again. I don't know how much of it was drugs or morphine, but this is what he was really thinking about.' Her sense of what was on Rees's mind in his final days is a key to a letter from Micky Burn, dated 2 December, which I found among his papers: 'It was wonderful to find you so serene and looking so young and – I can think of no other word – pure, and to know the reason. I do pray that it will continue to give you strength and hope and a kind of lightness in your heart and soul . . .'

Towards the end, my brother Daniel took a bottle of champagne into the hospital every day. Rees wanted his books with him, too. He asked for *The Brothers Karamazov*, Dostoevsky's story of suffering and salvation, guilt and freedom, good and evil, and Dante's *The Divine Comedy*. Daniel recalled: 'He was so ill and very drugged and I was very confused about what was happening. There was a German nurse who bathed him every day, and he spoke his beautiful German to her. She was amazed.' Daniel was with Rees when he died, on 12 December. He later told me: 'It was in the late afternoon and he said he was really not feeling very well and hurting a lot. I went to the sister and said that he needed something and she said that she understood. I held his hand, he hardly said anything except just before he died, he said, if I remember correctly, something along the lines of "What do I do next?" or "I wonder what happens next?" '

The handwriting is very shaky in the letter written from the hospital to Micky on 7 December, which was only five days before he died;

My dear Micky,

I'm at last able to write again and this is almost the first letter I've written, to thank you for all your messages of affection and sympathy, which have helped me to live even when things were worst. I can't tell you what your friendship has meant to me since we met again after Margie's death and it has very largely been your example in your own sorrow and loss which has helped me to accept my own. Nor can I say how much happiness I've had in coming to stay with you at Beudy Gwyn. I only wish I could come again soon.

I shall be leaving here soon, probably for a convalescent home near Sunbury, which sounds very pleasant. I don't know whether the children told you, but the doctors say I probably have a few more months to go, with luck perhaps a year, but now I'm no longer frightened at the prospect. The only thing to regret is all the very beautiful things the world contains and one shall never see again . . .

[*In an earlier letter to Rees, Micky had quoted Cromwell's reputed last words. He is supposed to have said to the minister, 'Can a man fall from grace?', to which the minister replied 'No.' Cromwell then said: 'Thank God, for I knew that I was once in grace.'*] I love the minister's remark to Cromwell. I was brought up a Calvinist and taught that if one was born one of the elect, one never ceased to belong – a doctrine which had strange effects on me . . .

No more now, as writing again makes me a bit tired and there is too much to say and talk about in a letter, but I hope I'll see you on your way to Greece. How I envy you and wish I were coming with you.

With much love,
Goronwy

I still have the final letter my father wrote to me, which he gave to my sister Lucy on the morning of the day he died. In it he wrote: 'Andrew Boyle has written two long pieces for *The Observer* based on my conversations with him. They will appear after Christmas and are,

I think, very good. Fortunately, we divide the proceeds which produces a bit of money . . . Did you know the doctor's prognosis of the course of my disease? They give me three months to, at best, a year. It's a bit of a shock but I am not unhappy about it, nor must you be. The others all know, so I thought you should too. But I should like to see one more spring or summer, which are so lovely, and shall try to make the best of whatever time is left. I shall be leaving here next week and we have found a very nice nursing home at Nettlebed, near Oxford, where I could stay till the end . . . No more now, though there is much to say. Writing makes me a bit tired . . .'

Rees was cremated at Mortlake Cemetery, and my brother Thomas was entrusted with his ashes. After my mother died, I waited for low tide on the river and walked, with the little box containing her ashes, along the muddy foreshore in front of the house at Strand-on-the-Green until I found a weeping willow on the bank. Under its branches I scattered her ashes on to the surface of the water. Just over three years later, Thomas, carrying his little box, found the same place and scattered Rees's ashes there, too. In our earthly way, we had tried to ensure that they were together.

# 13

'Anthony Blunt cast a long shadow over my life, just as I may well
have cast a long shadow over his . . . even from beyond the grave.'

Goronwy Rees to Andrew Boyle, November 1979


It was an eerie sensation to see Rees's face again in a photograph
accompanying Boyle's 'conversations with a dying man', which
appeared in *The Observer* on two successive Sundays in January 1980.
Much of what he was reported to have said did not sound a bit like
Rees. In the first interview, he said it had 'sickened' him to hear Blunt's
'well-bred' voice again, when he had appeared on the television. 'I
felt a little pity for his predicament at first but not for more than a few
moments. His sheer nerve continues to amaze and haunt me . . .' The
second interview focused on the weekend of Guy's disappearance and
Rees's disastrous decision to write the articles for *The People*. According to Boyle, Rees told him: 'I had hoped that my disclosures might
lead to public demands for an enquiry into the conspiracy in which
others besides Blunt, Philby and the two known Foreign Office spies
had been implicated. Instead, I was hounded down. I could only
surmise the extent of Blunt's involvement and wondered how far and
how persistently the security services were seeking to unravel it. Blunt
must have rejoiced at my discomfiture . . .' There was to be no RIP
for my father. After his death, it was open season for those who had
condemned him to say what they could not say while he was alive.
On one or two occasions, I became so angry that I wrote to newspapers
that persisted in bringing up his name. I knew that any further details
of his 'complicity' in the spy ring could come only from the security
services or from Blunt.

Anthony Blunt died in March 1983. Before he did so, he had given
one of his very few interviews to Robert Cecil, the retired diplomat
and writer, who was engaged in research for a study of the Cambridge
ring that appeared in a book called *The Missing Dimension* in 1984.
Cecil had excellent sources and his introduction to the notes on the
chapter he contributed struck a particular cord with me: 'The writer
claims good authority for all unqualified statements; he has not in all
cases been able to disclose what it is. He wishes to express his thanks
to all those, named and unnamed, who have helped him in verifying

a series of events, some of which necessarily remain shrouded in darkness . . .' I was in Berlin in the summer of 1984 when I received a telephone call from Peter Hennessy, then working for *The Times*, who wanted my reaction to Blunt's allegation, made in this book, that Rees was in the spy ring. I said I did not believe that my father was an agent and that Blunt's accusation was part of a 'settling of an old score'. My words did not get into *The Times*, even after Hennessy's shrewd tactics in tracking me down, and I later wished I had told him that I was about to cross to the 'other side'. Hennessy's story went like this:

Writer who 'exposed Blunt, also a spy'

by Peter Hennessy

Anthony Blunt, the art historian and former MI5 officer who spied for the Soviet Union, shortly before he died accused the late Goronwy Rees of having been a Soviet agent in the 1930s. Mr Rees exposed Blunt's activities to MI5 in 1951 after the flight of Burgess and Maclean to Moscow.

The deal that Mr Rees allegedly made with Blunt and Burgess in 1939, that neither would betray the others as agents of the Comintern, is disclosed by Mr Robert Cecil, a retired diplomat, in a book published today. Mr Cecil interviewed Blunt in the spring of 1982 while preparing his study of the 'Cambridge Comintern', which forms part of a collection of essays in *The Missing Dimension*.

Mr Cecil said yesterday: 'I asked Blunt if it was true, as Rees writes in his book, *A Chapter of Accidents*, that Burgess was shocked by the news of the Hitler–Stalin pact of August, 1939. He said: 'No. It was Rees who was shocked and said he could not work for the Soviet Union any longer.

'Faced with this awkward situation,' Mr Cecil continued, 'Blunt and Burgess decided to appear to go along with this; all three would end their careers as Soviet agents and agree never to give one another away.'

Asked if it was right to break a story of this kind, Mr Cecil replied: 'Not in the ordinary way. But espionage seems to me to come into a special category.

'Too much has been covered up and this has only stimulated speculation. The sad story of Goronwy Rees is a cautionary tale and this is surely a time when we need cautionary tales.'

Rees's death had the most curious effect on me. I felt stunned by the speed with which so much seemed to have gone, disappeared. I had lost my mother and my father within such a short period of time. How I could have felt so alone, with my children and my sister and brothers, I do not know, but I did. Rees and my mother had, in their passing, taken most of my life with them, I felt as if it had been torn from me, leaving a sharp, jagged edge. We took great comfort from the many letters we received from Rees's friends and admirers all over the world.

Shortly after his death, we received a delightful letter from the Warden of All Souls, Sir Patrick Neill, who offered to organize a memorial service for Rees in the college chapel. He told my brother Daniel that he had known Rees quite well in the fifties. He remembered a 'convivial' evening in the Warden's Lodgings, after it was known that he was to succeed John Sparrow as Warden. 'Your father had an enormous sense of fun and was a most entertaining companion,' he wrote.

Among the letters was one from Isaiah Berlin; we later asked him if he would give the address at the memorial service, but he said he did not feel he could; it was too difficult to know how to deal with the spy aspect of Rees's life. We quite understood. On the day after Rees's death, Isaiah wrote to Daniel: 'Your father's death is a deep grief to me. I had thought that he was to be moved to a nursing home not far from Oxford on Friday; and so I was arranging to see him today; and this morning someone from *Encounter* telephoned to say it was no good. Of course, you must have gone over every aspect in your mind about how it might be – you knew as I did that he could not live long – but no matter what one imagines one's state of mind would be, when it happens it is always much worse; and nothing is ever the same; and the thought that I will never see him again – he told me so when I went to him ten or so days ago – is one I cannot get used to at all. I first got to know him when we were both undergraduates – in 1931, I think – and we became great friends: I became deeply fond of him and remained so through thick and thin – the thick used to occur more than the thin – things always looked brighter, gayer, and delightful when he was there: I loved his company more than anyone's in the thirties and the forties and the fifties – and really at all times, even when difference divided us, as happened in the mid-fifties – and when I saw him again … all the old feelings returned and his marvellous life-enhancing, exhilarating qualities, his imagination, his affectionateness, his vitality and bright qualities made up for everything. I knew he was going through a difficult time after your mother was no more: and I used to have lunch with him, and see him in Oxford, and it was always, always a source of unique delight to me; nobody ever made things sparkle more . . .: his voice, his laugh haunt me now. I ought to have taken more trouble; seen him oftener. He was a genuine lifelong friend: and he thought so too. I must not go on: words are useless when really frightful things happen – they are like matchsticks and convey nothing. I am terribly distressed . . .'

If there were to be a memorial service, he wrote, he did not want to be asked to give the address: 'Too much painful feeling.'

In the end Rees's friend, John Sparrow, gave the address at the memorial service and not a word about spies was mentioned. It was a Saturday in the March following his death and many friends gathered in the beautiful chapel of All Souls to remember him. It was a very simple service, and ended with the prayer: 'O Lord, support us all the day long of this troublous life, till the shadows lengthen and the evening comes, the busy world is hushed, the fever of life is over and our work done. Then, Lord, in Thy mercy, grant us safe lodging, a holy rest, and peace at the last.' Sparrow's address was masterly. Remembering Goronwy, he said, was not quite like remembering other friends, who changed with the years, so that the older man will seem, when recalled, a different person, at least in some respects, from the man he was when he was young.

This was not the case with Rees, Sparrow continued: 'For me, whenever I think of Goronwy, it is always the same image that presents itself: it is Goronwy as I first knew him, when we were undergraduates together at New College, I have come to accept the fact that it was fifty years ago: what I find impossible to accept is that Goronwy was seventy years old when he died. And I don't think that this is due to a failure on my part to perceive a manysidedness in the man, or changes worked upon him by the years. Goronwy was – so to speak – all of a piece; and I don't think he ever changed, I don't think he ever grew up.'

Sparrow described his own memory of Rees: 'Let me try to reproduce the picture that presents itself to me when I think of him. He is talking – probably arguing; lively, with bright, intelligent eyes; his words come bubbling out unrestrainedly; he is never solemn; never, never pompous; laughter, or the possibility of laughter, is never far away. This does not mean he is not serious; indeed, he easily becomes indignant. He is warm-hearted; he doesn't calculate; he doesn't – perhaps – stop to consider. If he is unreliable, it is because he is at the mercy of his emotions, and because his emotions are so strong...'

A Peter Pan? A romantic? Mad? Bad? Dangerous to know? A disaster? Frivolous? Irresponsible? *A Spy*? What was my father? In the years that followed, I struggled to work out the puzzle, to no avail. I felt I could not let him go until I had, somehow, caught him in my hand so that I could study him, like a butterfly, on my palm. I was plagued by a riddle. He had told us he had not been a spy. This was either the truth, or, because he was a spy, he had lied.

When young, I never questioned my father and my love for him was the unconditional love of a child. I did not like myself for questioning him after his death. I felt I was challenging him. But somewhere, deep inside me, there was this insidious doubt. I could not be absolutely sure of him. Even towards the end of my quest for the truth of his 'other' life, I was still haunted by this sense of something unresolved.

I turned back to the piles of papers I had collected on my journey to see how others had interpreted the strange course of Rees's life. I had to know the truth about him. 'He was often described as a rogue,' Noël Annan had said. 'He was not reliable, he enjoyed making mischief, I don't know that he deliberately threw away his life, it is sometimes accidental and it is sometimes due to inner failings, weakness, irresolution. He was a man who let things happen to him...'

Isaiah felt that Rees had ruined his life through 'inconstancy': he wandered from one thing to another, enjoying himself. 'Goronwy was a source of life and pleasure to a lot of people. But there was no steady line in him,' he said. 'He did not really know what he wanted. He only wanted to enjoy himself; he was involved in some kind of stream of vitality. I don't think he was amoral, he knew perfectly well the difference between right and wrong. Guy was immoral. But Rees denounced those innocent people, for no reason at all, he accused people without evidence because he felt like it.' Isaiah thought it was because of 'something Welsh' in him and that Rees was like Lloyd George – 'also delightful and also charming and also a source of instant life'. He had a story for me that he thought illustrated Rees. 'Once, when I was visiting Palestine,' he said, 'I went to a trial where one Arab was accused of stealing sheep from another Arab. It was proved that the first Arab had not lost any sheep, so that what he said was false. When he was asked, "Why did you accuse him of stealing the sheep when you knew he had not?", he replied, "Maybe I was very angry." That could have been Goronwy.'

Isaiah thought that 'scamp' might be an appropriate word for Rees. It made him sound like Sergeant Troy, in *Far from the Madding Crowd*. I looked the word up in the *Shorter Oxford Dictionary* and selected the second definition as the one I was probably seeking: 'A good-for-nothing, a worthless person; a rogue, a rascal. Now also, a mischievous person, esp. a child . . .' Stuart Hampshire told me that Maurice Bowra had always said that Rees had a compulsion to 'stab somebody'.

At the start of my quest I had turned to those closest to my father to see if they could enlighten me on what had happened all those years ago to give him his unenviable reputation. It seemed to me that I could go on talking to people for ever without anyone producing any proof of my father's complicity in the spy ring, proof I had to have. I needed more than speculation before crossing the line between believing him and not believing him. I had to widen my net.

One of those to whom I wrote next was Lord Greenhill, who, when he was Permanent Under-Secretary at the Foreign Office and head of the Diplomatic Service was involved in tidying up the mess left behind by Burgess and Maclean. Many of my letters to people I hoped could help me went unanswered and I did not count on hearing from him. But early one morning in March 1993 the telephone rang and a cheery voice announced itself as that of Denis Greenhill. Taken by surprise, I mumbled something about being interested in his views on my father's possible involvement in the spy ring. He said he could not tell me much as he had never met Rees, though he could tell me what was said about him. 'He was said to be a communist,' he told me, 'He was a buddy of theirs and it was inconceivable to me that, whether paid or not, he did not, either consciously or unconsciously, help them. He was said to be somebody to steer well clear of. There was a black mark against his name.'

Was I getting closer to something in the 'wilderness of mirrors'? I did not know. I felt as if I was going round and round in circles, like a dog chasing its tail. 'No one,' my father once said, talking about the importance of reading novels, 'can ever really know what goes on in someone else's head.'

Over the months, as I pursued my work of detection, I had, very slowly, come to the realization that I might never find what I was looking for. I had hoped that by discussing Rees's character – the one he said he did not possess – his failings and his virtues with his friends and his critics, and by putting all the pieces together, I would ultimately arrive at a point where I could, with some certainty, reach a kind of truth about his life. But although I had learned more than I ever expected, and, in the process, had built up a portrait of the father whom I felt I did not know, there remained at the back of my mind a sense that the answer to the remaining unsolved mystery could not be found here, in these islands. With some foreboding, I came to the conclusion that there was only one place where Rees's 'Secret' was to be discovered: Moscow. I had to go over to the other side. But how could this be done? The more I considered the prospect, the more remote seemed my chances of any kind of success.

Then, in one of those strokes of fate that are the stuff of dreams, I was given a telephone number . . .

# 14

Every man shall bear his own burden

Epistle of Paul the Apostle
to the Galatians, 6:5

When *Deadly Illusions* by John Costello and Oleg Tsarev was published in July 1993, I was about to set off on a tour of Wales to look up Rees's connections there. I could not shift the sense of anxiety and fear that always overcame me when yet another spy book appeared, expecting that it was going to disturb and upset me with yet more allegations about Rees. But this book was different. It was the first history of Soviet espionage operations to be written with direct access to the KGB files: a collaboration between an English historian who had written a book about Anthony Blunt and a former KGB colonel who had become historical consultant to the newly-named Russian Foreign Intelligence Service. It was a large, fat volume, with a shiny black cover marked, sensationally, 'Top Secret: The KGB secrets the British Government doesn't want you to read.'

I looked up my father in the index; there he was, but this time with a code name, GROSS. As usual, there were few page references beside his name but, looking them up as I always did, I came to page 245 and saw something I had never seen before in an extract from a report sent to Moscow Centre by Guy's control officer in 1938.

It read: 'The kind of work which he [*Burgess*] would do with great moral satisfaction and with absolute confidence in its success and effectiveness is the recruitment by us of young people graduating from Oxford and Cambridge Universities and preparing them to enter the Civil Service. For this kind of work, he has such assistants as TONY in Cambridge and GROSS in Oxford. MÄDCHEN [*Burgess*] always returns to this idea at every meeting, motivating it by the argument that only this kind of agent can give us truly trustworthy information.'

Costello and Tsarev went on to explain: 'The references to TONY and GROSS are the original code names given to Anthony Blunt and Burgess's friend, Goronwy Rees. That neither bore German cryptonyms like the 'Three Musketeers' [*Philby, Maclean and Burgess*] indicates that Blunt and Rees were not among the first generation of Cambridge recruits. Blunt's rather too obvious code name was later changed to JOHNSON in wartime cryptograms from the NKVD *rezidentura* in the Soviet embassy. But it was as TONY and in collaboration with Burgess that his induction coincided with the second phase of the expansion of the Cambridge group into a network...'

According to the records, Blunt was recruited by Guy at, or around, the beginning of 1937. In his debriefing by the KGB in 1952, Burgess had pointed out that Blunt evolved from a 'talent scout' to a key source for the Soviets during the war, when he was in MI5. Blunt wrote to Moscow in 1943: 'To characterize my activity in the period since 1937 up to the beginning of the war, I did almost nothing. I started to do our work and also tried to do a rather difficult task – that is to create the impression that I did not share the views of the left wing, while on the other hand to be in the closest contact with the undergraduates of the left wing so that I could spot talent – the people who were of interest to us ...' There were no details about my father's role, but the book stated that Rees, who had been recruited by Burgess, had 'broken away' in 1939 in protest against the Soviet–German pact.

I turned the pages to the final reference to Rees. This was in a footnote relating to the KGB 'illegal' undercover agent in London, Arnold Deutsch, who, with his colleague, Ignaty Reif, recruited Philby, Burgess and Maclean, on the directions of the masterspy, Alexander Orlov, the *éminence grise* of the Cambridge spy ring. Deutsch, a Czech by birth, who operated under the legitimate cover of being an academic researcher attached to London University, enlisted and ran seventeen British spies before he was obliged to leave England at the end of 1937, leaving no control officer in charge of the group until spring 1938. The footnote explains that Deutsch included Rees as part of what he defined as the 'Cambridge Group', as opposed to a separate 'Oxford Group': 'This was because this Welsh socialist, although a Fellow of All Souls, Oxford, was recruited in 1938 through recommendation and his close association with Guy Burgess.'

The book included a letter from Donald Maclean to an officer at Moscow Centre dated 25 April 1938, which caught my eye because I saw the name of Lord Halifax mentioned in it. Then working at the Foreign Office, Maclean wrote:

Dear Comrade,
    This is to say first of all how glad I am to be in touch and working again.

As you will have heard, I have no reason to think that my position is not quite sound, and I think the arrangements which we [*Burgess and Philby*] have made for work should be all right ... With regard to the work, I will let you have, as before, all I can, which will be chiefly the printed dispatches & telegrams, & such secret reports and particularly interesting papers as come my way. This time we are sending some dispatches & a good many telegrams; it would be useful to know how many of the latter you would like – a lot of them are I think of little value. We have also sent a memorandum by Collier, head of the Northern [*Russian*] Department about British policy generally in regard to Spain, together with the comments thereon of the high Foreign Office authorities. The document is, I think, of considerable interest. Collier takes the more or less left-wing anti-Fascist line, which, as you will remember, he has long followed, but all the rest of them who comment, Halifax, Momsey, Plymouth and Cadogan, are as was to be expected, unanimously in favour of the present policy of conciliation with Italy & consequent acceptance of a Franco victory ... I heard yesterday that the 3rd Musketeer [*Burgess*] has had a breakdown of some kind and has had to go away for two months. I have not seen him myself for many months so do not know if this is likely to be true, but I shall be sorry if it is ...

There was also a psychological profile of Guy, written by Deutsch in Moscow in 1939. Deutsch, according to the records, found Guy a 'very temperamental and emotional man and ... easily subject to mood swings'. He was 'well-educated', 'extremely well read', but 'superficial'. Deutsch remarked: 'He speaks very well, willingly and a lot.' He reported: 'Many features of his character can be explained by the fact that he is a homosexual. He became one at Eton, where he grew up in an atmosphere of cynicism, opulence, hypocrisy and superficiality. As he is very clever and well educated, the Party was for him a saviour. It gave him above all an opportunity to satisfy his intellectual needs. Therefore he took up Party work with great enthusiasm. Part of his private life is led in a circle of homosexual friends whom he recruited among a wide variety of people, ranging from the famous liberal economist Keynes and extending to the very trash of society down to male prostitutes. His personal degradation, drunkenness, irregular way of life and the feeling of being outside society was connected with this kind of life, but on the other hand his abhorrence of bourgeois morality came from this. This kind of life did not satisfy him. His homosexuality he explains is not inborn because he can also live with women. He learned it at Eton because everyone is engaged in homosexuality there, so he simply joined in ...' Burgess, as a probationary candidate for the ring, was asked to produce a list of friends and contacts; in a four-page letter he provided the names of two hundred people.

I had to know more, and set my sights on Oleg Tsarev. In his foreword, he explained that he had joined the First Chief Directorate of the KGB in 1970, after studying at the Moscow Institute of International Relations, when he had attended lectures given by Kim Philby. He came to London as an agent in 1974, working under the cover of being a journalist for five years. He related how, in 1989, four years after the beginning of *Perestroika*, the KGB publicly admitted for the first time that there was an intelligence service that operated in peacetime; he took a job in the newly-established press office of the service, which was besieged by requests for information from foreign journalists when it was decided to open up the archives. However, when he searched through the steel cabinets filled with the records of seventy years of Soviet intelligence work, he discovered that any research project would not be easy.

Tsarev pointed out that intelligence records could not be considered 'archives' in the traditional historiographic sense of the word because they are collections of operational documents compiled to serve the practical needs of running agents. Some of the reports in the files are not even stitched into the bound volumes in chronological order; others have been placed in files relating to particular operations or even turn up under an entirely different subject. Soviet intelligence officers never thought that their files would become historical source material: many reports are undated, or misdated, as well as misfiled.

Naturally, I had reservations about making a personal approach to Tsarev. Would he tell me more about my father? Could he tell me more about my father? Could I believe him? There were those who were highly sceptical about the credibility of the information coming out of the KGB files. There were stories of researchers wandering about Moscow with huge wads of money. There had already been a muddle over Hiss, of whose guilt Whittaker Chambers wrote in his extraordinary book, *Witness*. In 1992, General Dimitri Volkogonov, chairman of the Russian government's military archives, said that recently opened records contained no evidence that Hiss spied for Russia. Hiss, who was jailed for perjury in 1950, was delighted. But, two months later, the general said he could not be so sure; he had not made as thorough a search of the files as he first implied. I turned it over and over in my mind and decided that I did not really care any longer about what other people said; I had come so close to my goal and I *had* to know.

It was on 16 July 1993 that I picked up the telephone and dialled the number I had been given for Tsarev. It was, oddly, the day that Stella Rimington, Director of Security Services, announced that MI5 was going to reveal some secrets about itself in an HMSO publication.

I had already spoken to the intelligence historian, Christopher Andrew, in Cambridge about whether the word 'recruit' – used, to my knowledge, for the first time in the context of Rees, in *Deadly Illusions*, – could possibly be right. 'Using "recruitment" is difficult', he said. 'They weren't so much recruited as dying to volunteer. It was such fun. Rees could have been a "sub" agent. Those who were fully recruited had to fulfil two conditions – willingness to take instructions and acceptance of clandestinity.'

When I rang Tsarev's number in Moscow, a voice told me that he would not be in until 4 p.m. I went out to Sainsbury's and wandered about in a daze, standing in front of the shelves deep in thought. My younger son, Benjamin, was moving into a new house the following day, and I found that I was talking to myself as I walked around with the trolley: 'Should I take some Flash to clean the bath? . . . I'd better take a bottle of wine so that we can celebrate . . . what did Christopher Andrew say about files? . . . did Rees *really* agree to take instructions?'

I picked up the telephone again and rang the Moscow number. Tsarev was in. I told him I was concerned about seeing this word 'recruited' in his book. His English was perfect, his voice smooth and reassuringly accustomed to intonations. It was all those years he spent in London, 'Oh, no,' he said, 'he did not co-operate. Nothing happened actually.' He told me that my father was supposed to provide political hearsay but that he did not co-operate and after the Soviet–German pact nothing more was heard of him. At that time the Cambridge ring was out of touch with Moscow, agents were being recalled and assassinated. The references to my father, he said, were in the Burgess file.

Tsarev said he knew no more; he had seen no file on Rees and, as 'nothing had happened', it was possible that none existed. Would it be possible to find out if there was a file, I asked? Tsarev replied: 'I don't know, but you can see it if we have it . . .' I was stunned. But surely, I said, that would not be allowed. The smooth voice continued: 'It would be. You are entitled, as his daughter, to see what we have.' I imagined months of tortuously difficult correspondence ahead of me which would never come to anything. 'How do I go about this, then?' I asked, realizing how ill-equipped I was for such a mission. He answered, as if it was the most obvious thing in the world: 'Well, you send us a fax . . .'

The formalities over, I thanked him, said goodbye and sat down for what seemed like a very long time on the chair by the telephone in the hall. Tiny things became very important; I needed to open a communication channel, I needed a 'safe' fax machine, far from prying eyes. I did not want intimate details of my father's life to come chattering through a public machine. I rang a friend: 'I wonder if I could send a fax to the KGB from your house and give them your number so that they can reply?' He took it in his stride. 'Of course, come round.' I sat at the table in the dining-room and wrote out a letter to Yuri Kobaladze, head of Tsarev's office. It went something like this:

Dear Mr Kobaladze,
I have been speaking today to Mr Tsarev about references made in his book, *Deadly Illusions*, to my late father, GORONWY REES. I was very shocked by what I read, because my father always said that he had not been a Comintern agent and I hoped I could believe him. It is impossible to find out anything here, but many books have been published which have accused him of complicity. This has been very distressing for my family, as I am sure you can understand . . . Mr Tsarev suggested I should make an official application to you to request your help on this matter. Could you assist me to find out the truth about my father's exact role? . . . I know that you will appreciate how important this is to me on a personal level . . .
                                        With all best wishes . . .

As I faxed the letter through, I thought over what Tsarev had said about Rees not co-operating. That seemed more than possible, even probable. Why should Rees, who had never really applied himself to anything by that time in his life, suddenly become terribly serious and committed? It almost made me laugh to think that Guy might have relied on him. It was not until two weeks later that I received a fax from Tsarev, informing me that the search would involve time and effort as some of the required data was scattered over a number of files. He would be in touch again when he had found something.

It was not until October that Tsarev told me he had completed his researches and was ready to talk to me. Before I could really take stock of what had happened, I found myself standing in the queue outside the large shabby house in the Bayswater Road, which is the visa section of the Russian Embassy. It was not an easy country to get into, and in view of the siege of the White House in Moscow earlier in the month it looked as if the situation might become even more complicated. We were an odd collection standing on the pavement. In front of me was a young man from Gerrard's Cross who wanted to visit St Petersburg to see a girl he had fallen in love with and there were some rather grey businessmen with battered briefcases. The storming of the White House had frightened off potential tourists and the couriers from the travel agencies, applying for group visas, were complaining about the lack of business. My first application was a flop; the clerk behind the little glass window told me I would have to wait three weeks for a visa and that my 'support' document was not in order. As I did not want to sit miserably in a Moscow hotel room after being told something shaming about my father, I had decided that I would take my son, Benjamin, with me. But we were caught in the Catch 22 situation that used to be such a feature of travelling during the Cold War: no visa, no ticket; no ticket, no visa.

I asked Tsarev for help in cutting through the red tape and, the next time I presented myself at the embassy, I was not asked to join a queue but met by an official, who, if not exactly smiling, appeared to want to give the impression that he was pleased to have been of service as he handed me our passports, complete with visas. There was no charge, he said. One of Tsarev's faxes had done the job.

On our first morning in Moscow, Ben and I set off from the hotel to keep the appointment at Tsarev's office. It was cold and the sky was overcast. We followed his instructions and passed the big Lubyanka building – the former KGB headquarters – on the way. The blue-grey house with the shiny black door to which he had directed us was once the residence of Viktor Semyonovich Abakumov, a former NKVD chairman. I felt very detached from reality as we walked along, with one half of me looking at what was going on in the Moscow streets and the other half thinking of Rees in the thirties. We stopped on the corner of Dzerzhinsky Square to watch the new market economy in action; a small 'enterprise zone' had been set up on the pavement and people had arranged themselves behind wooden boxes to sell whatever they had to sell; home-grown tomatoes, packets of American cigarettes, two or three candles, bananas. It was noisy and bustling. There was some impromptu foreign-exchange dealing in progress, too; Ben worked out the rates. I wondered what Tsarev had managed to find for me and what he looked like; it was difficult to tell from the blurred photograph on the dust-jacket of *Deadly Illusions*.

When I rang the bell of the blue-grey house, it was answered by one of two men who were speaking to each other in Russian and had been disturbed, I realized, when they sat down again at a table in the hall, smoking and talking. We sat on a sofa and waited, looking around at our surroundings. I felt we could have been waiting in the entrance hall of a doctor's or a dentist's house in Paris or in Kensington. There were some fur hats hanging on the hat stand and it was warm and centrally heated. A man I recognized as Tsarev came down the wide staircase to meet us, and we went up with him to the first floor where he showed us into an interview room looking out on to the street which, he said, was not his office. There was 1950s functional furniture, a personal computer and two telephones on the desk. Tsarev was doing all the talking and, I realized, trying to put me at my ease. As a present, I had brought him a bottle of malt whisky which I put on the desk. I took out my packet of cigarettes and sat down; he took out his and sat down opposite. He was immaculately dressed in a style that was a mixture of European and East Coast American: navy-blue blazer with gold buttons, grey flannels, black brogues and an Oxford striped shirt with a buttoned-down collar. He was short and stocky, built like the hooker in a rugby football team. We were both a little nervous.

I began by asking him about his next book, which I understood was about Soviet intelligence operations in Britain. He told me that he was writing it chapter by chapter and his daughter, Xenia, who went to school in Kensington for five years while he was based in London, was translating it into English. I mentioned that Costello had told me that this book would reveal the existence of an 'Oxford' spy ring but that it was RIS policy not to divulge the names of agents who had not confessed themselves: the 'caring' face, so to speak, of the new Russian Intelligence Service. There was another aspect to it, Tsarev said. 'If we go giving away names, we shall lose the co-operation of those who have co-operated with us in our research … I've not yet decided how to present the Oxford ring. Probably we will just give the code names, but not in circumstances which will lead to identification …'

We spoke briefly about code names and then I pounced. I asked: 'At the end of your book, you said that my father had been recruited in 1938 and that he broke in 1939 ... Was "recruited" the right word? I understand that there were various stages they went through before becoming a fully-fledged agent ...' Tsarev said: 'Fully-fledged agent, no. But he knew he was co-operating with the Soviet intelligence service. They were recruited for the cause, the communist cause.' I told him that I had established, through tracing my father's article about South Wales in *The Spectator*, that Guy had told Rees in November 1937 that he was working for the Comintern, and asked whether there was any reference to this incident in the files. I needed verification, if that were possible.

Tsarev said that the files were in not in good order: many Soviet agents were recalled from London at that time because of Stalin's purges. The information he had uncovered was that Rees was recruited by Burgess, with the authority of Leonid Eitingon, code-name PIERRE, who was in Paris at the time. (Eitingon, I was to learn later, was chosen to lead the team that murdered Trotsky in Mexico in 1940,) All was turmoil in London then, he said. He was not sure of the date of the recruitment, but felt it must have been 1938 because that was the year Eitingon was moved from Paris to Spain. Burgess had his contacts with Soviet intelligence in Paris, and Eitingon used to travel from Barcelona to see him. This was all in Burgess's file, Tsarev said, but added that one always had to be a little careful about Burgess. 'He often acted on his own initiative ...' It might well have been that Burgess approached Rees in 1937 and asked for Eitingon's consent to recruit him later. The British networks, he explained, were 'put on ice' in 1937 and, without a control in London, acted independently of Moscow. Burgess's report on the recruitment of Rees was also on file. Tsarev continued: 'Rees wanted to join the Communist Party and asked Burgess about it. Burgess said "Oh, no, don't do that, stay outside, you can do more outside." It was the same old story. He said their talk was simple and straightforward.' Rees, he had most probably made a commitment to the cause in the hope that the Russians were going to fight the Germans.

Tsarev's book stated that from October 1937, Burgess was out of direct contact with Moscow for nearly ten months. His NKVD file shows that the Centre's link with him was restored in Paris in August 1938 through Eitingon, then serving as deputy to Alexander Orlov who masterminded the recruitment of Philby, Maclean and Burgess. Eitingon continued to run Burgess from Spain, requiring both to travel to Paris, until the Centre decided, in March 1939, that a new

London 'legal' *rezident*, Gorsky, should take over Burgess's control. According to *Deadly Illusions*: 'It irked the chiefs in the Lubyanka to learn that MÄDCHEN [Guy's code name] had chosen to act entirely on his own initiative during the hiatus after the recall of Mally and Deutsch had left the Cambridge group temporarily without a control officer.' It was very difficult, Tsarev said, to establish exactly what had happened between 1938 and 1939, because reports did not reach Moscow. Lavrenty Beria, the deputy chief of the NKVD, would, he said, 'close down the London station and then he would open it up again and he would recall people and send them back. Everything was topsy-turvy, people were nervous.' Nobody cared very much for intelligence work at that time; everyone was preoccupied with the impending war.

So, I had established, somewhere there was a piece of paper on which Guy had recorded 'recruiting' my father, at a time when he was not being closely 'managed' by a control officer in England. What did Rees provide, as a collaborator? I asked. Tsarev did not know: 'But, for the moment, we can assume it was political hearsay.' Guy, he said, had written a long paper on how Soviet intelligence should work in British universities, especially in Oxford and Cambridge. He told Moscow that he had got TONY in Cambridge and GROSS in Oxford, as talent-spotters. But, Tsarev pointed out, GROSS never 'realized' himself in the role that Burgess singled out for him. 'We know he did not, because the talent-spotter was somebody else ...' Rees, he explained, could not be described as an 'agent' – with his consent, he was a 'source', and 'operational contact' – although he knew what the cause was and he knew that any information he gave Guy would go to the Soviet Union. In Tsarev's view, Rees's agreement to co-operate with Guy could be put down to 'romanticism and to ideological conviction'.

Guy, according to the records, came to believe he was playing a central part in the evolution of the scheme to recruit 'moles' who could be sent to burrow in the Civil Service and the intelligence services. In a memorandum he compiled, 'Work Among Students for the Preparation of Them for the Civil Service', which was forwarded to Moscow in March 1939, he wrote: 'The organization of work among university students is of the greatest importance because, through this work, we could control the regular inflow of people who are going to enter the Civil Service and whom it would be possible to recruit before they become too well known and to arrange for them to secure posts in one or another branch of the Civil Service. Two of the most important universities are, of course, Oxford and Cambridge. To conduct such work there we need somebody who is in close contact with students.'

I now had proof that there was a definite, and recorded, start to the collaboration between Rees and Guy, though aspects of it were still frustratingly elusive. At the time in question, Rees had only his links with All Souls, which did not involve mixing with undergraduates, and he spent nearly all his time in London. Tsarev had said that 'someone else' was, in fact, the talent-spotter and Rees's role remained shadowy. He had two pieces of information for me, he had said. I wondered what else he could tell me.

The second item turned out to be about the Soviet–German pact, which had persuaded Rees to break with communism. There was a report, said Tsarev written by Burgess just after the Pact was signed, informing Moscow that Goronwy Rees said he was 'disappointed' and that he did not want to go on. In this report, Guy had told Moscow: 'I said the same to him, just to cover my activity, and kept on working.' It was an operational report, Tsarev explained, which stated that Rees, a British journalist, who was recruited by MÄDCHEN, refused to co-operate after the pact. 'We hear no more of him after that' said Tsarev.

So, according to the files, Guy told Rees that *he was not going to continue either.* I knew from Robert Cecil's interview with Blunt in March 1983 that Blunt had said he had finished, too, at the time of the Pact. I thought of all those people who had condemned my father as weak, easily led and impressionable. I could see no reason why Rees should not have taken Guy at his word and believed that the little gang of three – himself, Burgess and Blunt – had, together, abandoned the cause in August 1939. This would explain why he went on seeing them throughout and after the war; the shock and the panic he felt when he discovered that Guy had defected was sincere and understandable, as was his reaction to Blunt's attempt to dissuade him from telling MI5 of what he knew about Guy's activities.

Tsarev had yet another piece of information, but not for me. It was, he said, information of a 'strictly personal and intimate character'. This is how our conversation went:

JR: You know something else, do you, about Rees that you are not going to tell me?

OT: (*after a long silence, a sigh*)

JR: Yes?

OT: Yes, but that is his business. We shouldn't talk about it.

JR: Is it something about homosexuality?

OT: (*looking very uncomfortable*) No.

JR: Is it to do with his love affairs . . . Rosamond?

OT: Well, she is mentioned and some other lady is mentioned. But it is our policy not to tell and it should not go into your book.

JR: Can you remember the initial of her Christian name?

OT: I can't remember, actually.

JR: Would the ladies in the love affairs have been of interest to you?

OT: No, it has nothing to do with us.

JR: How do you know about it?

OT: I just came across this information . . . in the late thirties.

JR: Late thirties . . . meaning after 1936?

OT: Yes, the report is at about that time. But I am not sure the events took place then.

JR: Has it anything to do with communism?

OT: (*shaking his head*) It is strictly personal. It has nothing to do with the intelligence services. It is just that somebody mentions this . . . and that's all. It was not exploited in any way. There are all sorts of bits of information in our files which have no relation to intelligence work. This is intimate business which should be buried . . .


When I walked out of the house with Ben, the crows were still busy in the snow, but I had no interest in them. In the drab interview room, where we had sat and talked and smoked a large number of cigarettes, I had learned everything I wanted to know about my father; the mystery had been solved. It was as if I had been let out of a trap that had been holding me, painfully, in one place for so long. It was an exhilarating sensation. I felt liberated. For, although I had not wanted to hear what I heard, a great weight had been lifted from me. All at once I seemed to have been released from the numbing hold of a predicament which had prevented me from letting go of my father and putting his life behind me. At last I could move forward, which he and my mother would want me to do, and, at last, I would be able to give my own children an account of their grandfather's life.

Talking to Tsarev had been like visiting a healer, I later realized. For the first time in my life I had managed to find someone to whom

I could speak about this area of my father's life, who had no personal interest in it whatsoever. Tsarev had not known Rees. He did not feel himself tricked or deceived or let down or involved. He did not cast judgments. His interest was detached and academic. I also realized that I had never been able to discuss this subject with anyone with any success before. It had even divided me from my sister and my brothers. Talking about our father led to arguments because we each saw him in a different light. I had tried to bring up the subject of his 'other life' with friends many times and in many different ways, but no matter how I approached it, the first mention of the word 'spy' proved a conversation-stopper. Strange looks always followed or nervously told jokes, often about John le Carré. With Tsarev, however it was as if I had come in from the cold. I felt there were no barriers between us; there were no questions I could not ask. I did not have to choose my words carefully; he knew I was not just indulging in a private fantasy. I am sure he did not wish to be comforting, but he was. In years to come, there may be many more disclosures about Rees, but my fear of further surprises disappeared in that interview room in Moscow. My uncomfortable and unpleasant sense of shame for not believing Rees had gone. I did not feel angry with him any longer. I knew why he had deceived me; he could not have done otherwise. At last I could think of my father with love, understanding and compassion. I felt a very great sadness about all that he and my mother had been through together.

At last I had discovered The Secret. *This* was my father's burden. I thought of the many people who had told me that my father was a man with a burden. I also remembered an incident at All Souls after the war which Isaiah had mentioned to me. One day, when he was with my father, they met a politician carrying a copy of Whittaker Chambers's *Witness* that had just been published in the United States: 'Rees said to him "Can you lend me that book?" as if it were very important. I thought he identified himself with Chambers ... by which I assumed he had been a communist.'

And I remembered something that my brother Daniel had said to me when we were sitting in the garden of a pub in Norfolk, talking about Rees. He said he thought Rees suffered from a sense of guilt, guilt that he had made the terrible mistake of backing the wrong side, and that he had carried that guilt to the end of his life. Rees had considered himself to be one of the enlightened few who embraced communism but, instead, he had found himself horribly mistaken.

Rees had spoken to Daniel of all those thousands of people killed by Stalin: deaths, to which he had, as it were, given his consent. This was the prison, almost, in which he was confined and from which there was no escape. Alcohol made it go away for a bit, but the burden was always there. Seven years before he died, Rees had written of Stalin: 'He was so . . . successful that, whatever his victims may have thought, large numbers of people were to be found in the West who accepted his claims without question. It is one of the greatest ironies of history that, at a time when Stalin's terror was at its height, the prestige of the Soviet Union, as the last best hope of mankind, never stood higher in Western radical and intellectual circles . . .'

Turning Tsarev's words over and over in my mind, I walked, with Ben beside me, back towards the Kremlin. The winter light was already beginning to fade. Tsarev had told us that we should walk along the avenue where Pushkin took his constitutionals, but it was time for a late lunch. We went into the ornate Metropole Hotel, opposite the Bolshoi Theatre, where the Central Executive Committee met in the years immediately after the Revolution. There is a new restaurant in the hotel, called the Teatro, with plastic palm trees and little café tables, pretending to be Mediterranean. They were longing to give us some coffee from their huge shiny Italian cappuccino machine. We ordered pasta and some wine from Georgia, and next to us there were four very smartly-dressed young Russians, the new rich, who would not have looked out of place in New York, with Georgio Armani glasses and Rolex watches. One of them had a mobile telephone. I thought how much this scene would have amused and interested Rees and how much he would have enjoyed being there with us.

Back in our hotel room, I listened to Tsarev's voice on the tape I had recorded, just to be sure I had correctly heard what he had told me. It seemed to add up to so little, yet it meant so much.

In A.J.A. Symons' words: 'Nothing was left to be discovered; the Quest was ended.'

# Bibliography

Annan, Noël, *Our Age: Portrait of a Generation*, Weidenfeld & Nicolson, 1990

Ayer, A.J., *Part of My Life*, Collins, 1977

Berlin, Isaiah, *Personal Impressions*, Hogarth Press, 1980

Bowen, Elizabeth, *The Death of the Heart*, Gollancz, 1938

Bowra, Maurice, *Memories*, Weidenfeld & Nicolson, 1966

Boyle, Andrew, *The Climate of Treason: Five Who Spied for Russia*, Hutchinson, 1979; revised edition, 1980

Costello, John, *Mask of Treachery*, Collins, 1988

Costello, John, and Tsarev, Oleg, *Deadly Illusions*, Century, 1993

Crossman, Richard (ed.), *The God That Failed: Six Studies in Communism*, Hamish Hamilton, 1950

Driberg, Tom, *Guy Burgess: A Portrait with Background*, Weidenfeld & Nicolson, 1966

—— *Ruling Passions*, Jonathan Cape, 1977

Ellis, Dr E.L., *The University College of Wales, Aberystwyth, 1872–1972*, University of Wales Press, 1972

—— *T.J.: A Life of Dr Thomas Jones CH*, University of Wales Press, 1992

Freeman, Simon, and Penrose, Barrie, *Conspiracy of Silence: The Secret Life of Anthony Blunt*, Grafton, 1986

Glendinning, Victoria, *Elizabeth Bowen: Portrait of a Writer*, Weidenfeld & Nicolson, 1977

Grant Duff, Shiela, *The Parting of Ways: A Personal Account of the Thirties*, Peter Owen, 1982

Green, Martin, *Children of the Sun: A Narrative of 'Decadence' in England after 1918*, Constable, 1977

Humphreys, Emyr, *The Taliesein Tradition: A Quest for the Welsh Identity*, Black Raven Press, 1983

Kristol, Irving, *Reflections of a Neoconservative*, Basic Books, 1983

Lees-Milne, James, *Harold Nicolson: A Biography*, Vol. 2: 1930–1968, Chatto & Windus, 1981

MacNeice, Louis, *The Strings Are False: An Unfinished Autobiography*, Faber and Faber, 1965

Muggeridge, Malcolm, *Like It Was: The Diaries of* (ed. John Bright-Holmes), Collins, 1981

*New College, Oxford, 1379–1979*, ed. John Buxton and Penry Williams, published privately for the Warden and Fellows, 1979

Nicolson, Harold, *Diaries and Letters, 1945–1962*, Collins, 1968

—— *Vita and Harold: The Letters of Vita Sackville-West and Harold Nicolson, 1910–1962*, Weidenfeld & Nicolson, 1992

Podhoretz, Norman, *Breaking Ranks: A Political Memoir*, Weidenfeld & Nicolson, 1980

Quennell, Peter, *Customs and Characters: Contemporary Portraits*, Weidenfeld & Nicolson, 1982

Roberts, Andrew, *The Holy Fox: A Biography of Lord Halifax*, Weidenfeld & Nicolson, 1991

Rowse, A.L., *All Souls in My Time*, Duckworth, 1993
Shelden, Michael, *Friends of Promise: Cyril Connolly and the World of* Horizon, Hamish Hamilton, 1989
Skelton, Barbara, *Tears Before Bedtime*, Hamish Hamilton, 1987
Spender, Stephen, *World Within World*, Faber and Faber, 1951
——*Journals 1939–1983*, Faber and Faber, 1985
Sudoplatov, Pavel, *Special Tasks* (with a foreword by Robert Conquest), Little, Brown, 1994
Symons, A.J.A., *The Quest for Corvo*, Cassell, 1934
Wharton, Michael, *A Dubious Codicil*, Chatto & Windus, 1991
Wright, Peter, *Spycatcher*, Viking, 1987
Yorke, Matthew (ed.), *Surviving: Uncollected Works of Henry Green*, Chatto & Windus, 1992

BOOKS BY GORONWY REES

*The Summer Flood*, Faber and Faber, 1932
*A Bridge to Divide Them*, Faber and Faber, 1937
*Where No Wounds Were*, Chatto & Windus, 1950
*A Bundle of Sensations*, Chatto & Windus, 1960
*The Multi-Millionaires: Six Studies in Wealth*, Weidenfeld & Nicolson, 1961
*The Rhine*, Weidenfeld & Nicolson, 1967
*St Michael: A History of Marks and Spencer*, Weidenfeld & Nicolson, 1966
*The Great Slump: Capitalism in Crisis*, Weidenfeld & Nicolson, 1970
*A Chapter of Accidents*, Chatto & Windus, 1972
*Brief Encounters*, Chatto & Windus, 1974 (*Encounter* columns)

*Translations*

*Danton's Death* by Georg Büchner (with Stephen Spender), Faber and Faber, 1939
*Conversations with Kafka* by Gustav Janouch, Verschoyle, 1953; revised edn, André Deutsch, 1971

# Appendix

It was with some consternation that I learned from Jeremy Treglown's review of the hardback edition of this book in *The Times Literary Supplement* that there were some letters from my father to Rosamond Lehmann in the archives of King's College Library, Cambridge, of which I had been totally unaware. I was anxious to see them; would these letters tell me more about what had happened over the summer of 1940, when my father, then a second lieutenant in the Royal Welch Fusiliers, fell in love with my mother, Margie, bringing to an acrimonious end his affair with Rosamond Lehmann?

At King's, I was handed four letters and three poems, all carefully preserved between sheets of paper in folders, which, I was told, were given to the college archives by Miss Lehmann in the 1970s, with the instruction that they were 'sensitive' and should remain closed to the general public. Her instructions were not altered on her death in March 1990, though I was given to understand that any interested scholars have been given access to them.

The four letters are undated and I have attempted, by looking for clues and hints, to put them in chronological order. They appear to cover a period beginning in the spring of 1940 and ending in the summer of 1941. What is significant about them is that they are letters chosen by Miss Lehmann to be kept in posterity as a record of that part of her life.

I was aware, when I was writing the book about my father, that the affair was already floundering before he and my mother met and that Rosamond was devastated when she learned of their marriage. However, very little about her feelings has been recorded in the various published appreciations of her work. But Frances Partridge, in her most recent volume of diaries, *Good Company*, which came out in 1994 (published by Harper Collins), supplied a valuable insight to Rosamond's attitude towards my father.

In April 1967, Frances Partridge and Rosamond Lehmann took a holiday together in Italy. On 27 April, Mrs Partridge recorded in her diary: 'Gradually Rosamond relaxes with me and her personality unfolds. In spite of having been left by at least four men (Leslie Runciman, Wogan, Goronwy Rees and Cecil Day-Lewis), she clearly nourishes in her heart a conviction of being universally beloved and desirable, and I think these defections appear to her like astonishing mistakes or just incomprehensible folly . . .'

A little later, while still in Italy, Frances Partridge observed: 'Episodes from Rosamond's past come out in the course of conversation and I am gradually joining them together. The impression I got of her being an unconfident blushing girl when she was at Girton and I at Newnham was only partly correct. She must already have been a spoiled beauty and her father's darling. Some innocent but unhappy love-affair was the basis for *Dusty Answer*; then came marriage with Leslie Runciman, about which she says little or nothing. Wogan and Day-Lewis were the great passions of her life; Goronwy Rees, another Welsher, was also passed over in silence (not *once* mentioned) though I remember how she had confided in Ralph and me at the time of his defection that it had been an appalling and "incomprehensible" blow to her, she felt "he still loved her though he didn't seem to realise it." '

In the first letter of the collection, all appears to be well:

Wynnstay Arms Hotel,
Wrexham

Darling Rosamond,

Thank you for your sweet letter; but I'm very sorry about Hugo[1] and hope he's better and you aren't too worried by your children's diseases. Wogan's message delights me; and so do David Cecil's compliments which you must know are deserved. I've started to try and read the book but have hardly the heart or the interest to go on. I've been very occupied since I saw you. Monday is an 'officers day' in which we do model exercises in the morning, erect barbed wire in the afternoon, and end up with night operations, during which I fell into a river, lay flat on my face in a bog & ended as a casualty, wiped out by the enemy. Yesterday I took about 250 men for a 15 mile route march which was extremely beautiful. It was a warm sunny conservatory day, and the country like a greenhouse, with trees in blossom and young green grass and leaves, and the earth pink with ploughing, like a landscape by Renoir, all the colours new and soft and bright. At the head of my 250 men I strolled through the countryside, in a poetical daze, and wished you were there to see it, and talked to the sergeant who was getting

1 Rosamond's son, Hugo, was born in 1929.

283

married in Cardiff this Saturday. I asked him if he would be going away for his honeymoon and he said sternly 'She'll be lucky if she gets outside Cardiff' and added in a resigned happy way, 'She means to have a spree on Saturday night. I suppose she'll get drunk.' I enjoyed myself enormously. Then we had a lecture and in the evening I was asked with some other officers to a party in the hotel where the ATS live – a very odd party. About 20 sex starved girls, slightly brutalized by military life, making desperate efforts at gaiety in a rather squalid boarding house; occasionally about 4 of them would throw themselves on a man & begin to take his shoes or collar and tie off while he was held down – mysterious departures into upstairs bedrooms – some of them beginning to get maudlin on beer & confessing to secret passions for Rupert Brooke (in 1940) & higher things. Only one girl seemed quite nice, a plump, plain, determined girl with rather fine eyes who suddenly looked perfectly agonised and said violently 'I hate it all', with great sincerity and rushed away, obviously to cry. By being extremely polite I succeeded in convincing everyone that I was a) dull b) cynical c) not suitable for such orgies. And I am not. Today I've had physical training and five lessons on the Bren gun & have prepared, for tomorrow, a lecture on Regimental History, designed to inspire pride in the regiment by recounting its victories and defeats. I feel like Homer.

Darling Sunday was lovely & I was absolutely happy, as I am always with you when I feel I'm not concealing anything; only always it seems difficult that I should cause you pain by being truthful, I feel little twinges like toothache at some of the things I say. Only it is better like this, I love you more genuinely, & when I cease to lie, I see you truthfully too, and don't have to invent imagined grievances to compensate my guilt. In Llangollen and driving home through that green country I felt peaceful and happy for the first time for so long and have remained so since, & I think of you with increasing love and affection. It should have been a symbol that Spring really burst out that day – relating human love with flowers, like Aziz.[2] Darling write to me again soon. Next week we take to tents and leave this hotel. I love you & more & more you astound me by your love,

darling, with all my love<br>Gony

In the second letter, things are not going so well:

Wynnstay Arms Hotel,<br>Wrexham

Darling Rosamond,

I've been brought rather low for the last two days by an inoculation and have been excused duty and felt rather ill and very depressed. I don't even

---

2 As in *A Passage to India*.

feel very much, only a dull and horrible void. Your letter came this afternoon and destroyed any pity I might have for myself; your state is so much worse than mine, which is simply that of the ennui and spleen I so much fear. And once the happy surprise has passed at finding that my fellow officers are human beings, as they are, I begin to feel again that none of them can have any real interest for me or I for them. Now of course they all hope childishly to be sent to Norway, but it is extremely improbable, and there is no need for you to worry, and I of all people am very unlikely to go anywhere for the moment. I don't know whether to be glad or sorry, having made such a wreck of everything; I look around with fear and dread at the ruin I've made & wonder if I shall always behave in such a way. Most of all I fear the kind of hysteria which overcame me & is really the source of the brutality you rightly resent.

Yet I have a profound affection and love for you, not of Dadie's[3] kind, nor of your literary admirers nor of the kind that merely brings happy memories. I think of you as close and living & part of me that I want to be with again when I can. It seems improbable that I shall be, because I cannot get more than one night off ever from here, which seems far away from everywhere. If I could manage it, I should like to come and see you. Until I can, I hope you will try to believe that there is, or can be, something permanent and valuable between us.

Perhaps you will wonder why then I should have behaved as I have. I find it hard to say, though I have tried to explain. But now I see how much guilt & anxiety weighed me down and wonder why there should have been so much concealed hostility. What is true is that I did, & do, love you so much that I used to repress all that hostility completely so as not to hurt you; I suppose that is why I was so anxious. Equally I suppose there was the fear of the end I thought must come one day, which made me foresee always a terrible catastrophe; I should have been less afraid if I'd thought I could have [word missing possibly] all the suffering of it.

Now it has come, it seems as if it might not be the end but a new beginning, if you think we can meet & be happy together. Only I have hurt you so much that I wonder if such wounds can heal. I know I have humiliated you; yet now I think such things may be unimportant when compared with loving you. With me I think that sex is dominated by fear and breeds hostility; it is a kind of disease in me & I think everyone is infected when it touches & I transfer to them the hostility I feel towards myself. I only wish you would believe that no-one has given me as much pleasure & happiness as you. We were happy, sometimes completely so, because you could make

3 George 'Dadie' Rylands, Cambridge don and life-long friend of Rosamond's who, according to her own account, started off her writing career when he sent her first novel, *Dusty Answer*, to Chatto and Windus, where it was immediately accepted and published in 1927.

me feel as if all my fears had disappeared & didn't exist any more & that I was as I would be if they had never existed. But one isn't so easily released from oneself; & since my fears are a part of me I suppose they were driven deeper and [illegible] down, they are like Furies that pursue one & cannot be evaded & in the end have their revenge, the worse the longer they are postponed. One reason why I so often want to live by myself is that then I can live with my fears and my guilt, because in the end that is the only way to overcome them.

I should like to see what you have written. Your letter doesn't seem like an attack & gives me no guilt that I haven't had already. Will you send it? Darling, don't think of winter, there can be great happiness for us still.

With my love<br>Gony

My father met my mother, who was then only 19, in the early summer of 1940 at Parkgate, on the Wirral, and they were married at the end of December.

Headquarters,<br>38th (Welsh) Division

Darling Rosamond,

I'm sorry I haven't written before, you can believe it wasn't from lack of love, but simply because of the doubt and fear and bewilderment after our weekend together. I do remember every minute of it, I've never been happier with you, or loved you more, or known better that you want my happiness as much as yours. Thank you for Guy's[4] letter, I have had one from Hester[5] too, each as admirable as the other, and both repeating the same doubts, which so nearly convince me, so much that I thought the only thing I could do, before making any decision, was to see Margie again, in case, after all, I found that I wasn't mistaken. So I managed to get 48 hours leave and she came to meet me, & in spite of everything I couldn't any longer think I was mistaken. I've hardly ever been really alone with her before; & when alone I find that she is even better than I have any right to expect; she makes me happier than I've ever expected to be & I know that my happiness isn't merely a temporary fancy. I need her as much as she needs me, & I can't think of myself without her any more.

My darling, I know that this is cruel, it isn't meant to be so, but I must tell you only the truth I've been able to discover. I shall marry Margie as soon as I can. I know what this will mean to you, and I know it will mean my losing you, which is the greatest loss I shall ever have had. I love you and shall always love you, & never will be able to forget how happy we have

---

4 Guy Burgess.
5 Hester Chapman, one of Rosamond's close friends and an historical biographer.

been; and but for you I should never have been able to love anyone, though this will be no satisfaction for you. My darling, you are better and more beautiful than anyone I have ever known, and you always will be.

I try not to think of your unhappiness, but it haunts me; only there is nothing I can do. There's nothing I can say except that I shall never be able to forget you for a moment and shall never stop wanting to see you.

With all my love,

Gony

Because of a reference to a letter from Rosamond published in *The Spectator*, the last of the four letters at King's College must have been written sometime shortly after 18 July 1941:

Hawks Club,
Cambridge

Darling Rosamond,

I was very glad to see you again & that you look so much better and were so much happier. You know I like Cecil[6] very much, and he is a very good person; more so than I. I hope very much you can go on being happy together. I lost the train, as you know, and caught the 4.35 and arrived here at 7 rather tired but otherwise very well. Guy didn't seem to me to be very happy, perhaps it is one of his periodical depressions, or perhaps it's love. I'd like very much to see you again; at least I feel now we can meet without merely hurting one another. Only I feel nervous about causing trouble, either for you or for anyone else. I hope very much I didn't involve you in difficulty by sending for my map; I couldn't leave it & had to have it and couldn't come myself, it would have been much worse. I feel that now you can be happy again, & perhaps if at last you have some luck, it might be a permanent kind of happiness, and I shouldn't like to do anything to spoil it, and it seems to me that at this moment seeing me might cause difficulty or at least distress to someone; but if we wait until everyone was more sure, then things might go well; you'll know, I hope, that I really only think this because you may in the end be happier. So tell me what you think. I may be in Cambridge another two months, not longer anyway; after that I may go to the Staff College, there's just a chance I may go to the Middle East.

Have you seen your doctor, & what was the result? I can't believe it is true that you are ill, it is your looks that make them think so; they don't seem natural and never did.

6 In April 1941, Rosamond had re-met Cecil Day-Lewis, whom she first encountered in 1936; by the end of the year they were living together and their relationship was to last nine years.

I have been reading a book of De Vigny's[7] which I think is the best book of military life there is, *Grandeur et Servitude Militaire*. Have you read it? You would like it. I read your letter[8] in the *New Statesman*; it filled me with a desire to see Margaret Rutherford; yet I do hate Noel Coward, though not for Graham Greene's reasons, which appear to be pure Catholic nonsense.

I saw Dadie on Saturday night. Maurice[9] was dining with him; M. waved at me wildly and affectionately, D. sat embarrassed and disapproving, it was an absurd scene.

Will you give my love to Hugo? He's the nicest little boy I know, and one day I hope I may even see him again.

You know, I have almost lost interest in myself which leaves a large gap to fill one's mind; it's fortunate there are other things to take my place. Only it leaves one rather dumb. Being in Cambridge is rather like being on a river, one floats & floats & floats, even the war seems distant; I suppose this will not last for long; in Cambridge nothing seems to change; only the walls of the colleges have Vs with hammers and sickles inside them. So far I have spoken to no-one who thinks Russia will win the war. I appear to be alone.

Darling look after yourself as well as you can. I hope you will be peaceful at Fieldhead[10] & Sally[11] at least will be blissful, which must give you a lot of happiness. Write to me; I'm very happy that we can meet & can at least speak to each other again.

Very much love,
Gony

7 Vigny, the Romantic poet and novelist, began to write when he was an army officer. Published in 1835, the correct title of this book – three short stories about the devotion to duty of Napoleon's forces – is *Servitude et grandeur militaires*.

8 In fact, it was a letter in *The Spectator* in July 1941, that Rees had seen. In it, Rosamond criticised Graham Greene's sober notice of Noel Coward's *Blithe Spirit* in which he objected to a joke about Joan of Arc. Rosamond also felt Greene had not properly appreciated the performance of Margaret Rutherford, whom she described as a 'phenomenon of the first artistic order'. She said she had enjoyed 'a riotously exhilarating evening' at the theatre and chastised Greene for being 'portentous' about Coward's new play. Margaret Rutherford had appeared in Rosamond's own play, *No More Music*, which was performed in the summer of 1939.

9 Maurice Bowra, the most famous Oxford don and wit of his day, had been elected warden of Wadham in 1938.

10 The house on the Thames at Bourne End, Bucks, built by her father, Rudolph Lehmann, writer, Liberal MP and editor of *Punch*, where Rosamond grew up. Rosamond told an interviewer in 1982 that she had taken the children back to her mother 'who wasn't at all pleased to see me' in 1940 because she knew her marriage to her second husband, Wogan Philipps, was over. 'I was desperately bereft and lonely, trying to keep going for the children', she said.

11 Rosamond's daughter Sally, was born in 1934; she died of polio in 1958 in Jakarta, where she had been living with her husband, P.J. Kavanagh.

# Index

Goronwy Rees is referred to as GR: his daughter Jenny is referred to as JR